Ethnic Angst

Ethnic Angst

A Comparative Study of
Bapsi Sidhwa & Rohinton Mistry

Dr. Ajay Sahebrao Deshmukh

PARTRIDGE
A Penguin Random House Company

ISBN:	Softcover	978-1-4828-4154-1
	eBook	978-1-4828-4153-4

To order additional copies of this book, contact
Partridge India
000 800 10062 62
orders.india@partridgepublishing.com

www.partridgepublishing.com/india

For the maestros who are emblem of simplicity, greatness, humility, love, dedication and great human beings in my life

To

Dear Samad Sir for giving this dream

&

Dear Bhoomkar Sir
for giving freedom,
strength and vision to accomplish it

&

My dear parents and loving family
for everything that I am today

Acknowledgement

It is a great pleasure to acknowledge all the loving and caring people in my life who encouraged and supported me to complete this book.

This book is due to Dr. Santosh M. Bhoomkar and Dr. Shaikh Samad. Thank you sir for your love and blessings.

I offer my sincere gratitude to my family, without which this study was just impossible. I thank my parents Shri Sahebrao Shankarrao Deshmukh and Smt Saraswati Sahebrao Deshmukh for teaching me self-discipline, patience, sincerity and commitment to the work. I thank elder sister Sou. Shobha, brother-in-law Shri Yuvraj Shelke, elder brother Shri Vijay and sister-in-law Sou. Jayashri for their love and blessings. I thank my younger brother Shri Abhay and sister in-law Sou. Dhanshri and nephews Vishwas, Vishal, Shantanu, Anurag and niece Pratiksha and Mansi for their love and warmth.

Its pleasure to thank my wife, *Rajashri*, for being supportive and caring as well as my son *Hrushikesh* whose innocent smiles have sweetened my labors and my daughter *Gayatree* who gave me new aspirations and strength to achieve them.

I express my sincere thanks to my dear friend Dr. Suhel Shaikh and Dr. Shankar Gavali and Dr. Ramesh Shinde for being a great support system.

--- Dr. Ajay Sahebrao Deshmukh
"Guruvandan", N-9, L-46/4
HUDCO, Aurangabad - 431003,
Maharashtra, India

Foreword

Ethnicity and Cultural identity have become the major issues in the multicultural, multi-ethnic and pluralist nations. The all inclusive American Identity and Canadian Identity seem far from true, as the dominant culture is reluctant to absorb immigrant cultures. Hence, the caregorization of literature as Immigrant Literature, Minority Literature, etc… This book, thus, is a 'must read' for the students of Minority Literature in particular and Multicultural Literature in general. The writers, chosen discretely, are two preeminent and best known writers, who have made a mark on international literatures in English. They have become canonical writers within the canon of multicultural writers from different parts of the world writing in English, which is gaining wide acceptance and publicity at the moment. These writers are Bapsi Sidhwa and Rohinton Mistry. The former is a Pakistani female writer while the latter is an Indian male writer. Both are Canada based writers of Parsi descent.

The study juxtaposes the female-male discourse and successfully brings out the marginalization of the ever dwindling Parsi community on various counts in the turmoil ridden world. Sidhwa's novels *The Bride*, *Cracking India* and *American Brat* are equally important on the theme of women's liberation, particularly that of women in India and Pakistan, and in the societies on the subcontinent in which women are treated as chattels. Sidhwa's gynocentric perspective determines the narrative strategy, resulting in the production of a truly feminist work. Her novel, *The Crow Eaters,* portrays the Parsi community and their movement and migration to the UK, and their efforts to be like

British. As against Sidhwa's novels, Rohinton Mistry's works manifested a male discourse in which it is the men who are in command and it is they who occupy the centre of the stage for example Gustad in *Such a Long Journey* and Nariman Vakeel in *Family Matters.* However, both, Sidhwa and Mistry have the capacity to mix universal themes with the particularity of individual lives. Their works are an expression of a Parsi sensibility and are rooted in the community in which they have been raised. Parsis are the most colonized people as they migrate to different parts of the world, particularly, America and Canada. Consequently, Postcoloniality becomes a major theme and preoccupation in the works of the two writers, and they try to depict how Parsis interact with the rest of the populace around them, whether in India, Britain, America or Canada. The study compares and contrasts the narrative skills of these two writers, who have won accolades and many a prizes of honor, yet they feel disappointed as they have not been written about much. It seems to be the result of their being marginalized as Parsi writers – not quite authentic to India or to Pakistan and not included among American writers. Despite this fact, their works are timeless and tale of the culture conflict in the movement and migrations of the Parsis.

Literature is a powerful tool in the hands of creative writers to modulate and change the societal framework, and Sidhwa and Mistry through their extremely absorbing and interesting work seek to contribute to the process of change that has already started the world over, involving a reconsideration of minorities' rights and status, and a radical restructuring of social thought. These writers wish to build a world which is free of dominance and hierarchy, a world that rests on the principles of justice and equality and is truly human.

Thus, Dr. Ajay Deshmukh deserves all congratulations for this commendable work that would stir the consciousness of the researchers and help them understand the problems faced by the immigrants, particularly the minorities, in the nation states.

Dr. Shaikh Samad
Former Principal, Vasantrao Naik College, Aurangabad
Member, Board of Studies of English,
Dr. Babasaheb Ambedkar Marathwada University, Aurangabad

Contents

I

Introduction: Breaking the Ice

In the age of space odyssey when man has landed on the moon and mars, humanity has retreated into the dark ages. When human beings are exploring the infinite potential of mental, physical, intellectual, spiritual and emotional powers, it's high time to search the *divine being* in the man who is lost amid the buzz of power, greed, hatred and violence as well fanaticism, racism, religious zealotry and terrorism.

At the turn of 21st century, world has seen reign of terror disturbing the human psyche. The terrorist attack on Twin Towers of World Trade Center, terrorist attack in London, terrorist attack on Indian Parilament and recently on Canadian Parliament, war in Iraq, Afghanistan, Jasmine Revolution all over African continent, Greece, fall of Al-Quaida, emergence of ISIS (Islamic State of Iraq & Syria) in recent times, fall of LTTE in Sri Lanka, insurgencies in Pakistan, terrorist attack on Hotel Taj, Godhra Carnage, disturbance in China and necular radiation in Japan etc and the socio-political, religious-cultural upheaveals all over the world have increased threats to the idea of *utopian world sans boundaries*.

I feel the urgency to follow the inner voice of that supreme power residing in each individual who has charismatic power to create new world order of humanity, initiate peaceful co-existence and freedom from all fears and anxieties. It can be put aptly in the words of Ben Okri, one of the great poets and novelists of our time, in his poem *Mental Fight*:

Will you be at the harvest,
Of freedom, realizers of great dreams....
Only free people can make a free world....
Our future is greater than our past.
(Emphasis added) [62-63: 1999]

Its crucial time to raise our heads and look into the future direction as life offers great opportunities to human beings there. It is necessary to overcome the barriers of boundaries of nation, religion, culture, language, ethnicity and race. As it is rather difficult to erase these identities permenantly from our life, human beings are trapped into these compartments. Kamleshwar in his magnum opus novel *Kitne Pakistan* aka *Partitions* dexterously comments as:

> Nations might die out, Naim Sahib, but race and ethnicity never do. Did Christianity succeed in wiping out the different races? No, the conceptual framework of race is at variance with religion? Could the advent of Buddhism alter the racial and ethnic realities of China, Japan, Cambodia, Burma, Sri Lanka and Indonesia? Many people in these countries embraced Christianity or Islam. But could the hold of religion weaken their racial bonds and customs? [2006:113]

Today, world is divided into religious zones like Christian world and Islamic World. Movements like Pan-Islamic world and terrorist groups like ISIS aim to establish the idea of Islamic State. Idea of national identity based on religion or culture has not worked any where in the world. Kamleshwar argues on identities based on such nominclatures as:

> Religion does not establish the parameters of national identity. If the whole of America embraces Islam today, does that mean it loses its identity as a nation? Will its culture turn Arabic or Iranian? Religious identities had always emerged from within a nation. [Ibid 112-113]

It is necessary to steam out the hatred, misconceptions on the proper occasions through proper channels. It is observed that race, ethnicity or majority are the controlling factors on ideology and cultural make up of the particular place. The drift between ethnic culture and majority culture gives rise to unrest in national life. David Lloyd has made the difference between ethnic culture and minority culture as:

> An ethnic culture can be conceived as turned, so to speak, towards its internal differences, complexities and debates, as well as to its own traditions or histories, projects and imaginings, it transformed into a minority culture only along the lines of its confrontations with a dominant state formation which threatens to destroy it by direct violence or assimilation. Minority discourse is articulated along this line and at once registers the loss, actual and potential, and offers the means to a critique of dominant culture precisely in terms of its own internal logic. An ethnic culture, strictly speaking, is inassimilable; minority discourse forms in the problematic space of assimilation and the residues it throws up. [1994: 222]

In such times of crisis, it is necessary to come to terms with reality by admitting and respecting the *difference* as a vital aspect of human existence by inculcating tolerance towards *other i.e. religious, cultural, national, ethnic and lingual etc..*

It can be possible by spreading awareness amongst scholars, academicians and every sensible human being who has ignited his mind with sacred fire of truth, knowledge, freedom, love and compassion for fellow human beings. This vying for love, bonding, compassion and quest for peaceful co-existence has laid the foundation of this book.

The aim of present book is to make a comparative study of the two Parsi writers - Bapsi Sidhwa and Rohinton Mistry in relation to the ethnic anxieties reflected in their fictional worlds. Both differ from each other as they belong to two different geographical locations, Pakistan and India respectively. However, both are now settled in Canada. Since they belong to the sub-continental countries which were once united before acquiring their status as independent states, they share the common element of religion and culture. Bapsi Sidhwa and Rohinton Mistry are the two crucial Parsi writers who focus on the problems of their microscopic community. They highlight the problems of survival in the cultural milieu they live in. Bapsi Sidhwa confronts the Muslim society in Pakistan and Rohinton Mistry experiences the Hindu ethos in India. The discussion here is aimed at the vivid facets of their skills as writers and the issues they deal with. Both the writers write about their community at a different point in time. So the problems faced by them are also rather different, though not completely.

Every creative genius has his own world-view which is reflected in his/her works. The artist deals with his socio-religious, cultural, political, economical and environmental aspects of his/her contemporary society, because all these factors are sources of development of his/her imaginary world. It is influenced by the writer's sense of survival in a hostile environment and identification with the problems and issues following the hostility. At the same time a writer is concerned about the way in which others recognize him/her and place himself/herself in a particular socio-cultural context. So the characters created by the writer are fictional realities. If the writer belongs to a minority ethnic group living on the edge, certainly his/her imaginary world is obviously occupied with the problems that his/her ethnic group faces. S/He deals with the subsequent anxieties of his ethnic group and obviously demonstrates the need for the continuation of the race of that ethnic group. Here the discussion is focused on two Parsi writers. So their world view obviously reflects the Parsi community. It deals with the various anxieties --- psychological and existential that Parsi community suffers. It should overcome *the sense of an ending.* Parsi as a minuscule community should focus on its future and not on the past. Past is the history and imperfect memory as Julian Barnes comments in his Man Booker Prize winner novel, *The Sense of an Ending* as:

> History is that certainty produced at the point where the imperfections of memory meet the inadequecies of documentation [2011:59].

It is necessary to re-write the history of *the sense of being together* by erasing this exaggerated sense of an ending.

This book is an attempt to understand the sources and reasons that cause anxiety as well as how it is expressed in various forms in human life. It also attempts to analyse the repucurssions of such ethnic anxieties on human life. For this purpose methods like Close Textual Analysis and Comparative

Analysis of the fictional worlds of Bapsi Sidhwa and Rohinton Mistry are used.

I hope it would enhance the human understanding of ethnic angst and assist to neutralize them to create a better world full of humanity, humility, mutual trust, tolerance and human understanding.

II

Ethnic Angst: Fire Burning Beneath the Ice

> Ethnic anxieties arise out of a sense of ethnic identity. Such identity may be religious or secular. Anxieties, however, are compounded when the secular interests of two differing identities are seen to be divergent or threatening to one another. The threatening aspect of the 'other' or majority community becomes more pronounced in the case of economic or social backwardness. [Chandra, 1989:398]

*

Today the world is celebrating the concept of global village. It has become more rigid and retreated to its primitive nature of group, tribal, racial and ethnic modes of behavior what Harold R. Isaacs refers to the 'House of Mumbi' [1971], the name of the progenital mother of the KIKUYU tribe of Kenya. It can be exemplified in the backdrop of 9/11 World Trade Centre Terrorist Attack, war in Iraq, fight against international terrorism, polarization of the world on the basis of Islamic and non-Islamic countries etc.

In Indian subcontinent, the scenario is grim. It has seen various insurgencies, Indo-Pak wars, Post Babri Demolition riots, Godhra Carnage, ethnic onslaught, religious riots, Terrorist Attack on Hotel Taj, and socio-political upheavals in the recent times. Nilufer Bharucha rightly reflects:

> **The current explosion of ethno-religious politics in the Indian sub-continent... has forced the recognition that racial/religious identities cannot be easily subordinated to indices of 'secular' modernity or postmodernist, post nationalisms. In the face of global market-economies and the cultural hegemony of satellite communication, [and mass media,] 'ethnicity is often the last refuge into which great massess all over the world are retreating.' [2003:47]**

Samuel P. Huntington [1996:21] has said that ethnic identities are very dangerous and have led to major military conflicts today. He emphasizes that cultural preferences, commonalties and differences are also important in shaping the behavior of nations. He has identified nine major civilizations in the world in the post cold war period- Western, Latin American, African, Sinic, Islamic, Hindu, Orthodox, Buddhist and Japanese. He feels that the real danger to world peace today is not clashes between nations but clashes between civilizations. The terrorist attack on New York's Trade Center Twin Towers, has also been seen as a civilization clash. President Bush of the USA, called it 'an attack on civilization', more precisely on the Western Civilization by Islamic Civilization. In India too there are clashes between Hindu and Islamic civilizations (Babri Mosque demolition, Godhra killings). Similarly, ethnic and racial problems have led to the conflicts between LTTE and Sri Lankan Govt. Kurds, Berbers, Lankan Tamils, Sikhs, Kashmiris, Palestinians, Tibetans, Crimean Tartars, African Sudanese, Basques, Saharwais are the ethnic groups who have always been in conflict with the government for its refusal to acknowledge its separate existence as an ethnic entity.

Ethnicity is one of the major issues emerging in contemporary discourses. The plethora of issues that have cropped up in the area of cultural studies needs to be closely evaluated. Hence a close look at the ethnic-related issues would serve the purpose better. According to CHAMBERS 21st century Dictionary the term Ethnic is: "Relating to or having common race or cultural tradition." It also defines an ethnic group as: "Associated with or resembling an exotic, especially non-European, racial or tribal group." Ethnicity is considered as: "Racial status or distinctiveness." The word "ethnic" was derived in 14th century as a noun and in 15th century as an adjective meaning heathen; from Greek word "ethnos" (nation). CHAMBERS 21st century Dictionary describes the term Ethnocentric as: "relating to or holding the belief that one's own cultural tradition or racial group is superior to all others." According to OXFORD Advanced Learner's Dictionary the term Ethnic, means:

1. **A) of or involving a nation, race, or tribe that has a common cultural tradition.**
   B) [Of a person] belonging to the specified country/area by birth or family history rather than by NATIONALITY.

2. **Typical of a particular cultural group esp one from outside Europe or the USA.**

It defines the term Ethnocentric as: "making judgment about another race or culture using the standards of one's own."

All these definitions reflect the aspects of ethnicity which underscores the similarity, oneness or commonness of culture, traditions, and race. The reference to the particular cultural group as "One from outside Europe or the USA", suggests that it is a European slang for the non-Europeans. It also connotes the cultural, racial, and spatial difference resulting into Orientalism. Further, it suggests that Western/Occidental (European and American) culture is superior to Eastern/Oriental culture and raises doubts about cultural identities. The word **tribal** connotes primitiveness which suggests the unrefined, uncivilized, violent, harsh and coarse patterns of behavior. It is **exotic** suggesting the grandeur of cultural or racial traditions or social mores of one's ethnic group. Tracing the origin of the term as an adjective, it means **heathen**, implying the pre-Christian pagan people. It also connotes the inferiority in a derogatory sense. In Greek, **ethnos nation** suggests the national aspect of identity and existence. It emphasizes on "[of a person] belonging to the specified country or area by birth or family history rather than by NATIONALITY", symptomatic of the importance of space where one is born, and ancestry one belongs to. It also shows the superiority of one's own culture or race over others which germinate into the existence or survival and identity struggle ensuing ethnic anxiety.

Bill Ashcroft and others have given detailed analysis of the term **ethnicity**. They have distinguished the term ethnicity and race**:**

> **Ethnicity is a term that has been used increasingly since the 1960s to account for human variation in terms of culture, tradition, language, social patterns and ancestry, rather than the discredited generalizations of race with its assumption of a humanity divided into fixed, genetically determined biological types. ....race emerged as a way of establishing a hierarchical division between Europe and its 'others'. [2004:80]**

Schemerhorn has referred ethnicity as: "the fusion of many traits that belong to the nature of any ethnic group: a composite of shared values, beliefs, norms, tastes, behaviors, experiences, consciousness of kind, memories and loyalties" [1974:2]. Bill Ashcroft and others have argued that the aspects of ethnicity are related to space and time. It can change itself as per conditions and circumstances. An ethnic group is described as:

> **A group that is socially distinguished or set apart, by others and/or by itself, primarily on the basis of cultural or national characteristics. [Ibid, 81]**

According to them the first use of ethnic group in terms of national origin developed in the period of profound migration from Southern and Eastern European nations to the USA in the early twentieth century. The name by which an ethnic group understands itself is still most often the name of an originating nation, whether that nation still exists or not (e.g. Armenia). The term ethnicity gets wide prevalence.

The phenomenon of migration has added another dimension to ethnicity. Nowadays immigrants are considered as 'ethnic'. Isajaw describes 'ethnicity' in its current context of immigration as:

> **...a group or category of persons who have a common ancestral origin and the same cultural traits, who have a sense of peoplehood and of group belonging, who are of immigrant background and have either minority or majority status within a larger society. [Isajaw 1974:118]**

Politically ethnicity has a very crucial aspect. Bill Ashcroft and others traced the political aspect of ethnicity. For them, it is not necessary that ethnic groups must be marginalized cultural groups. But ethnicity is a major tactic of political welfare. It is a preferred resolution to individual helplessness. The ethnic group is a prominent configuration in the proposition of political power in any society.

So it is clear that ethnic revolution is a direct result of the use of cultural identity and the affirmation of ethnicity in political conflict. Schermerhorn's definition of ethnicity encompasses all its aspects:

> **A collectivity within a larger society having real or putative common ancestry; a shared consciousness of a separate, named, group identity; and a cultural focus on one or more symbolic elements defined as the epitome of their peoplehood. These features will always be in dynamic combination, relative to the particular time and place in which they are experienced and operate consciously or unconsciously for the political advancement of the group. [1970:12]**

It highlights on the common past or history of that particular ethnic group. It may include the memories of a collective past, of genesis or of historical experiences like colonization, immigration, assault, or slavery.

The main characteristic of this definition is the usefulness of those 'symbolic elements' [Ibid, 12] that may provide a sense of ethnic belongings. Such symbolic elements are association patterns, physical contiguity, religious association, language or dialect forms, tribal affiliation, nationality, physical features, cultural values, and cultural practices such as art, literature, and music. Various combinations of these elements ('one or more') [Ibid, 12] may be privileged at different times and places to provide a sense of ethnicity.

Thus ethnic identities continue beyond cultural assimilation into the wider society and the determination of ethnic identity is not essentially related to the continuation of traditional cultures. It is not necessary that ethnic group must be completely unified on its aspects or features. It is possible that members of an ethnic group can be varying regarding such features or aspects. But it becomes prominent to identify such features or its dynamics as an essential function in the transnational, globalized and hybridized world where world has become a small village.

In the United States the collectivity of immigrants from a region of the world and their descendants are called **ethnic groups**. Immigrants are socialized into identifying as a member of one of the list of ethnic groups. Such groups have an appeal to some notion of the past. Thus Mexican nationals, upon crossing the border, become Hispanic ethnics. In the West, the notion of ethnicity, like race, and nation, developed in the context of European colonial expansion, when mercantilism and capitalism were cheering global movements at the same time when state boundaries were being more obviously and strictly defined. In the nineteenth century, modern states generally required authenticity through their claim to represent **nations**. Nation-states always embrace native populations that were expelled from the nation-building project and such people typically constitute ethnic groups. Thus, members of ethnic groups often understand their own identity in terms of something outside of the history of the nation-state-- either an alternate history, or in historical terms, or in terms of a connection to another nation-state. The status of these people can be defined in Linda Hutcheon's words as 'ex-centric' or in Derridian terminology 'outside' the margin. The biological race too, is frequently considered, and some believe it as a basic policy on which cultural heritage can be preserved and sustained via genetical persistence. This concept is however proposed by those who believe that the ethnic group can be accessed also by spontaneous choice or more- commonly- marriage (exogamy), and is not closed to a new member. Political connotations result into ethnic nationalism. Ethnic nationalism is the form of nationalism in which the state obtains political legitimacy from historical, cultural or traditional groupings or ethnicities; the underlying assumption is that ethnicities should be politically discrete. It was developed by Johann Gottfried von Herder, who introduced the concept of the Volk (German for folk). Anthony Smith uses this term to classify non-Western concepts of nationalism as opposed to western views of a nation mainly being defined by its geographical territory. Romantic nationalism is a form of ethnic nationalism infused with romanticism such as Nazism. The concepts homelands, fatherlands, and motherlands are often used as an ethnic nationalist concept. The concept of Ethnic Origin is an effort to organize people, not according to their existing ethnicity, but according to the place from where their ancestors arrived. Some common features are responsible for growing anxieties resulting out of ethnicities which challenge each other in cultural, political, social or any other way. The ethnic pointer generally indicates the marginal or the subaltern. The politics of ethnicity also operates within post-colonial spaces. In post-colonial societies, the dominant group develops into the norm and the ethnic minorities become noticeable. The Muslims in India have always had a strong sense of ethno-religious identity. Current ethno-religious discourse in India has gained foothold due to its increasing conflict with Hindu fundamentalism. In this reference some problems are posed as Sander L. Gilman points out: "Can successful ethnics still be ethnic? Do ethnics have to be Subaltern? Or can they be good bourgeois...?" [1998:23].

Nilufer Bharucha also highlights these issues with reference to Parsis as:

> **Can Parsis claim ethnic identity? If being ethnic means being oppressed, means living within the culture of victims, can Parsis be called an ethnic minority? [2003:54-55]**

Considering above assumptions, it is obvious that Parsis residing in India, Pakistan and in the Western countries are in minorities as per their demographic decline as well as they are ethnic due to their subjugation by the dominant cultures like Hindu, Islam and Christian respectively. Thus Parsis claim to be 'an ethnic minority' [Ibid, 54]. Bharucha also raises some other questions as Parsis of post-Raj India migrated to West to merge into the mainstream white-masters:

> **Then again can a successful minority like Parsis in India be ethnocentric in that country but try to 'pass' in the West as part of the white mainstream? Can ethnicity be flaunted in one context and denied/ hidden in another? Can the same people occupy ethnic space in postcolonial India and transcend ethnicity/nationality in the west? Can ethnicity and transnationalism co-exist? [2003:54-55]**

These are apt comments by Bharucha with reference to the Parsi ethnic group that is reduced to a minority ethnic group in post-colonial India. They preferred migration to the west but there too, they are clubbed together with other 'colored' people. Bhabha has related the dislocation while thinking about the identity, location, and culture of an ethnic group as: "specific conjecture of identity, location, and locution that most commonly defines the particularity of an ethnic culture" [1998:34]. Further, Bhabha comments:

> **...the anxiety of displacement that troubles national rootedness transforms ethnicity or cultural difference into an ethical relation that serves as a subtle corrective to a valiant attempt to achieve representativeness and moral equivalence in the matter of minorities. For too often these efforts result in hyphenated attempts to include all multiple subject positions -race, gender, class, geographical location, generation- in an overburdened juggernaut that rides roughshod over the singularities and individualization of difference. [1998:34]**

Whenever any culture or ethnic group or civilization has an advantage over all others, whether culturally or politically, their programs of self-glorification have usually directed to destruction of not just that ethnic group or civilization but also that of the other who have been drawn into that whirlpool of mass obliteration. Ethnic attachments often show the way to the gateways of cruelty and even bestiality. The psyche actively guides towards the self destruction. Extreme attention on ethnic identity can lead to fetishisation and essentialisation of identity. So these identities should maneuver in ever-widening spheres of belonging. Bharucha points out that, "Assertions of ethnicity come within the ambit of the first/primary circle and are only one of the parameters of identitarian consciousness. [2003:58]. The Nationalist identity operates with the wider transnational identity. These identities are such "...that the former and present lives do not match, they quarrel, even contradict, cancel each other out" [Kuortti 1998:62]. As ours is not the perfect world, these different identities could come in conflict with one another and could be placed within private and public spaces. There could be overlaps within these spaces and private and public histories could clash as Mudimbe said:

> **Historical deconstruction certainly robs identity based on ethnicity of the mythic sense of timelessness on which it thrives, but to say that ethnicity is artificially constructed does not give us license to dismiss it as illegitimate. Dismissal only begs the question of how far back in time**

> **we have to go in order to satisfy criteria of 'genuineness'. [Mudimbe 1988]**

Ethnic anxieties arise in the exercise of power. It is a clash of two different constructions, usually more ethnicities to be defined against each other. Silverman noted this as: "A group is ethnic only if there are 'outsiders' and if it exists within a wider political field" [Eds.Varma Sushma J. and Seshan Radhika 2003:127-128]. Thus, ethnic politics is the politics of marginality. Certainly, ethnicity materializes into being most regularly in just such instances when individuals differentiate a need to verify a communal sense of identity in the face of threatening economic, political or other social forces. Ethnic politics by its nature characterizes marginality and comparative weakness. Sometimes same weakness can be termed as strength. Hence, Ethnicity can be called as a relational notion in which the dominant are capable to describe the subordinate.

Thus various facets are responsible for the conflict of two different ethnic groups which cause ethnic anxieties. As Chandra says:

> **Ethnic anxieties arise out of sense of... ethnic identity. Such identity may be religious or secular. Anxieties, however, are compounded when the secular interest of two differing identities are seen to be divergent or threatening to one another. The threatening aspect of the 'other' or majority community becomes more pronounced in the case of economic or social backwardness. [1989:398]**

Such threats to economic or social existence may lead to insecure religious identity. Thus ethnic anxiety and its ramifications should be taken into consideration.

Parsis migrated to India after Arab onslaught in search of a safe place to reside. But in India, they were given conditional refuge. It was 'cultural onslaught' on the Parsis. Being a minority group, they agreed on all specified conditions. Consequently, they faced the prblmes related to migration and adjustment with the new land.

Culture is a means of creating its separateness from and defiance to other communities. Issues like exile, rootlessness, and cultural differences arise due to migration. Minority discourse leads to simplify the diasporic tendencies. Thus, diaspora has wider implication and is located within the discourse of ethno-cultural studies. Diaspora can be described as "practically any population that is considered 'deterritorialized' or 'transnational'" [Vertovec 1997:277]. It is obvious that geographically, "diaspora involves a radical... redefinition of place" [Stewart 2001:13]. Migration can be defined when there is an ethnic awareness, an active associative life and links with the land of origin in diverse forms, real or imaginary. Diaspora deals with the formation of new identities, spaces for development, resolution, clash and a new culture, either merged or plural. In lexical terms, the word 'Diaspora', with capital 'D', refers only to the dispersal of the Jews after 538 BC. Etymologically, it is derived from the Greek meaning 'scattering'. Migration brings the loss of "roots", "language", and "social norms" [IH 1991:429].

Landing on a new shore brings the question of assimilation. For this, La Framboise and others [1993:401] have given the models including assimilation, acculturation, alternation, and multiculturalism. **Assimilation** is the likeness of melting pot. It suggests the creation of a new culture by abandoning the past culture. Here the member of one culture loses his/her original cultural identity by acquiring a new identity in the second culture. On the other hand, **Acculturation** encourages the idea of belonging to two cultures at the same time. It implies that the individual, while becoming a capable participant in the majority culture, will always be identified as a member of the minority culture. **Alternation** highlights the sense of presence in two cultures. The individual has a sense of belonging to two cultures without compromising his or her sense of cultural identity and is capable of alternating his/her behavior according to the needs of a situation. In contrast, **Multiculturalism** promotes a pluralistic approach and offers the possibility of cultures maintaining different identities. In it, the individual maintains a positive identity as a member of his/her culture of origin while at the same time developing a positive identity by engaging in complex institutional sharing with the larger political entity comprised of other groups. It has been more often used, to create a sense of the equal importance of all cultures. Lastly, **the fusion** represents the assumptions of the melting pot theory. It suggests that cultures sharing an economic, political or geographical space will fuse together until they are indistinguishable to form a new culture. Thus, individuals and families who live at the juncture of two cultures can claim the possession of both the cultures. Yet for the reasons of being born into one culture and living in the second, they are considered as marginal people, very different to the norm set by the majority. Such marginality leads to the psychological conflicts of a divided self. The problem for these marginal people (migrants) is that Center does not accept them. They are always treated as *Mohajir*. Marginalization in any culture is an issue associated with what is not major, not central, and not powerful- in short, everything that is subordinate. Edward Said aptly described it as an "alternative" [Said 1994:392] in all the segments and facets of life. This loss of the self and fragmentation makes them subaltern. Thus, Diasporic discourse deals with 'minority' and marginal aspect. Thus, diaspora deals with various issues related with migration. One of the issues is cultural encounters. Since this thesis deals with the ethnic angst of Parsis, it is necessary to find out the notion of culture in the present scenario. The word **'culture'** acquired a new meaning in the 1960s and 1970s. Prior to that culture was associated with art, literature, and classical music. To have **culture** was to possess a certain taste for particular kinds of artistic endeavor. Gloria Anzaldua defined culture as:

> **Culture forms our beliefs. We perceive the version of reality that it communicates. Dominant paradigms, predefined concepts that exist as unquestionable, unchallengeable, are transmitted to us through the culture. Culture is made by those in power. [1987:888]**

The main dilemma with this idea of culture is that it brings about not only admiring one's own culture but also thinking of it as in some way separated from the daily world. Cultural structures are hybrid, mixed, impure too. Rushdie expresses his idea of culture and his notion of 'translated' individuality as he says:

> **The word "translation" comes, etymologically, from the Latin for "bearing across". Having been borne across the world, we are translated men. It is normally supposed that something always gets lost in translation; I cling, obstinately, to the notion that something can also be gained. [IH 1991:16]**

In such a perspective, transculturalism can be defined as a process of translation. It is in this sense that the boundary becomes the place from which something begins. It is impossible to acquire a clean and pure ethnic identity. It is only possible through death: "The hideous extremity of Serbian nationalism proves that the very idea of a pure, "ethnically cleansed" national identity can only be achieved through death" [Literary Theory 1998:936]. Thus, one has to accept transculturalism as one of the very basic and important factor of diaspora.

Another problem migrant group suffers from is that of nationality and national identity. The word 'Parsi' suggests the place Pars/Fars and to the people who migrated and adopted India as their Nation. The 'nation' is both historically determined and general. As a term, it refers both to the modern nation-state and to something more ancient and unformulated - the nation - a local community, domicile, family, condition of belonging. The British cultural historian, Raymond Williams highlights:

> **'Nation' as a term is radically connected with 'native'. We are *born* into relationships which are typically settled in a place. This form of primary and 'placeable' bonding is of quite fundamental human and natural importance. Yet the jump from that to anything like the modern nation-state is entirely artificial. [Raymond 1983]**

As Parsis left their native land of 'Pars' and came in search of new secure land in India, they became transnational. The process of transnationalization is described as: "an appeal for increasingly similar, ecumenical and universal values, or, to use the terms of Brezinski, 'a new planetary consciousness', a new 'harmony', a 'new world unity' and a new 'consensus'" [Mattelart 1983:57]. In its European origins, nationalism was also messianic, modeled on patterns of Judeo-Christianity. According to Kohn Hans, modern nationalism took three concepts from Old Testament mythology: "the idea of a chosen people, the emphasis on a common stock memory of the past and of hopes of future, and finally national messianism" [Kohn 1965:11].

In Indian context, Parsis were not 'chosen people' in Indian national milieu. They were forced to take refuge in India as a result of religious fanaticism of Arabs. Parsis became underdogs in their own nation i.e. Persia as well as their adopted nation i.e. India. But they never shared the memory of common past and hope for future in Indian socio-political atmosphere. Their minds were fixed into the deep roots of their primary roots, Persia/Iran. Hence, Parsi as an ethnic group became a stateless nation because ethnic groups are also generally defined as a Stateless nation not represented by its own unique, coterminous state. The concept has historically been notorious, and led to an abundance of wars, conflicts, and mass bereavement through history. This vague status of nationality can be described as:

> **The primary characteristic of the cyborg is that of a creature who transcends, confuses, or destroys boundaries... as the production of the intermixing...cannot claim racial or cultural purity. Their neither/nor racial status, their unclear genealogical relationship to the history of oppression... and their ambiguous national identity. [Haraway 1990:190-233]**

This ambiguity of the national identity is the outcome of the migration. This continuous travel from one geographical locale to other causes the problems of adoption. This translation results into the transnationality, or transnationalism. Vertovec highlights on this as:

> **'Transnational' generally implies migration of people across the borders of one or more nations. It also refers to the deterritorialisation of population along with their material and non-material cultural commodities. [1999: xx]**

The terms 'transnational network', 'transnational communities' and 'diaspora' are often used interchangeably. Transnational networks form a precondition to the emergence of transnational communities and the process of this transformation is generally selected by 'transnationalism' as Basch says:

> **...process by which immigrants forge and sustain multi-stranded social relations that link together their societies of origin and settlement. We call these processes 'transnationalism' *especially* to emphasize that many immigrants today build social fields that cross geographic, cultural and political borders. [1994]**

These transnational communities mould themselves according to the culture of the host country as these communities behave like chameleon. In this way this process of transcending the boundaries of nations, cultures results into multiplicity, hybridity and complete loss of self identity. Time and again, Parsis experienced trauma of uprootedness, loss of homeland and nation, cultural erasure, experience of 'othering' and being 'other'. Their subaltern, minority status forms the mental setup and related behavioral pattern which is an important factor to identify them as an 'ethnic group' or 'ethnic identity'. It is necessary to see some of the important issues focusing experience as the source of 'identity formation'. Experiences are crucial factors in creating the identity in the context of space and time. Any experience can contradict itself in a particular space and time. Hurston talks about her identity as a "colored" person. Her colored identity comes alive when she is thrown against a white background:

> **It is that sharp, white background or "whiteness", then, that mandates in African American (US) or other sharply polarized, racially defined contexts, the tactical assertion of Blackness. [Hurston 1979:152-55]**

Real identities are located in the locations in which experience and perception occur and individual acts. Robert Gooding-Williams proposes that "being racially classified as black- person" [1998:23] is not enough to be hailed as black by others alone. For him "*one becomes a black person only if, (1), one begins to identity (to classify) oneself as black and, (2), one begins to make choices, to formulate plans, to express concerns, etc., in light of one's identification of oneself as black*" [1998:23] (italics original). This definition highlights the individuals' negotiation and their subjectivity. Black identity includes both a public self and lived experience, which means it is produced out of the modes of description made possible in a given culture. It is also dependent on any given individual's active self-understanding. Identity is used not only to talk about how one is identified but also how one identifies oneself with something. Yet it is one that recognizes the social categories of identity that often helpfully name the specific social locations from which individuals engages in. Identity categories are neither stable nor personally homogenous. Identity categories offer way of expression and scrutinize important relationship between lived experience and social location, as reflected in the poem:

Going by my passport / They call me Indian abroad
But in my own land / I don't know who I am.
In South Africa I'm colored/ In the U.S.A. I'm minus red
I still don't know who I am./ Beyond the Vindhyas I'm a southie
Or more often a Madrasi/In Madras I am a Malayee
Does anyone know who I am? / To the Muslims I am a Hindu
To the Hindus I'm a Brahmin / Or some other caste name
Do tell me who I am / If I am to be known by language
Or worse by religion and caste / Sometimes even by my race
Who can say who I am? [V.S. Kumar 1996:171-172]

Identity has various aspects. It is not totally cognizant or unaware, although, it seems to be utterly the one or the other. At some place, it is "referred to as a conscious sense of individual uniqueness,... to an unconscious striving for continuity of experience, and at yet other places as a sense of solidarity with a group's ideal" [Sudhir Kakar 1991:16]. Therefore, it is a cognitive or physical anxiety of identity which comes through experience. That's why, it is essential to see the 'Experience' as a source of identity formation. Moraga proposes people to "deal with the primary source of [their] own oppression... [and] to emotionally come to terms with what it feels like to be a victim" [Moraga 1983:30]. Central to Moraga's understanding of oppression is that it is a physical, material, psychological, and/or rhetorical illustration of the appealing relations of domination that comprise our communal world. Hence, the object of oppression is the body or "the flesh" [Moraga 1983: xviii-xix], where oppression is experienced and through a process of understanding, it is theorized, understood, and eventually tackled. The different social facts - such as gender, race, class, and sexuality- form an individual's social location. These social locations are pertinent for the experiences. So the space and time are very important factors regarding individual's identity formation.

Thus this part of the book has highlighted on various critical imperatives regarding the ethnicity, ethnic group, migration, culture, nation, trans-culturalism, trans-nationalism and subsequent problems of adoption and identity crisis, experience and social location as the source of identity formation.

III

Parsi Zoroastrian Ethos: The Sacred Fire

> His (Zarathustra's) beautiful religion was for everyone who was prepared to join the fight of good against evil and live by three guiding principles – good thought, good words, good deeds. The fire which stands at the centre of the religion was considered only as the symbol of Ahura Mazda, the light and the truth. --- Nargis Dalal

*

Zoroastrianism is a beleaguered faith. In the process of modernization and extreme individualism, this tiny community is on the verge of extinction. Though less in number, Parsis have made significant contribution in all walks of life. They are pioneers in diverse fields like banking, shipping, atomic physics or Art. It is a triumph of their will power, an ability to rise above the limitation of numbers and enrich the life of the nations they reside in. Parsis in India demonstrate an amazing capacity for assimilation whereas their identity remains unbroken. There is a sense of gradual change of identity within and outside the community. To the majority of Indians, they are known for their philanthropy or for their comic appearance in some Bollywood films with their peculiar costumes or odd Hindi pronunciation. They are considered as the crazy community of Bawaji's. For many others, they are people of plenty, engrossed in the luxury and extreme individualism. Such isolation of India's Parsi Zoroastrians has resulted in their cocooned existence. Nani Palkhiwala writes about his community with pride:

> **History affords no parallel to the role of Parsis in India. There is no record of any other community so infinitesimally small as Parsis, playing such a significant role in the life of a country so large. [1994:317]**

Thus, it would be interesting to unveil the façade of this close and mysterious community.

It is believed that the Parsis of India are the only surviving Zoroastrians of the Common Era. The earliest Zoroastrians were just Indo-Iranians who embraced the ideas of Zarathustra. The conventional Indo-Iranian's religion was polytheistic. Zoroaster wanted its revision and reform, claiming that there is one supreme deity, Ahura Mazda, whose nature and will required modification in men's thought, worship, and manner of life. Once instigated, the renovation made its way slowly across Iran to become finally, as the good Mazdayasnian religion, the official faith of the late Achaemenid kings. The dominant Muslim invasion in the seventh century was not instantaneously disastrous for the followers of Zoroaster but for the centuries their position was of the second-class subject, occasionally tolerated, frequently persecuted, and almost all the time harassed by Muslims seeking their conversion. A few thousands endured by gathering together in far-flung areas where weather was cruel and life uneasy. But they espoused emigration as a more beneficial strategy to survive. Thousands of Parsis found shelter in Gujarat. They flourished there and then in increasing numbers moved to Bombay (now Mumbai). In Bombay, they found favor with the English administration. They were called Parsis - after the region which has provided an alternate name for Iran itself. Today, their descendants represent the great majority of the Zoroastrian fold. They have established themselves during the 20th century as a self-conscious community not only in several other Indian cities but also elsewhere in Asia, in Africa, and in almost every country of the English-speaking world.

Looking back in history of their migration to India, it is necessary to fix the point of time and place of their aggreavated life condition. It can be the Arab invasion on Iran. It was completely against the teachings of Prophet and

Koran. In Koran, there are codes of conduct for every person who believes in Islam. Entering into anybody's house without permission is prohibited:

> **Fa- illam tajidu fi-ha ahadan falatad quluhaa hattaa yujana lakum wa-in qeela lakumu ji- farji-u huwa ajka lakum, wallaahu bima tahmaluna allem.**
> **[Koran: Chapter 10: Sura 9 "Al Tauba", Verse 28]**

Translated it reads:

> **Seek permission before entering, anybody's house, if not given permission return back. It is for your own goodness. Surely, whatever you do, God knows everything.**

It indicates that Arabs didn't follow teachings of the Koran. They misunderstood teachings of the Prophet. Their behavior was contradictory to the verses in Koran.

> Chapter 10, Sura 9 "Al Tauba" Verse 5 says:
> **Fa-ijan Salaqal Ashhurul Hurumoo Faqtulul**
> **Mushrikina haisu wajattumuhom waqujuhom**
> **wahsuruhom waqudu lahum kulla marsadin**
> **fa-in taabu wa-aqaqmus salaata wa-atuj zakaata**
> **fa-qallu sabilahom innal-laaha gafurrur rahim.**

Translated it reads:

> **If non-believers believe in the oneness of God and start paying Zakkat, you should hail them.**
> **Otherwise, it is your duty to show them the right way.**

Zoroastrian do believe in oneness of God i.e. Ahura Mazda. They do believe in Charity. They help people who are in need of something. Zoroastrian never worshipped any idol. They profess faith in God. But still Arab attacked Iran which was cruel and brutal and against God's wish. As Koran says:

> **Ya ayyuhal lajina aamanu qaatilul lajina yalunakum minal kuffaari wal yajidu fikum ghilija waatamu annal laaha maa-al muttaqun.**
>
> **[Chapter 10: Sura 9 "Al Tauba": Verse 123]**

Translated it reads:

> **O believers! fight with the disbeliever. Remember, God is with those people who profess faith. (Try to show them the right way since they are ignorant)**

In Iran, Arabs didn't own anything. But they invaded Iran. It was their paradoxical behavior. As Koran says:

> **Laisa alaikum junaahun antad qulu buyutan gairaa maskunatin fiha mata-ul lakum, wallaahu yaahlamu maatubaduna wama taktumoon.**
>
> **[Chapter 10: Sura 9 "Al Tauba", Verse 29]**

Translated it reads:

> **You are allowed to enter any house if it contains your thing. Surely, God knows what you pretend and what you hide.**

Overall, Arab invasion was against Islam and contradictory to Prophet's teachings. But they destroyed Iran. Arab leaders set fire to every written document that they could reach. They banned Iranians from speaking in Farsi because they wanted to eliminate Iranian culture and make them subordinate to Arab language and finally to Arab culture. Commander Saad Ibn-e-Abi Vaghas wrote to Calipha Omar concerning the books at Ctesiphon. Omar wrote back:

> **If the books contradict the Koran, they are blasphemous, on the other hand, if they are in agreement, they are not needed.**
>
> **[Dr. Kevala 2004:01]**

All books were thrown into the Euphrate. Luckily, before Iranian language could gradually disappear, *Firdosi*, the great Iranian poet of all times, caused its endurance by his extraordinary literary work of *Shahnameh*. Arab leader imposed Islam forcefully on Iranians. In this regard, they committed genocide of Zoroastrians. This persecution was continued until Reza Shah Pahlavi, the Great, came to power and ended such a cruelty to Zoroastrians and other religious minorities. After the Arabs overran the whole of Iran, a small group of Zoroastrians left country and came to India seeking refuge. They landed at Sanjan, a place in Gujarat around 900 CE and have lived in India ever since. At Sanjan, King Jadav Rana gave them refuge. At first the king was hesitant giving shelter to the refugees from Persia. The King sent Zoroastrian refugees a messenger with a glass of milk, symptomatic of homogenous mixture that should not be tampered with. In reply, the Parsis dropped a lump of sugar in the milk, saying that they would merge in easily and make the culture sweeter. Wisdom and flexibility of Dustoor impressed the King. They were granted refuge in India because Parsis neither proselytized nor entered into politics. Parsis were given shelter on following conditions:

1. The high priest of the Zoroastrian would have to explain their religious belief to the king.
2. To adapt the Gujarati language.
3. The women would wear the sari.
4. Men should handover their weapons.
5. Venerate the cow.
6. The marriage ceremonies shall be performed at night only. No marriage with local people.

Parsis adapted Gujarati language loyally, forgetting their conventional language. In all modern day census reports, Parsis specify Gujarati as their mother tongue. But they accepted it maintaining their distinctiveness: "Though, the Gujarati spoken by Parsis is an idiosyncratic variant of the language. This is highly typical of the Parsi tendency to adapt but without surrender of their distinctiveness" [New Society, *Parsis: The Jews of India*: 22/01/1988]. Parsi women adopted Sari as the dress of the community. This sartorial norm has been devotedly followed. Parsis have a high regard for cow and due to this practice, Parsis still do not eat beef, though there are no religious prohibition against eating the beef. Parsis performed their ceremonies in the night. This condition was imposed to distract the local populace from the threat of conversion. Parsis do not allow outsiders in their *Fire Temples*, which is a further guarantee that they will not attempt any conversions to their religion. They do not allow insular marriage. The wedding ceremony is carried out even today after sunset, and at least a part of ceremony is reiterated in Sanskrit. Fidelity to the ruler of the day was a strong trait among the Parsis. They could safeguard their faith due to the liberal attitude of the Hindus. They could sustain their identity because Hindu caste system banned insular-marriage.

The Dastoor on behalf of the whole Parsi community promised to the King Jadav Rana in following words: "Hame hinustan rayr bashim."

Translated it reads: "We shall be the friends of all India."

[Dipanjali, June-December, 1996:11]

While accepting these conditions, the high priest was asked to reply by reciting 16 Sanskrit '*slokas*' or stanzas pledging loyalty to Hindu King. These conditions have great impact on the Parsi psyche ensuing ethnic anxieties even today, after 1300 years of their arrival in India. In this regard, it is also necessary to see the tenets of Zoroastrian faith.

Zarathustra developed his beliefs from the old Polytheism of Iran. The ultimate innovation he made in religious deliberation was to recognize Ahura Mazda, the Lord of Wisdom. Essentially, Zarathustra's religion was the product of conscious rebellion against the pre-existing polytheistic religion. The principal characteristics of the religion taught by Zarathustra are: its emphasis on ethics, its positive approach towards life, optimism about the future of the world, its stress on free choice and its catholicity. It is described as:

> **O Mazda, You placed life in the physical body and gave mankind the power to act, speak and guide. You wished that everyone should choose his or her own faith and path freely.**
>
> **[Yasna 31, verse 11,**
> **translated from the Avestan language.]**

It signifies that once human beings are given freedom, they can make right choice as they would face the consequences of that choice. Zarathustra believed that the universe is bound by the relationship on cause and effects.

His teachings are based on three basic principles: *Good Thoughts/ Reflection* (*Humata*), *Good Word* (*Hukta*) and *Good Deed* (*Huvarshta/Manashi*). He recognized that all the motives of human beings are based on action and reaction. It is highlighted as:

> **I recognize Thee as the First at the birth of life;**
> **for Thou hast ordained that all acts and all words**
> **Shall bear fruit-evil to evil and good blessings to the good. [Yasna 43.5]**

Zarathustra's God is benign. He initiates righteousness, compassion, and honesty. Zoroastrians should help each other to the transmission of science and education. Zoroastrianism becomes the messenger of knowledge and enlightenment. He pointed out a divine spark in every human being so as to comprehend its potential to reach the state of perfection.

Every religion focuses on essential features. It becomes imperative to highlight such key aspects of Zoroastrian belief as these characteristics underscore the basis of daily human life of a Zoroastrian.

Zoroaster preached the eternal and universal values and belief that transcends human life into divine one. He focused on Truth, *Charity, Purity, Dignity of Labor* and *hard work, Asha.* Zoroaster taught that one should be tolerant in thinking and should respect all that is good, true and beautiful. ***Truth*** is of prime importance in Zoroastrianism. The prayer Ashem *Vohu* focuses on Truth. It suggests that truth itself is happiness. Hence, Parsi-Zoroastrians in India and Iran are revered for their honesty. Herodotus has referred to "truthfulness" [Book One: Section 136] as a vital element of Zoroastrian existence.

Zoroaster also stressed to evaluate the truth and realiability of practical implication of his teachings in daily life. If people found it useless and impractical, they can abandon it. It exemplifies the flexibility and freedom Zoroastrianism provides to its followers. In the prayer *Yatha Ahu Vairya* the importance of ***Charity*** is highlighted. Charity is an integral and indivisible part of Zoroastrian life. Parsi and Charity have become synonym in India. Zoroastrian religion has always approved communal assistance. Consequently, it was proudly observed that there was no poverty in Parsis. ***Purity and cleanliness*** are virtues to be adhered and implemented in human life. It implies both body and spirit. It is considered as religion in Zoroastrianism. Purity of water, land, air, and fire is fundamental principal of Zoroastrianism. Herodotus has talked about the cleanliness of running water in section 138 of his first book in the ancient Iran. **Dignity of Labor** and **hard work** are living principles in Zoroastrianism. It is the duty of a good Zoroastrian to free people from the oppression and exploitation of others. A good Zoroastrian respects the labor and hard work of others as well as of his own. It is evident in the history of Parsi Zoroastrians that they progressed and attained a reputation for their entrepreunership and business all over the world.

It is crime to sacrifice animals in the name of religion. Idolatry, litholatry, and human made places of worship are rebuked in Zoroastrianism. It is believed that God dwells in the soul and heart of the human being. Equality between man and woman is recurring virtue in Zoroastrian Gathas.

Human beings could not survive if they are optimistic about their present and future. They can overcome their present cathartic conditions with the hopes of bright future. ***Hope or Asha*** is life and spriti of Zoroastrianism. Human life thrives on the wings of hope. **Asha Vahishta** symbolizes the divine experience intended in the divine design of things.

The natural elements of ***Fire***, ***Water*** and ***Earth*** have great significance in Zoroastrianism. **Fire** has multifarious meanings as the fire of motivation, love, justice, emotional empathy, commitment and life giving force in all forms of Ahura Mazda's creations. Fire symbolizes Asha. Fire can devour as well as change every thing it touches. Being purefying element, Zoroastrians started worshipping *Ahura Mazda* through fire. This has earned them the fame as *Fire Worshippers.* But the Persian poet Firdausi highlights the reality while speaking of Zoroastrians in his famous epic, the *Shahnama*:

> **Maa gui ke atash parastan budand. Parastandeh-e-pak yazdan budand.**

Translated it reads:

> **Do not call them fire worshipers. For they are worshippers of Ahura Mazda through fire. [Muncherji 2001:40]**

Fire, Earth and Water are revered with great religious importance. Efforts are taken to maintain their purity. Because of it, Zoroastrians do not cremate, bury or drown their dead.

Gathas revealed Zoroaster's *Weltanschauung* (World view). According to Prophet Zarathustra the whole universe is dominated by two primal forces, **Good & Evil.** There is perpetual struggle between these two. Mankind has to choose between them. Ahura Mazda (*Ormuzd*) the *Lord of Light, Wisdom of life represents Goodness and* righteousness. It brings human beings on the path of brightness. On the other hand, Evil is represented by *Angra Mainyu* (*Ahirman*). It is the *Hostile Spirit.* It misleads humanbeings on the path of darkness.

Avesta is the collection of the existing scriptures advocated by Zarathustra as well as the religious writings of his followers. Avesta is also the name of the language spoken in Iran. It comprises of two parts, the older Avesta and the later Avesta. The later Avesta is also known as Khordeh Avesta. Gathas or Divine songs are the most important part of these scriptures. It is in a dialogue form, dialogue between the prophet and God. They are credited to Zarathustra himself.

The Avesta is written in a number of languages. The Gathas were written in a Pre-Avestan language. Later scriptures were written in the Avesta language and in the Pahlavi and Pazand dialects. Today only a portion of the original scriptures is available. It was burned during Alexander's destruction of Persopolis.

There is great controversy over the use of Avestan language in prayer recitals. Reformers argue that they should be recited in the language of the believer or in English to understand the real meanings of the prayers. On the other hand, orthodox wants to continue the old practice.

Ancient Aryans believed that Ahura Mazda created the perfect world. There was no evil in the world created by Ahura Mazda. There was no disease, illness as well as hunger and thirst. But the evil forces of Ahriman attacked the world and disease, illness and old age. Thus death came into existence.

Fravahar is the symbol of Zoroastrians. *Fravahar* symbolizes the spirit of human being that continues before their birth and after their death. It is portrayed in human form. It represents two aspects of human existence Good & Evil. It highlights the eternity of the spirit. It hints at the values such as "struggle to thrive" and "loyalty and faithfulness" [Dr. Behram Varza 2004:06]

It implies Zarathustra's philosophy of presence of Good and Evil in every human being. It is necessary to encourage the positive force (Sepanta Minu) and to overcome negative force (Ankareh Minu). This spiritual struggle between goodness and evil helps human beings to keep away the evil. Naturally, it results in prosperity in all walks of life. Thus, Zoroastrianism stresses the freedom of choice and its consequences.

Parsis were cut off from their ancestral fellow citizens due to migration to India. They preserved their traditional manners and morals partly because these provided their self-identity as a community and strengthened the desires to be helpful. It was essential for endurance. It was partly because a certain amount of cultural separation was helpful in reassuring native Indians that they had come neither to conquer by force nor to dominate by influence. Simultaneously, they may well have been at pains to stress similarities between customs and by adaptation maintaining a low profile. They preserved their ethnic distinctiveness. Their integrity and enterprise won them a respect in Indian society. It was this kind of successful adjustment that helped them to flourish in colonial India. Among India's ethnic groups, Parsi-Zoroastrain is the only ethnic group without any caste system. Free from caste taboos, they made themselves useful to Europeans doing business in colonial India. Traditional virtues of the Parsis precisely led them to their employment. Honesty, business, good sense and sincerity towards India managed them to survive and propser modestly. They acquired fluency in English to become their employer's peers. Accepting every opportunity, they were soon trusted with responsibilities. It offered those positions in which they could exercise power and earn their own shares of profit alongside the British. Parsis were one step away from entrepreneurship. During the nineteenth century, they took that step and changed the history of India. The history of India could not be written without account of the Parsis's phenomenal enterprise in the fields of business, manufacturing, building, construction, education, medicine, law, government and social welfare.

Personal ethics is also very important to Parsis. Smoking is a taboo for most Parsis because they believe that the smoke, mixed with the poisonous carbon dioxide of exhaled breath, pollutes fire. Contradictory to this, it is observed that relations with a cross-section of several communities provided Zoroastrians sufficient opportunity to indulge in smoing. Priests and lay members of governing *anjumans* as well as laity are observed smoking. Wearing *Sudreh* and *Kusti* at Navjote denotes conscious pronouncement of Parsi-Zorastrian identity. In spite of everything, it is more important what a person desires to be and strives to do in his life.

Intoxication is considered as an act of disloyalty. It is believed that liquor is an enemy to clear thinking and right aspiration. It shows loose moral character. On the other hand, it is not considered as a moral imperative willingly with self-discipline or with legal prohibition. Whereas moderate drinking is enjoyed at home or at community get together.

The sexual ethics of Zoroastrians have been shaped in colossal measure by their constant disapproval of asceticism and the threats to their endurance posed by historical obligation. Marriage is a holy responsibility and parenthood is through as an ideal state in The Avesta. To make priesthood as a hereditary profession, Priests are allowed to marry. Both polygamy and concubine were allowed from earliest times. But Zoroastrian should avoid it to beget a healthy and surviving progeny. By the 17th century "polygamy by males was.... [still] prevalent" and "child marriage quite common." [Bulsara 1938:17]. There are many reasons of late marriages in Parsi community. The spread of poverty is one of the reasons of late marriages. Marriage was delayed to take pleasure in the better economic safety. New generation Parsis preferred to marry outside the community. It resulted into the disappointment of the orthodox who believed in the genetic superiority of Parsis. Pillo Nanavutty said that "intermarriages are becoming the norm rather than exception." [1977:174]

Wadia claimed that the ancestors of Parsis in India "freely mingled by marriage...with the people of the land," [Wadia P.A. 1949:140] and they "managed to survive" [Ibid, 140] because of it. He added if they could expect now to survive by "a policy of rigid exclusivism and in-breeding, by becoming a caste when the whole idea of caste was being discarded by all their neighbors." [Ibid, 140]

In Zoroastrianism, the main reason for the protection of endogamy is identity, both ethnic and religious, which is inherited from father. Therefore, Parsis have thought the children of non-Zoroastrian fathers as ineligible for Navjote or inclusion in the community. Simultanesouly, the marriage of a Zoroastrian male to a non-Zoroastrian is not acceptable. It is believed that children receive their religious instruction from their mother in the home. It is observed that mother's religious commitment is habitually stronger and her practice of religion is more faithful. Consequently, the inheritance of identity from the father is likely to be drawn to the mother's faith. So it is clear that the Zoroastrian community stands to lose potential members whenever insular marriage occurs. Dabu has firmly stated that "preservation of their blood from getting mixed with that of other races is a necessity" [1959:16]. Mixed married people are "an asset to the community" as "outcastes" [Paymaster 1975:30]. The Parsis in India had decided to maintain friendly relationship with native population. They cause no threat to the peace by interfering with basic social structures suh as family and religions of native people. They consciously followed it for the sake of settlement after seeking refuge in India. Therefore, from the time of arrival of their first ancestor in India, Parsis gradually maintained their ethnic purity and the reliability of their religion by endogamy and an anti-conversion policy.

It is aptly reflected as:

> **The mission of Zoroaster was to rid the Mazdayasni religion of the evil of devayasni and restore it to its pristine purity. [Karkhanavala, 1971: 94-95]**

Thus, Zoroastrianism is basically a part of "the process of evolution within the Mazdayasni religion… Because Zoroaster did not convert, conversion of non-Mazdayasnan[s] is forbidden in the religion. That [moreover] is why marriage of Mazdayasni with a non- Mazdayasni is tabooed and is considered a grave sin..." [Karkhanavala 1971:94-95]

But modern day Parsis have some other reasons to defy the conversion. Conversion as an open-door policy would allow "a steady stream of people" to choose the faith "not out of love, conviction or understanding, but merely to take advantage of ... [Parsi] funds or charities." [Dhalla H.B 1971:138] Dr. Shernaz Cama, points out:

> **Conversion is controversial. In Zoroastrianism all are welcome- all can enter the most ancient shrines at Yazd/ Kerman in Iran. In India a promise was given (condition made to Jadhav Rana) that no proselytizing will occur- hence the ban on conversion or entry into temple. It has become a very heated ethnic debate not religious… Today it has become a point of rigidity between orthodox**

and liberals. Even most of the Parsis cannot accept the Zoroaster openly welcomed *all* to join the faith. [1997:12]

Nanavutty says that an anti-conversion policy is directly contradicts the teaching of Zarathustra. It is pointed out as:

...every Nyaesh and every Yasht in the *Khordeh Avesta*, the Book of Daily Prayers, ends with... 'May the knowledge, extent and fame of the commandments of the excellent religion of Mazda ever increase in the world, over all its seven regions. So may it be. I must attain this goal; I must attain this goal; I must attain this goal.' [1977:174-175]

Mr. Keki J. Gandhi, Secretary of the Federation of Parsi Zoroastrian Anjumans of India and editor of the Fed Newsletter, wrote in the April 1995 issue on the major consequence arising from inter-faith marriages. He raised an important question: "Does a Parsi Zoroastrian (male or female) lose the rights of a Parsi Zoroastrian merely because of marriage to a person belonging to another faith?" [1995:1]. He continued his questions regarding the debate whether a Parsi Zoroastrian ceases to be either a Parsi or a Zoroastrian because of interfaith marriage. He highlighted on the explanation of the two terms, **Parsi** and **Zoroastrianism.** Both these terms were defined in the Bombay High Court judgment delivered by Honorable Justice Daver and Honorable Justice Beaman in Suit 689 of 1906. The word Zoroastrian indicates the religion of the person whereas the word Parsi signifies his nationality or community.

Later in the judgment, Justice Daver focused on that a Parsi born is a Parsi. It is irrelevant what other religion he or she afterward espouses and acknowledges. The orthodox section of the community denied to accept such legal points and have withdrawn behind the protection of the sentiment that Ahura Mazda would look after them in future too as He has done before. The division between the orthodox and the reformists has resulted into a generation gap in attitudes to marriage and life. Ava Khullar in her article in the Parsiana of November 1994 highlights this change as:

From the mid 60s what was apparent was that in their individual capacities, Parsis were adapting to a changing socio-economic situation for their economic and emotional

> **satisfaction by seeking educational and occupational opportunities abroad, marrying outside the community when suitable partners could not be found etc. [Parsiana: Nov.1994:26]**

Lovji Cama highlights that the offspring of "interfaith marriages have either the religion of the other faith or have no religion at all" [Parsiana: Nov.1994:42]. But this unwillingness to change with time is harmful to this tiny community. Nargis Dalal condemns this Parsi tendency of genetical purity:

> **To claim that after nearly 1,200 years in India, Parsis are ethnically pure is absurd... Only small groups escaped to India after the conquest of Persia by Islam and the forced Islamization of the people. Through the centuries Parsis have intermarried with the natives of India with or without the approval of the priests. Therefore, the concept of ethnic purity is a myth. [Times of India: 24/01/1995]**

Farrukh Dhondy in **Bombay Duck** bitterly criticizes the attitude of racial purity:

> **There is evidence to show that the first settlers had no woman with them and must have inter-married with the natives, the Hindus, so the first claim of the Parsees to be racially pure is suspect. [1991:190-91]**

Such voices clearly reflect the modern Parsi psyche that distrusts the original story of racial purity, an excuse to cancel out the inter-religious marriages. Ava Khullar analyzed that the highly westernized and freedom seeking young generations gave more importance to their individual progress. They did not mind whether community cease to exist.

According to a notification of the trustees of Parsi Punchayet that declared their policies regarding this issue:

> **We, the undersigned trustees of funds and properties of the Parsi Punchyet, do hereby notify for the information**

> **of the public that we are advised by the learned counsel that the funds and religious properties under our charge- such as Towers of Silence, dharamshalas, masakhanas, fire-temples, etc. are held by us for the benefit of those only, who are Parsis by birth and at the same time Zoroastrians by religion. Such only are entitled to the benefit of the funds and properties. The benefit of the funds and above said properties, in our charge, cannot be given to those who are not Parsi Zoroastrian as described above. [February 9, 1905]**

It is pathetic that with the madness of racial purity, learned people, anjumans, punchayets are not ready to see the possibility of extinction of their ancient religion and culture. This is what Pangborn expresses rightly:

> **In any case, the concern of the traditionalists is that the name could be saved but the substance of their religion lost. [Pangborn 1982:146]**

These are the controversies regarding the conversion, inter-faith marriage depending on social, financial and religious grounds. Other issues leading to controversies are dokhma, recitation of prayers in its original language as composed by the prophet.

Zoroastrian traditionalists have acknowledged the futility in ancient rituals and rites. But with certain rituals like prayers are firmly followed in traditional pattern. The major orthodox group insists on the Avestan prayers and recitation in the original language. As Jal Rustamji Vimadalal expresses it:

> **These Manthras are a protection ... from superphysical evil influence... also from any physical evil or misfortune or difficulty in this mundane world... they forget the power of sound, they forget that these prayers were composed not by ordinary men... but by seers and sages to whose vision the effect of these Manthras was open... any attempt to substitute Gujarati must be nipped in the bud... it would toll the knell of our age-long connection with our ancient**

> **traditions, our glories and our ancestors, our religious rites, ceremonies and prayers. [1971: 6-8]**

According to Dabu, Parsis must use the words of the prophet exactly because "...these are considered to be sacred and powerful incantations, used by Magi, who knew the art of composing potent spells." [1959:174]

The problem of disposing the dead is also very serious. Zoroastrian scholar, Dr. Shernaz Cama in her letter to the editor informs:

> **In Iran too burial is common as in Delhi etc. Theologically and environmentally the *Dokhma* was the best system. First, because it was the last good deed performed even your very flesh fed birds of carrion. Second, there is no pollution of earth and it does not involve using up of valuable good earth for burial - so environmentally sound. Today, logic has lost out in Iran. Logically burial is done because of lack of carrion birds in cities and towns. Here it has become an ego issue. [1997:9-10]**

Tremendous decline in the numbers of vultures is another blow to Zoroastrianism. Lack of these birds has bereft the final rites. In India and Pakistan vultures are dying due to their eating habits of dead animals. These birds are mainly facing death because of kidney problem. *Maharashtra Times* reports that in "India three species of these birds have declined by 90%" [23 April, 2005]. With the decline in the number of vultures, Bombay Parsi panchyet has taken a scientific step by installing giant solar reflectors to hasten the process of decomposition of corpses.

Under Muslim rule, Zoroastrians became a disadvantaged minority. In India they are still a minority. This minority status was shaped by their sieged mentality. Under such conditions, energies are exhausted in struggling only to survive, and no investment in the task of re-shaping the world. But with the first chance under the British rule they flourished economically. It was resulted in great visibility of many institutions built and funded by Parsi philanthropists. There are schools, colleges, and institutions for students at all educational levels, hospitals both general and specialized, housing colonies for co-religionists who might otherwise not find decent homes and amenties available for social gatherings or festivals, bunglis and dokhmas for the dead.

But in post-colonial period their status was degraded under independent India's Hindu majority. The economic fitness of the Parsis had been in decline well before it was noticed that the community was dwindling. K.D. Umrigar summarized many Parsi grievances about their financial decline. He observed that flourished business, industries of previous century, were "getting smaller year after year" [1971:35]. Rise of unemployment despite of the spirit of entrepreneurship is disturbing the community. Lack of specialized variety pointed to their economice decline. It gave rise to middle class white-collar workers. Wadia P.A. wrote about increasing poverty in Parsi community:

> **...poverty is not only an economic phenomenon but has become a general social phenomenon, affecting a substantial majority of families within the community. [1949:9]**

Causes for financial decline are still being searched after many years. Minchoer concluded:

> **The rich of yester years became the upper-middle class traders of today; the upper-middle class became the middle-class fixed income earners; and the lower-middle class became the new poor of the community. [Minocher H.H.B 1978: xii]**

Housing conditions were another facet of the emerging poverty among Parsis in India. It caused slow damage in the quality of life. At the turn of the century, first housing colonies were built with the help of community funds for the poor Parsis. In present times, those colonies have become slums. New construction has never kept up with the requirement of standards. Due to price hike and scarcity of housing places, it became impossible for single persons and families to own their own housing complexes. It resulted into over-crowding, over-burdened facilities, and deterioration as a consequence of lack of proper maintenance. These colonies became "a breeding ground of organized beggary and hooliganism" [Wadia P.A. 1949:33] for the children. Parsi funds have not published audited accounts or annual reports of their financial expenditure. In present times, a Parsi applicant can go from one Parsi trust to another for relief or educational assistance. In this process, he may get a little or too much from either. These circumstances have created the new class of the "professional applicant" and "professional beggars" [Parsiana, Welfare, Feb.2004]. The Parsiana report highlights it as:

> **This indiscriminate, unscientific, beggar-producing-charity is the worst. It is obviously of the greatest importance that the children of those receiving charity should not grow up in turn into the 'application complex'. [Parsiana, Welfare, Feb.2004]**

Thus, one can see the downgraded conditions of Parsis in India. The community once well-known for prosperity and charity is trapped into financial crisis and corruption.

Parsis were instigated into political passivism as the result of the centuries-long segregation of Zoroastrians from the political system. Parsi immigrants in India found it viable stance for survival. They were given status of unwanted refugees depending on the kindness of Indian rulers for the survival. With emergence of British rule in subcontinent, Parsis were introduced to some connection with political system. They were classified with the British. The magnificence and alliance with British set them apart from most Indians. It was crucial time in history when Indians passionately desired for independence. National Independence in 1947 changed the Indian scenario. It exchanged the roles of ruler and to be ruled. It gave Hindus (in case of India) and Muslims (in case of Pakistan) first opportunity in centuries to exchange the role of servant for that of master to dominate the political arena. Parsis were thrusted on the margins of new socio-political order. It reinforced the minority status and apolitical consciousness on Parsis. But the preservation of elite consciousness helped Parsis to "forget the actual dangers to the community's future" [Kulke 1974:268].

There is no Zoroastrian theory of war or of the rights of the individuals versus the rights of the state. There is lack of proper description of the nature of relationships like religious institution and state. In Iran, political weakness was the cost readily paid for the peace and safety under the ruling Arab rulers as a result of being a religious minority maintaining a low profile. Kulke has concluded that the necessary substance of the Zoroastrian's political belief has been "strict loyalty to the ruling authority in the interest of survival." [Kulke 1974:133-134].

After the Arab assault, the anxieties of complete destruction of the Zoroastrian religion were at last reduced by seeking refuge in India. In India they enjoyed toleration and equal status with native ethnic groups. Freedom provided the favorable climate for the achievement. Their ambition was given proper expression. Consequently, the prospering Parsi community shook off the siege mentality. Thus, subjugation had encouraged to attain glory in its capacity to survive in hardships and rise again. With this attitude, they turned blind eye towards the problems within the community. This issue was voiced aptly by a Pakistani Parsi in the 1970s:

> **...so blinded ourselves with our self-woven cocoon of past glory, that we are unable to make a rational judgment on our own degeneration... because we... survived Alexander and the Arabs, we [think we] shall survive into the distant future by the Grace of Ahura Mazda, even if we sit with folded arms, and do nothing... [Minocher H.B.H. 1978: x]**

As a result of negligence towards the demographic decline and internal controversies, Parsis are suffering from the sheer survival problem. Nani A. Palkhiwala observes:

> **A hundred years ago the fertility rate among Parsis was the highest in India. The highest figure of the Parsi population in India was the 1, 14,890 recorded in the Census of 1941. But over the last fifty years the number has been dwindling. Today the total number of Parsis throughout the world is estimated to be a little over 1, 00,000. Of this number about 70,000 live in India, 18,000 in Iran, a little over 3,000 in Pakistan, and another 15,000 are scattered over Europe, America, Africa and the Far East. [1994:317]**

The Register General and census commissioner of India J.K. Banthia gave the warning of a significant demographic decline at both the PARZOR meet Bombay in October and the Federation of Parsi Zoroastrian Anjumans of India (FPZAI): "The time may come when the birth of a Parsi child will be a cause for national celebration." [Parsiana, Feb. 2004]. Zoroastrians suffer from the severe population decline. The demography of Zoroastrians all over the world was increased as late as upto 1941. But it was blocked:

> **Twenty years later, their number had diminished by nearly 14%, and after another ten years, by 9% leaving a total of 91,266. [Marshall R.R. 1977:28]**

There are various reasons for decline in Parsi demography over the years and difference in decline is vast as given in the report: "The principal causes of death over the last half of the decade were accidents, cancer, cardiac failure, haemorrhage, influenza-pneumonia, old age, senile debility, and uremia" [Report 1970:21-23]. From 1940-1990 the Parsi/Irani population in India has declined from a peak of 1,14,890 in 1940 to 76,382 in 1990, a loss of around 38,500. The 2001 figures will be less than 70,000 [Parsiana, Feb. 2004]. As per the 2001 census, the total Parsi-Zoroastrian population in India was 69,601, with around 45,000 residing in Mumbai. [Hindustan Times Mumbai, February 21, 2013]

Health issues and genetical problems in Parsi community are of grave concerns. Desai mentioned the diseases among Parsi causing increased death rate. His focus was on types of life-shortening illnesses tending to be hereditary or syndromes related to the living surroundings in terrible housing. Thus, tuberculosis, respiratory diseases, diabetes, mental illness, and retardation were special foci for his concern. The next real prospect of their extinction is always in their consciousness, intensifying the poignancy and urgency of each individual concern.

In spite of being a tiny ethnic minority community, Parsis have contributed a large amount to the growth of India. Though they are one of the fast retreating communities of the world, yet they face their marginalization with the ability to laugh at cruel complexities of life. The Parsi writers are also very sensitive to the various anxieties experienced by their community. Their works endorse the anxieties and aspirations, fears and disillusionment of their community, its scrutiny of human position in a family, in a country, and in the Indian-sub-continent.

Thus, this book aims at investigating the ethnic anxieties in the fictional worlds of Bapsi Sidhwa and Rohinton Mistry. Both writers belong to countries which were one before Partition. Being Parsis, a minority in both countries, they suffer ethnic anxieties. The Parsi-Zoroastrian is a Ethno-religious/Minority.

Dharan has aptly described the portrayal of this tiny community by Parsi writers regarding various problems their community suffers at present. He says:

> **Obviously then, their literature is characterized by both ethnocentric and minority discourse features. It depicts all the concerns of the modern-day Parsis. Being the minuscule minority in India, the Parsis do experience ethnic anxieties. They feel insecure, experience identity crisis and feel threatened by possible submersion in the dominant Hindu culture... The factors which contribute to... ethnic atrophy are the Parsis's single-minded pursuit of prosperity, extreme individualism, craze for urbanization, late marriages, low birth rate, the rather high incidence of cancer, Alzheimers disease, osteoporosis, mental illness, and low fertility rate. [Dharan 2001:100-101]**

In this way both the writers have portrayed various anxieties of their community facing on the marginal existence. Bapsi Sidhwa portrays the undivided India in her two novels- **The Crow Eaters** and **Ice Candy Man**. Her depiction of Western part of India (now independent Pakistan) is the picturization of composite cultures which was undivided India and the vital role played by her community as 'mode of social change' [Kulke 1978]. Though, both independent nations have different political ideologies and religious majorities, Parsi community of Mistry and Sidhwa is always categorized as a minority. In Mistry's fictional world, Muslims are aligned with Parsis as a minority. These writers have dealt with different periods, and locales but the central focus of their discourse is their minuscule community and various 'ethnic anxieties' it suffers from in the course of changing time. Parsi community suffers from the problems of ethnic anxieties due to marginalization, subaltern position, and cultural hybridity. It faces the troubles of decline in membership, some of the religious rigidities like – ban of conversion, inter-faith marriages, problems regarding their final rites as there is decline in the populations of vultures, and unavailability of Tower of Silence in the various parts of both these countries. It has raised the debates for the reformations in the community. These facets of Parsi ethnicity are studied in this book. It examines the way these writers have dealt with these issues and priorities they attempted to give as a member of minority community in their nations. Though both the writers are not living in their countries, their engagement with the country is that of diasporic writers. It is necessary to admit that one can't deny the authenticity of their experiences and expressions of realities their community faces in their fictional world. In such way their community has emerged as the protagonist who, against all odds, is desperately trying to survive in the coming millennium. A.K. Singh points out, "Their works exhibit consciousness of their community in such a way that the community emerges as a protagonist from their works though on the surface these works deal with their human protagonists" [1997:66]. The quick possibility of their annihilation gives the sense that the works of all these Parsi writers would serve the need of future generation. They can understand this great religious heritage through their fictional works. Rohinton Mistry said in an interview that his fiction will "preserve a record of how they lived to some extent," [Lakhani: 25] when the Parsis will disappear from the earth. It is a genuine remark Mistry has made as all the Parsi writers are portraying their community. Writers like Perin Bharucha, Nargis Dalal, Boman Desai, Ardashir Vakil, Farrukh Dhondy, Dina Mehta, Firdaus Kanga, Sohrab Homi Fracis, Thrity Umrigar, and Meher Pestonji who are constantly portraying the predicament of their minuscule community.

Recent novels by Parsi writers stress on the Parsi identity as a separate ethno-religious minority in India. **Perin Bhraucha's** *The Fire Worshippers (1968)* highlights the dilemma of insular marriage. Pestonji objects to such marriage as it would bring the disintegration of the community. **Nargis Dalal's** '*The Sisters*' exemplifies the 'Parsi paradox' to explore attitudes to marriage and social relationship. **Bapsi Sidhwa's** *The Crow Eaters (1978)* opened all the doors and all the windows of Parsi world to the readers. She has created an array of delightful, idiosyncratic Parsis. Parsi death rites, insular-marriage issue, neutrality towards Indian freedom movement, loyalty to rulers, and future of minority problems are discussed. *Ice-Candy-Man (1988)* portrays the horrible story of partition through a Parsi perspective. *An American Brat (1994)* deals with the problem of insular marriage of Feroza and David Press. It underscores that cultural differences does matter. It also consciously or unconsciously talks for the favorable changes if community wants to survive. **Rohinton Mistry** in his story collection *Tales from Firozshah Baag (1987)* focused all the problems of Parsi community. The problem of identity crisis degraded social status in post independence India, uprootedness, and problems of extinction of the community. *Such a Long Journey (1991)* deals with Parsi beliefs, death rites, identity crises, Nagarwalla Case through the fictitious character of Jimmy Billimoria. It problematizes the ethnic anxieties of his minority community in Hindu majority. *Family Matters* depicts the problems of insular-marriage and Parsi social-status in post-Ayodhya India. **Boman Desai's** *The Memory of the Elephants (1992)* is an honest introspection into the strengths and eccentricities of the Parsis. It is thus a culturally rooted fantasy with a strong desire to record the history of the Parsi-exodus and to restore it from the cultural memory. It raises the questions of Parsi identities. **Farrukh Dhondy's** *Poona Company (1980)*, a short story collection, focuses the Poona Parsi milieu in Poona. The Parsis in these stories are from the lower middle class who are better integrated into the Indian context. They are the Parsi bookies, conmen and even 'khandian', the Parsi corpse-bearers. Their Parsi identity has not been threatened and hence does not have to be overtly affirmed. The Parsi nostalgia for the British Raj is noted as are the Parsi death rites. His *Bombay Duck (1990)* celebrates the bi-cultural identity of expatriates and moves between the two worlds of Bombay and London. It is a novel of fitting in, of the breaking down of cultural boundaries. **Firdaus Kanga's** *Trying to Grow (1990)* portrays the Parsis from upper-middle class from Bombay. It asserts the Parsi identity and the clash between this identity and encroaching Hindu spiritualism, which contemporary Parsis, in spite of their elite consciousness, find it very attractive. It highlights the nostalgia for Raj, 'anglophillia', and gay relationship of Brit and Cyrus. It also deals the insular marriage. **Dina Mehta's** *And Some Take a Lover* delineates the Parsis's apprehensions and political crises in the wake of the Quit India Movement and the Naval Rating Mutiny. This novel also deals with the insular marriage theme. There is dilemma of the minority community and its identity crisis. Parsi, understandably an anglicized community, would find it extremely difficult to identify with other Indian communities. **Ardashir Vakil's** *Beach Boy* deals with Cyrus Readymoney, a Parsi and his fostered Hindu family. It highlights the cultural and religious differences. **Meher Pestonji's** *Mixed Marriages (1999)* deals with the various issues regarding Parsi identity. It highlights the insular marriage problems and subsequently Parsi alienation in Indian milieu. **Sohrab Homi Fracis's** first story-collection *Ticket to Minto (2001)* is most apparent in the specifically Parsi stories of collection. The Parsis of his stories are doubly alien, both within the explicitly Western realm and within the predominantly Hindu and Muslim landscape of India. They remain a small, intermarried minority in both US and

India, fighting for survival, which is the subject matter of a number of pieces. The title story *Ticket to Minto* illustrates how alien-ness can be found *within* a country, as well as without. These stories are about being "**Other**", being an alien, an outsider. **Thrity Umrigar's** *Bombay Time (2002)* traces the ambition and disappointment in the lives of several inhabitants of a Parsi neighborhood in Bombay (Mumbai). It deals with characters having a love-hate relationship with Bombay and India in general as it is pronounced in the Parsi community. There is a segment within this community that has never quite reconciled to thinking of itself as cent percent Indian which adds to their ambivalent attitude.

IV

Bapsi Sidhwa: Glory of the Bygone Age

Bapsi Sidhwa is an important voice in Commonwealth as well as in Parsi Fiction in English. She was born in Karachi in 1938. Apart from being a writer, Bapsi Sidhwa's interest in *social work* includes active participation in Women's Rights and Social Investigation. She was a member of in a women's delegation to Iran and Turkey in 1970. In 1975, she represented Punjab at the Asian Women's conference at Alma-Ata, in the republic of Kazakhstan, (then in the USSR). She worked on several social work committees and was actively involved in setting up the Destitute Women's and Children's Home in Lahore.

Sidhwa's literary career began with ***The Crow Eaters (1978)*** which focuses on Parsi community, its values and paradoxes. ***The Bride (1982)*** has feministic overtones, as it deals with the woman's search for human-status and liberation from cruelties of Muslim patriarchy. ***Ice-Candy Man (1988)*** portrays the horrors of partition and political passivity of the Parsis towards contemporary political movements. ***An American Brat (1994)*** paves new experiences in Sidhwa's fiction related to migration to the West, and identity crisis as a result of migration.

Bapsi Sidhwa has mirrored her community brilliantly in her writings. Her novels aptly reclaim her fame as a Parsi writer. She deals with the predicament of her tiny microscopic community in the colonial and post-colonial era. Her fiction highlights various aspects concerning beliefs, ceremonies, death-rites, attraction for white-skin and the dilemmas that Parsis face on various occasions. Her fiction records the ethnographic history of her community. This chapter deals with her novels in a chronological order to trace the ethnic angst of Parsi-Zoroastrian community as reflected in her writings.

I

The Crow Eaters: Parsi Idiosyncrasy

The Crow Eaters being a pleasant comedy, human vulnerabilities and follies are treated with tolerance and meek curative irony. Sidhwa presents the hilarious saga of Parsi family. Her immediate concern is to present the marginality of Parsi community.

Sidhwa has shown peculiar traits of the Parsi community as exemplified in the beginning of the novel itself:

> **Because of a deep-rooted admiration for my diminishing community- and an enormous affection for it - this work of fiction has been *a labor of love* (emphasis added). The nature of comedy being to exaggerate, the incidents in this book do not reflect at all upon the integrity of a community whose honesty and sense of honor- not to mention its tradition of humor as typified by the Parsi *natak* (emphasis original)- are legend. (7)**

Most Parsis in the novel are shown as cultural hybrids, living and sharing intimately the cultural life, traditions, languages, moral codes, and political loyalties of two distinct peoples, "which were never completely interpenetrated and fused" [Park 1978:135]. The novel is about the Parsi community and all the major characters are Parsi Zoroastrian. Their ethnic peculiarities are focused in the novel. The characters and their tendencies are satirized, exploiting those ethnic features that are conducive to such satire. But at the same time, these characters are universal beyond any religion and ethnic group as such absurdities and characteristics can be found in a member of any religion or ethnic group as aptly commented by Makrand Paranjape:

> ***The Crow Eaters* is not a novel particularly about Parsis; instead, it is a novel where characters happen to be Parsis. The characters could well have been Hindu or Muslim and a good deal of satire would still have carried; each ethnic group, after all has its peculiarities and absurdities. [1996:90]**

In this novel, *The Crow Eaters*, Bapsi Sidhwa attempts to find out the answers of the queries of her microscopic minority community. Being the first ever novel about the Parsi community, she has tried to give the authentic account of the workings of Parsi mind, social behavior, value system, customs, and ethnic mores. Sidhwa has, very minutely and carefully, pictured the Parsi community. At the same time she has not let it degenerate into a mere sociological discourse. The characters make the novel an amusing piece of fiction emphasizing the harshness and gravity of the paradoxes of the community.

The novel opens with Faredoon Junglewalla's depiction as a well-known Parsi patriarch who has created such a niche in his community that he is listed in the local "Zarathusti Calendar of Great Men and Women" (09). His name is recited in "all the major ceremonies performed in the Punjab and Sind" (09) as an acknowledgment to the accomplishment of his "charming rascality" (09).

The ethnic element of the Zoroastrian community and related tribulations can be traced in the novel. Zoroastrianism has its belief and value system. One of the most important Zoroastrian value is *Charity*. The novel contains ample references to the Parsi Charity. Freddy while preaching the importance of Charity gives his own examples. He has donated funds for the constructions of orphanage, hospital and installed a water pump. With ulterior motive he dedicated it to his English friend Mr. Charles P.Allen.

But his charity is promoted by his selfishness or self-promotion as these English officers were useful for him to develop his business. Parsis allow their dead bodies to be consumed by vultures which is the last act of charity. Jerbanoo's reminiscence of the final rites of her husband focuses on how charity is an integral part of Parsi life: "It was his final act of charity!... As my beloved husband Jehangirjee Chinimini said, *Our Zarathusti faith is based on charity*" (47) (Emphasis added). After Soli's death too, Freddy made the proclamation of charity by constructing a school in Karachi. Charity also evokes the sense of community and binding duties for the fellow-Parsi which is described as:

> **An endearing feature of this microscopic merchant community was its compelling sense of duty and obligation towards other Parsis. Like one close-knit family, they assisted each other, sharing success and rallying to support failure. There were no Parsi beggars in a country abounding in beggars. The moment a Parsi strikes it rich he devotes a big portion of his energies to charity. He builds schools, hospitals and orphanages; provides housing, scholarships and finance. Notorious misers, they are paradoxically generous to a cause. (21)**

Extremity of the charity can be seen in the character of Yazdi. He treated servants with extreme humanity. He took care of his grandmother. He offered all his possessions as well as of other's to the poor and needy. After Soli's death, he retired from routine life. He just wanted to serve those all who were humiliated by human beings, by God, or by destiny. He acquired the *stoic* status. These developments in his character turned him modern day *hippie.* On sea-beach when Billy saw Yazdi, Billy asked him:

> **'Are you a communist?'**
> **'Maybe', said Yazdi. 'Perhaps I'm a follower of Mazdak.'**
> **'Who's he?'**
> **'The first communist. A Zarathusti ancestor. He realized centuries ago that all material goods, including women, had to be shared! (214-215)**

The dictum, 'Parsi thy name is charity' [Pestonji 1999:31] is an embodiment of their virtue of charity. Yazdi's character reaches the heights of humanity where it doesn't remain just a Parsi as aptly put in the words of Novy Kapadia: "The characterization of Yazdi adds the variety to the novel. It tells that Parsis are not *types,* nor do they have stereotyped reactions" [1996:133] When Billy got married "Two hundred Parsi families living in a charitable housing scheme and not invited to the party were each given a sack of flour, a ten pound canister of rarefied butter, lentils and a box of Indian sweets" (224).

Being the minority minuscule community, Parsis have a great sense of community or brotherhood which helps them to establish strong bond among fellow Zoroastrians. In Lahore, visiting Parsis was rare. But when they came into the city station, fellow Zoroastrian would provide them with breakfast, brunch, lunch, tea, drinks and dinner including boiled eggs and roasted chickens.

Another Parsi virtue is *cleanliness* that underlines the importance of purity of one's environment. Purity of the self enables the communion between Ahura Mazda and oneself. This obsession for cleanliness and ignorance about adult life created embarrassing situation for Billy. Billy and Tanya went to Simla by train. When he kissed her, she pushed him back and bit his tongue:

> **You are a filthy sweeper fellow! Haven't you studied hygiene? Poking your germs into my mouth! (227)**

In London the problems of sanitation services and uncleanliness, were criticized by Jerbanoo. The common bathrooms, toilets and lavatories of the hotel restricted Jerbanoo from bathing twice a day. The tiny cubicles offered flush bowls and toilet paper. Jerbanoo was not used to these systems. She scolded Freddy for his "dry-clean" (267). She was brought up to believe that "cleanliness is Godliness, and she refused to fail her religion" (267). Thus, Jerbanoo is a stereotype traditional Parsi woman who clings to her culture steadfast and finds it difficult to adjust to an alien culture.

Parsis are famous for their love for food and excessive eating habits. Sidhwa highlights such Parsi gluttony. Freddy suffered the gluttony of his mother-in-law Jerbanoo who is a typical Parsi:

> **...pulling all the dishes close to her plate, proceed gluttonously to help herself to second favorites.... Jerbanoo appropriated huge quantities of chocolate, biscuits, perfume and wines. (24-26)**

Freddy's helplessness caused him great pain. He complained about her. Freddy thought himself as guilty as Jerbanoo for her glutoony. He felt that she ate like horse and can "give an elephant diarrhea" (27).

Parsis are famous for their honesty. Sidhwa portrays the paradox in the character of Freddy when he planned to set fire to his store and encash the insurance policy. Sidhwa very brilliantly focuses on the portrayal of oriental people. Sidhwa highlights Freddy's shrewdness and cunningness exemplified in contemporary society which is inherited from their colonial masters.

Here Sidhwa portrays Freddy who very cunningly opted all the ways of the *rulers,* and wanted to be benefited from it at any cost. Freddy very acutely and effectively executes the plan and receives the insurance policy after due inquiry. He bribed the police officer to acquire the policy. Thus, Freddy becomes 'truly colonized' as he adopts the ways of the colonizers.

Parsi customs, ceremony and beliefs can be traced throughout this novel. Sidhwa tells about ethnic clothing of the Parsis. Parsis always cover their heads with a white kerchief or cap.:

> **...his wife and mother-in-law never appeared in public without *mathabanas* -white kerchiefs wound around the hair to fit like skull caps. The holy thread circling their waist was austerely displayed and sacred undergarments, worn beneath short blouses, modestly aproned their sari-wrapped hips. Stern-visage, straight-backed, the two women faced the world with such moral temerity that Hindu, Muslim or Christian, all had profound respect for the man and his family. (23)**

In Zoroastrianism, ladies wear mathabanus and men wear caps to avoid the evil attractions towards the hair. Hairs are used to spell black magic. Due to bad luck, Freddy's business suffered and he lagged behind as never before. He thought it as the curse of his mother-in-law. On consulting, a mystic advised him to snip the coil of Jerbanoo's hair himself. He successfully did the same. But he didn't like the dismal transformations in Jerbanoo after the black magic.

Sidhwa comments on some other aspects of Parsi family concerning woman. Putli retires to the "*other room*" (70) during her menstruation cycle. It is believed that even the sun, moon and stars are polluted by menstruating woman's impure gaze as per a superstition which has its basis in primordial man's fear of blood. But it was the time for women to take complete rest without guilt consciousness. Putli, too, enjoyed her retiring to the other room as "It was the only chance she ever had to rest. And since this seclusion was religiously enforced, she was able to enjoy her idleness without guilt (70). Thus, Parsi women were confined to the separate cells during their menstruation. Women followed the tradition without any complaint, thereby showing their attachment to the Parsi customs and beliefs.

Zoroastrians believe in the Good and Evil aspects of the life. There is constant struggle between these two and every Zoroastrian has the freedom of choice:

> **Freedom of choice is a cardinal doctrine in the teaching of Zarathustra. A child born of Zoroastrian parents is not considered a Zoroastrian until he has chosen the faith at the *Navjote* ceremony. Zarathustra in his Gathas says:**
>
> > **Give ear to the Great Truths. Look within with enlightened mind (lit: flaming mind) at the faith of your own selection, man by man, *each one for himself (emphasis original).***
>
> **And this freedom of choice extends also to Good and Evil aspects of God Himself. Evil is necessary so that good may triumph. Yet Evil by itself does not exist, it is relative, depending upon the distance from God at which the individual stands upon the Path of *Asha* - the Eternal truth - the grand cosmic plan of God. (124)**

Every Parsi household and its old women spun the sacred thread and shirt in leisure time. The initiation of Parsis into Zarathusti faith is completed with the Navjote ceremony where every Parsi is "invested with the outward symbols of faith- the undershirt, *sudreh* and the *kusti* they were girded to serve the Lord of Life and Wisdom"(124). Zoroastrians deeply believe in the prayers. For them the Parsi prayers are so strong that non-Parsi could not listen to them. There are many prayers for each occasion. Sidhwa narrates Billy's kusti *prayers:*

> **He dexterously undid the knots of the sacred thread and held the unravelled *kusti* in both hands. Billy did not understand a word of the ancient Avesta text, except the bit 'Shikasta shikasta, sehtan' which roughly translated means, 'I shall conquer evil.' When he came to this bit he whipped the tasseled ends of the thread so that they cracked thinly at the back. Once again he wound the *kusti* round his waist, tying it in a reef knot at the front and**

> **back. Each twist of the knot was meant to remind him that God is One Eternal Being, that the Mazadyasni Faith is the true faith, that Zarathustra is the true Prophet of God and that he should obey the three commandments: *good thoughts, good words and good deeds.* (139)**

At the end of the novel Freddy contemplates on his life. He talked to his children at length cleverly introducing the lessons of his experiences and his reflection on Evil and Good:

> **'It has taken me a long time to comprehend Evil- and Good- and a lifetime to catch just a glimpse of the Path of Asha, God's grand plan for man and the Cosmos. Yes, the strength of God comes to the man of Good Mind, the *Vahu Mana,* God's own mind... Thus spake Zarathustra!' (281)**

Zoroastrians are often called as *Fireworshippers*. But they worship Ahura Mazda through the fire as His most sacred and purified aspect: "The fire, which stands at the centre of the religion, was considered only as the symbol of Ahura Mazda, the light and the truth" [Dalal 1995]. So to violate its purity in any way is sacrilegious. Smoking is considered as Cardinal Sin. When the household servant was caught smoking in the house, it caused great distress in the family. Sidhwa describes the religious importance of the fire and its sacredness:

> **In a house fragrant with sandalwood and incense the smell of tobacco is an abomination. Fire, chosen by the Prophet as the outward symbol of faith, is venerated. It represents the Divine Spark in every man, a spark of Divine Light. Fire, which has its source in primordial light, symbolises not only His cosmic creation but also the spiritual nature of His Eternal Truth. Smoking, which is tantamount to defiling the holy symbol with spit, is strictly taboo- a sacrilegious sin. The cooking fire was never permitted to be extinguished; it was politely preserved in ashes at night, and fanned alive each morning. To blow upon fire is vile**

> **thing. Priests tending the temple fires cover their mouths with cloth masks, lest spittle pollute the *Atash*. (49-50)**

Parsis follow the tradition of religious tolerance. They respect all the religions and show a sense of tolerance towards all religion which is noteworthy:

> **The muezzin's cry, suppliant, plaintive and sensual, rose in the hushed air among the domes. Bells tinkled in a diminutive Hindu temple, snuggled in the shadows of the mosque. A Sikh temple, gold-plated, gleamed like a small jewel in the shadows and Freddy, *responsive to all religious stimuli*, surrendered his heart to the moment. (20) (Emphasis added)**

Freddy had a collection of religious scripture and literature. He had a great respect for all religions in the world. On the shelf he had scriptures of all religions. In this way Freddy's heart discovered an affinity with all religious thoughts. This can also be seen when Soli's death ceremonies were being completed by the priest. Non-Zoroastrians could not witness the ceremonies as well as could not see the face of the dead once final rites were performed over the body. Freddy keeping his voice steady said:

> **'They had stood all this while to see my son: let them. What does it matter if they are no Parsis? They are my brothers; and if I can look upon my son's face, so can they!' The bier moved slowly through the hushed, bowed heads lining the street. (179)**

Here one can remember how Freddy cajoled Yazdi and tried to persuade from the Rosy Watson issue. The same Freddy at his son's death preached the human love and brotherhood which is sans-religion.

There are many ceremonies related to marriage that Sidhwa has described at length. The process of marriage begins with the 'token money' ceremony. Sidhwa gives the details of marriage and related ceremonies particularly of *Mada-sara* ceremony:

> **This entailed much stepping on and off the small, fish-patterned platform. After the prospective bride and groom stepped off and planted the mango sapling that was to guarantee their fertility, the sisters hopped up to be garlanded, stained with vermilion and presented with their set of clothes and thin strings of gold. The gummy-mouthed aunts and uncles, eagerly awaiting their turn, came next. They were also garlanded, stained with vermilion, and given small envelopes containing cash. (218)**

Sidhwa very minutely narrates the wedding ceremony of Billy. Faredoon and Putli stood behind Billy and Sir Easymoney and Lady Easymoney stood behind Tanya, as witnesses:

> **The officiating priest eventually recited, '... Say whether you have agreed to take this maiden named Tanya in marriage to this bridegroom in accordance with rites and customs of the Mazda worshippers, promising to pay her 2000 direhems of pure white silver and two dinars of standard gold of Nishahpur coinage?'**
>
> **'We have', answered Freddy and Putli.**
>
> **'And have you and your family with pure mind and truthful thoughts, words, and deeds, and for the increase of righteousness, agreed to give for ever and aye, this bride in marriage to Behram?' the priest asked the bride's witnesses.**
>
> **'We have agreed,' they replied.**
>
> **Then the priest asked, 'Have you desired to enter into this contract with pure mind and until death do ye part?'**
>
> **'I have so desired,' answered Billy and Tanya in unison.**

> **After this the priest invoked the blessings of God on the married couple and advised them on how to conduct themselves properly. (223-24)**

The details of the Parsi wedding depict the cultural hybridity of the Parsis. Parsis are "a cultural hybrid" sharing the "cultural life and traditions of two distinct peoples" [Park 1978:892]. They partake of Hindu and Muslim ceremonies. The details of *Mada sara ceremony* have Hindu overtones and the wedding ceremony has Muslim overtones. The blending of both 'Contract (Muslim) and 'Commitment till death' (**until death do ye part)** (Hindu) can be seen.

Parsis have their own methods of final rites. They observe the purity of Fire, Earth, and Water. They neither offer their dead bodies to the fire nor bury in the earth nor drown in the water. Their final rites are called as Dokhma. They feed their dead bodies to the vultures as the final act of charity. These rites are performed at the Tower of Silence which is also called as *Doongarwari.* Sidhwa discusses about the 'Tower of Silence':

> **Parsis are a tiny community who leave their dead in open-roofed enclosures atop hills- to be devoured by vultures. The British romanticized this bizarre graveyard with the title 'Tower of Silence'...the marble floor slopes towards the center where there is a deep hollow. This receives the bones and blood. Underground ducts from the hollow lead to four deep wells outside the Tower. These wells are full of lime, charcoal, and sulphur and provide an excellent filter.**
>
> **The outer rim of the floor is made up of enough marble slabs to accommodate fifty male bodies, then comes accommodation for fifty females, and the innermost space, around the hollow, is for children. It takes the birds only minutes to strip the body of all flesh.**
>
> **Now, the height of the Tower is precisely calculated. The vultures, taking off at a full throttle, are only just able to clear the Tower wall. If they try to get away with anything**

> **held between their claws or beaks they invariably crash against the wall. (45)**

In Zoroastrian religion common Parsis are not allowed in *Dungarwari* because, "only professional pall-bearers are allowed to witness the gory spectacle inside the Tower" (45). Dokhma is considered "both practical and hygienic" (45). It originated in the "rocky terrain of Persia" (45). Parsi population is concentrated in the cities of Bombay and Karachi. There the Parsis have Doongarwari following traditional *dokhma,* but Parsis living in "far-flung areas have to be content with mere burial" (46). In Lahore too, there were no *dungerwarees.* It caused great panic in Jerbanoo as she did not want to be buried like a Muslim or a Christian. She blamed Putli and Freddy for damning her soul in "an eternal barbecue in hell" (46). She was not in favor of polluting the sacred earth by her remains. Jerbanoo expressed the deep regret for the vultures on the top of a green tree:

> **"What a pity. What a shame. These poor birds are permitted to starve despite all the Parsis we have in Lahore ...'all these vultures are going to waste - such a pity'." (50)**

Freddy laments the absence of Tower of Silence and dokhma ceremony thus: "Vultures, vultures everywhere and not a body to share!" (51). Sidhwa gives the vivid details of final rites of Soli. Dead body was bathed and dressed in white cotton. Prayers were recited and then dog was called to detect the life in the dead. It is believed that dog's four eyes can sent off evil spirits and can perceive the slightest clue of life. It was "a precious faculty in premedical days when corpses were inclined to recover and sit up" (177). Once again prayers were recited for the dead. The burial of the dead is not allowed in the Parsis as it violates the sacred earth. But the lack of the Tower of Silence made them adjust with burial. Even Jerbanoo too wished to get buried next to Soli which was an "unexpected…wanton act of sacrifice" (180). This "act of sacrifice" (180) wantonly brings to light the predicament that any expatriate or migrant faces in an alien land.

Parsis were given refuge on certain conditions. They were not allowed to marry local people and conversion of the masses to their faith was banned. Sidhwa deals with this issue of insular-marriage. Sidhwa points out that the desire to marry is conveyed by dropping "a fistful of salt into the drinking water" (111). Yazdi expressed his desire to marry Rosy Watson. Freddy was shocked to learn that his son wanted to marry an Anglo-Indian.

Sidhwa, in a paradoxical manner talks about the cardinal doctrine of *Freedom of Choice* and how Parsis oppose to the insular marriages just as they promised the king. Yazdi's narration of Rosy's story without embarrassment was very innocent. Freddy called her "a mixed-breed mongrel" (128). Freddy's abuse highlights the paradox of Parsi loyalty as well as racial and moral superiority over British. This is a paradoxical situation to what Tanya Luhrman said: "the moral qualities of the Parsis must be classified as more European than Indian, and, like the British, as superior to the moral qualities of the native Indian [1996:100]. Yazdi was shocked the way his father talked about her. Yazdi pleaded on humanistic ground. He argued that Rosy is a human being, a fine person and "Better than any Parsi I've met" (128).

This emotional and righteous appeal suggests that "His (Zarathustra's) beautiful religion was for everyone who was prepared to join the fight of good against evil and live by the three guiding principles- good thoughts, good words, and good deeds. In Zoroastrianism, rites are less important than ethical conduct." [Dalal 1995] Hearing such humanistic pleading, Freddy calmed down. Freddy very cunningly expressed him his great philosophy of *tiny spark of race and purity:*

> **'I believe in some kind of a tiny spark that is carried from parent to child, on through generations.... a kind of inherited memory of wisdom and righteousness, reaching back to the times of Zarathustra, the Magi, the Mazadiasnians. It is a tenderly nurtured conscience evolving towards perfection.'**
>
> **'I am not saying only we have the spark. Other people have it too: Christians, Muslims, Hindus, Buddhists... they too have developed pure strains through generations.'**
>
> **'But what happens *if you marry outside our kind?* The spark so delicately nurtured, so subtly balanced, meets something totally alien and unmatched. Its precise balance is scrambled. It reverts to the primitive. You will do yourself no harm- you have already inherited fine**

> **qualities- you have compassion, honesty, creativity- but have you thought of your children?'**
>
> **'In case of the Anglo-Indian girl the spark is already mutuated. What kind of a heritage are you condemning your children to? *They might look beautiful but they will be shells- empty and confused; misfits for generations to come. They will have arrogance without pride- touchiness without self-respect or compassion; ambition without honor... and you will be to blame.'* (Emphasis added) (128-29)**

Yazdi was disappointed by his father's orthodoxy. His father was like anybody else, prejudiced, biased, ignorant and stereotyped. This generation gap increased the distance between a father and a son. Contradictory to the Yazadi's case Sidhwa has given the typical Parsi methodology of the 'Bride-hunting' and importance of "accomplished Parsi girl of good family" (193) for a "Parsi bachelor" (193). After an advertisement in a newspaper they received hundreds of letters and then selected a girl from Bombay. Billy married Tanya. In the colonial period Parsis were at the height of their richness. They were able to spend lavishly on their ceremonies like wedding. Junglewalla family gifted Easymoney family with costly gifts like "chain of gold…a ruby-and-gold set necklace, earrings and ring… pearl studs and diamond tie-pins" (211). Then Sidhwa narrates the grandeur of the Parsis who lavishly spent money on their celebrations:

> **It was a memorable wedding. Years after people still talked about it. Hedges had been levelled in the compound of the Taj Mahal Hotel to clear parking space for carriages and limousines. Openings were dug in the walls dividing the banquet rooms, reception rooms, and lobby of service. Flowers were commissioned from Banglore and Hyderabad, cheeses from Surat, and caviar from the Persian Gulf. There was lobster and wild-duck and venison. There was a bottle of Scotch and Burgundy for each guest; and ambulances, their motors idling, stood ready to convey the inebriated or overstuffed to their homes or to the hospital… There was a**

> **Police Band, a Naval Band, a dance orchestra and an orchestra that played chamber music. There was singing. (224)**

Parsis identify themselves with the superiority of British, with whom they enjoyed superior status. But at the same time, they, too, have funny notions about the land of the rulers and rulers. So this fascination for white-skinned rulers is described as *'gora complex'*. The feeling of such *'gora complex'* can be seen at the end of the novel where Freddy took Putli and Jerbanoo on the tour of London:

> **Putli and Jerbanoo had almost identical fantasies about the land of their rulers. Their thrill was imaginative. They envisaged an orderly kingdom under the munificent authority of a British monarch based on their knowledge of the gigantic statue of Queen Victoria, cast in gun-metal and protected by a canopy of marble, in the centre of the garden on Charing Cross in Lahore. (252)**

This illusion of the rulers and their homeland was shattered as soon as they landed in the great land of their white masters. They faced disillusionment and confronted the *English reality*. They witnessed that English people are also very poor, dirty, working on deck. English people seemed very ordinary just waiting for the orders of Jerbanoo and Putli to follow as Sidhwa portrays:

> **They saw meek, unassuming men with mournful, retiring eyes; and men with the sly, cheeky eyes of street urchins. They saw seedy looking Englishmen sweep roads, clean windows and cart garbage. They met sales girls, clerks and businessmen; all English, all white-skinned and light-eyed, on a footing of disconcerting equality. And the expression on the faces of Londoners was no different from that stamped on the faces of cross-section of India. Where were the kings and queens, the lords and ladies and their gleaming carriages? Where were the men and women with haughty, compelling eyes and arrogant mien? They realized in a flash that the superiority the British displayed**

> **in India was assumed, acquired from the exotic setting, like their tan. (253)**

Jerbanoo and Putli were shocked to see Mr. & Mrs. Allen just as a middle class family. Jerbanoo could humiliate Mrs. Allen only in England after witnessing their degradation in their own homeland. However, they were treated with great respect and awe in India as the representative of the Raj.

The close contact with the British brings in the westernization of the Parsis which can be aptly described as the disease of *Anglo-mania*. The first reference in the novel of this is given when the Parsi gluttony causes Jerbanoo's illness. Jerbanoo cries out in her illness: "'Get an English doctor. Oh I'm dying. Get an English doctor'"(28). This shows fascination for everything which is English. They believed that whatever is English is the best and worthy to be followed and adopted. Mr. Easymoney entertained his guest by his stories of Sudan. He hailed his Parsi community as "the original… kafirs!" (221). Then he narrated the incident how he helped his soldier who was dying of thirst. '…though he might be a sir, and accustomed to the ways of British aristocracy, he was first and foremost a loyal and down-to-earth Parsi!" (221) This is an adequate remark where he admits their adaptations of British ways as well as maintaining the distinct identity as a Parsi community.

Freddy received the invitation cards from Government House for the parties along with his wife. Here Sidhwa has shown the interaction of two cultures. It created tensions when Putli, Freddy' wife, resists change. She was against walking "a step ahead of her husband" (188) as "a dutiful and God-fearing wife" (188). She condemned it as "hypocritical and pretentious, and most barbarous" (188). Putli means a puppet, she is controlled by her husband. Putli adapted to what she considered new-fangled customs, when she along with her husband were invited to the formal tea-parties on the gracious lawns of the Government House. She is persuaded to attend these functions by her husband, for whom it is an opportunity for advancing contacts and consolidating friendships. The Parsi milieu of Putli had a different value system. But "their deportment was as painful to Putli as being marched naked in public" (188). As regards adapting customs of the British the novel shows the gradual assimilation of British value systems in the Parsi milieu. Putli tried to preserve certain Parsi customs, like walking behind her husband. However, her daughter Yasmin after marriage considered such notions as old-fashioned and violently protests at the servile attitude of women:

> **Anyway it's stupid to walk behind your husband like an animal on a leash- Oh mother! Hasn't Papa been able to modernise you yet? (190-91)**

Putli, the earlier generation Parsi, is shocked by Yasmin preceding her husband down the steps and into the carriage and her seeming equal relationship with her husband. Initially adapting the manners and customs of the ruling colonial power was gradual and Putli's inability to understand change is seen as the '*generation-gap*.' As N.S. Ginwalla aptly points out: "These dressed up dolls of Parsi ladies pretend to be highly civilized and refined, and better socially, morally and intellectually than everybody else, simply because they are able to speak English and have a glimmering idea of English society, life, dress and manners" [1880:73]. But Putli's traditional attitude results in a comic situation. Putli had been instructed not to speak their Gujarati vernacular in the presence of Englishmen. As a devoted wife she started her conversation in typical accented English: "How doo doo?'(189), 'Home! I go. You go!" (190) Such fascination for the English resulted into caricaturesque portrayal of the Parsis. This is described as "Anglophilia…the Parsi disease" [Kanga 1991:161]

Sidhwa highlights the attitude of new generation Parsi youth towards life. Billy and Tanya entered their new home in the better localities of Lahore. Their new home and its atmosphere and life were completely different. This young generation wanted to throw off the yoke of old traditions and value system. Their eagerness to adopt western ways and assimilation into the changing social atmosphere compelled them to make friends with "modern couples equally determined to break with tradition" (245) who had "… a fanatical faith in the ways of English society in India, and a disciple's knack at imitation" (245). These young people would speak in English fluently. Sidhwa also highlights that this young generation is ashamed of its own culture and traditions:

> **They were utterly ashamed of traditional habits and considered British customs, however, superficially observed, however trivial, exemplary. They entertained continuously at small, intimate, 'mixed' parties where married couples laughed and danced decorously with other**

> **married couples. 'Mixed' parties were as revolutionary a departure from Freddy's all-male get-togethers at the Hira Mandi, and Putli's rigid female sessions, as is a discotheque from a Victorian family dinner. These parties were fashionably cosmopolitan, including the various religious sects of India: Hindus, Muslims, Sikhs, and Christians, the Europeans, and the Anglo-Indians. (245)**

This broadening of the views and frank manners of assimilation were adopted from the British. Migration and identity crisis are the other problems which Parsis often suffer. Though the novel does not have these overtones, there are certain moments in the text which reveal these issues. Mr. Easymoney in the course of discussion very briefly comments on the bigoted attitude of the natives which mirrors the Parsi attitude too: "...Now take you and me: One leg in India and one leg in England. We are the citizens of the world!"(222) These are apt comments of Easymoney, because after the independence Parsis migrated in large numbers to the West. This made them *cosmopolitan citizens*. Freddy's visit to London enabled him to understand immigrants' problems of adjustment with the new locality and culture. Jerbanoo felt uneasy with toilet papers so carried brass jar which embarrasses Freddy. He forbade her to use it. She scolded Freddy for his "'dry-clean'...Jerbanoo was brought up to believe that cleanliness is Godliness, and she refused to fail religion" (267). This way Jerbanoo faced basic problems of cleanliness highly recommended by her religion. Later on she faced the problem of bathing too but overcame it. She used the balcony as a bathroom where she can bathe twice a day. But it didn't work for long. People came to know about it. On the fifth day she heard a furious voice: "Bilmey! God, we're being flooded!" (268). The matter grew worse and immediately Freddy decided to return to India. This failure of adjustment in a new locality and culture depicts the problems of migrants.

Political ethos of the Parsi is always related with loyalty towards the Ruler. In Pre-independence era they readily sided with the British. They fully co-operated with the British and invited the wrath of the Indians. They were looked upon as traitors and despised since then. The Parsis proved indifferent and disloyal to the country they had adopted. The Indian attitude towards Parsis changed drastically and they were considered as the different, or to quote

Simone De Beauviour "the other". Parsis had to side with the British since they were in power and decision of the Parsis was politically motivated. Thus, the Parsi community found themselves in a strange dilemma; of facing the hostility of the people of the country they adopted during pre-independence. However, they relegated themselves to the 'margin' ever after the independence of India. They remained on the periphery, allergic to mingle into the mainstream of the society, probably due to their guilt-conscience. Freddy preached the law of necessity (need) and success to the younger generation. He taught them how flattery and submission help man to fulfill his needs. Here 'need' can be seen as the peaceful survival and progress of this tiny community. He believed: "Need... will force you to love your enemy as a brother!"(10). He himself has buttered people from whom he wanted something. This attitude of Faredoon is symptomatic of the behavioral pattern of Parsi community. He also pointed that how humble nature helped one to make progress despite of the hostile nature of others and surroundings. Faredoon's charity did not make him a paragon of virtue but was tinged with self promotion. His generosity was mixed with the self-interest. He developed his philanthropic image to increase his business contacts and to appear selfless and contradict the impression of being *toddy* of British. He tells his young listeners:

> **'I have never permitted pride and arrogance to stand in my way. Where would I be had I made a delicate flower of my pride- and sat my delicate bum on it? I followed the dictates of my needs, my wants- they make one flexible, elastic, humble.' "The meek shall inherit the earth", says Christ. There is also a lot of depth in the man who says, "Sway with the breeze, bend with the winds". (11)**

Parsi community needs the meekness as prescribed by the Christ if they want to survive as well as submerge and bend their wills to the rulers.

Sidhwa highlights the anxieties of Parsis regarding decline in their populations. She comments on the demographic status of her minority community and how it has survived and has created and maintained its own identity:

> **There are hardly a hundred and twenty thousand Parsis in the world- and still we maintain our identity- why?**

> **Booted out of Persia at the time of the Arab invasion 1,300 years ago, a handful of our ancestors fled to India with their sacred fires. Here they were granted sanctuary by the prince Yadav Rana on condition that they did not eat beef, wear rawhide sandals or convert the susceptible masses. Our ancestors weren't too proud to bow to his will. To this day we don't allow conversion to our faith- or mixed marriages. (11)**

These comments of Freddy Junglewalla aptly describe the Parsi behavioral pattern of adjustment, commitment, truthfulness and loyalty to rulers, and to the country which has given them refuge at the time of need. Being in minority demographically Freddy has made friends, loved them with "ulterior motives" (11). He assures his young listeners about their survival under the British Raj because other Indian communities would throw them on the fringes of slavery or second-rate citizens, so he declares:

> **For us it rises - and sets- in the Englishman's arse. They are our sovereigns! Where do you think we'd be if we did not curry favour? Next to the nawabs, rajas and princelings, we are the greatest toadies of the British Empire! These are not ugly words, mind you. They are the sweet dictates of our delicious need to exist, to live and prosper in peace. Otherwise, where would we Parsis be? Cleaning out gutters with the untouchables- a dispersed pinch of snuff sneezed from the heterogeneous nostrils of India! Oh yes, in looking after our interests we have maintained our strength- the strength to advance the grand cosmic plan of Ahura Mazda- the deep spiritual law which governs the universe, the path of *Asha*. (12)**

Here Freddy appears very selfish who knows how to extract desired things from others but actually it was the need of the hour, for one's survival and existence. His preaching seems bitter but it is based on the factual conditions and naked reality. So the sycophancy is shown as a "need to exist" (12). The tone of the author is ironicintended to balance personal inadequacies against the contradictions of life itself. Since the Parsis settled in India, they realized they could only survive as a minority by being strictly loyal to every ruling authority and avoiding tensions and conflicts between various groups and powers in the state. At no time in the subcontinent was the community itself a power that would have been able to enforce its own interests against the will of the rulers. Hence, Parsis learned to realize that only loyalty to the ruler generates that political climate in which they could remain undisturbed as a minority. The only condition for their loyalty was that they were not held up in the practice of their religion. Hence the exaggerated servility of Freddy, his son Billy and other Parsis towards the British is revealed as an act to ensure the legal security, peace and economic prosperity. With her ironic perspective the flattery of the Parsis is humorously revealed in the novel, but it also expresses an underlying identity crisis and quest for security among the community as a whole. Freddy travelled from North-India to Lahore. After reaching there, he visited Government House to show affinity and loyalty to the British Empire for secure future.

When Freddy came to Lahore there were only thirty Parsis in the city. After twenty years the number of Parsis swelled to almost three hundred. He became the undisputed head of his community. He was also spokesman and leader of the Parsis scattered over the rest of the Punjab and the North West Frontier Province right up to the Khyber Pass. Freddy's willingness and ability to help to give his time, to intervene and intercede, were proverbial; his influence with men who wielded power was legendary:

> **'Oh, he has the police in his pocket.' They boasted, 'He has the English Sahibs tamed so that they eat out of his hand.' And this was no mean accomplishment for the aloof, disparaging and arrogant British rarely became pally with the 'natives'. (150)**

Sidhwa ends her novel with the Parsi neutrality towards politics where Freddy abuses the Parsis who took part in freedom fighting. He was stirred by the talk of rebellion, self-rule, and Independence from the British- and most of all by the role of a few Parsis in all this. He stated his opinions with a vigor and prophetic emphasis that infected his listeners:

> **'Do you know who is responsible for this mess?'... I'll tell you who: that *misguided*(emphasis added) Parsi from**

> **Bombay, Dadabhoy Navroji! Things were going smoothly; there has always been talk of throwing off the British yoke - of Independence- but that fool of a Parsi starts something called the Congress, and shoots his bloody mouth off like a lunatic. "Quit India! Quit India!" You know what he has done? Stirred a hornet's nest! I can see the repercussions. (282)**

Parsi attitude of loyalty to British rulers is aptly reflected as, "They, my children, shall be taught that fidelity to the British crown is their first duty- loyalty the first virtue" [Kulke 1978:139]. It is ironic that Parsis like Dadabhai Navroji began the freedom fighting and his community blames it as an act of betrayal to the rulers. But at the same time Parsi community betrays the land that has given them refuge after being driven out from Persia. This attitude of the Parsis' is the direct result of the sieged mentality as they have suffered during the reign of Hindu and Muslim rulers of India. British Empire bestowed elite status, first class citizenship on them. Hence, the loyalty to the British rule is more important here. Children raised the doubt of future survival and predicament of the Parsi community in the independent India. Answering the question, "But where will we go? What will happen to us?"(282), Freddy assured the future security and existence:

> **Nowhere, my children… We will stay where we are... let Hindus, Muslims, Sikhs, or whoever, rule. What does it matter? The sun will continue to rise- and the sun continues to set - in their arses…! (282-83)**

His promise of secure future indicated the neutral positions Parsis would take in times of ethnic erasure. It is like: "Small fish must leave big fish alone, if they want to survive."[Pestonji 1999:83]. Freddy's last remarks leaves one with many questions, specially the Parsis, who are a minority community struggling for existence and individual identity, concerning their destiny in recent time. As per his comments Dadabhoy Navroji initiated the freedom fighting in an organized form, but the credit of all the great triumph of independence was taken by Gandhi and Nehru. No one has remembered the sacrifices or contributions of minorities particularly Parsis in the independence movement. That's why Freddy calls Dadabhoy Navroji a "misguided Parsi" (282). Parsis do not have any political identity in independent India or in independent Pakistan. That's why his neutrality is not wrong. He predicated the future of the Parsi community in independent nations which were based on religion and more on languages. As Parsis are in minority, Freddy says: "If there are any rewards in all this, who will reap them? Not Sidhwa! Not Dadabhoy Navroji!"(282). He knows that as long as British are ruling the country, Parsis have that royal stature. So he doesn't want to betray their true friends who treated them on equal terms. Because Brahmins too in India regard them as untouchables:

> **Freddy bumped into a sauntering, decorated cow. The Brahmin priest accompanying the sacred animal cried, 'Watch your step, *babooji*', and sidestepped nimbly to avoid the preoccupied Parsi's contaminating touch. (35)**

It aptly describes the post-colonial predicament of the Parsis and their degenerated social and political status. Tanya Luhrmann aptly writes:

> **They [Parsis] were remarkably successful during the Raj. But their success came at the cost of jettisoning their adopted Indian identity in favour of western one. As a native colonial elite, Parsis were more westernized than most other Indian elites, and as displaced Persians, they committed themselves thoroughly to a non Indian sensibility. Now they feel marginalized in a postcolonial world, with an aching sense of loss of status, of cultural genius, of their historical moment.[1996:81]**

That's why Freddy charged Rustom Sidhwa and Dadabhoy Navroji as: "Making monkeys of themselves and of us! Biting the hand that feeds! I tell you we are betrayed by our own kind, by our own blood!"(283). Freddy refers to the Independence movement as a kind of prostitution and jail, a brothel, by comparing it with Hira Mandi and its prostitutes.

On superficial level these statements look very comic or notorious but they aptly expressed the anxiety and agony of all the Parsis at that time who had no '*homeland*' once again. They were once again in limbo, in the enigma of existence. But at the same time, Freddy consoles himself and children that it doesn't matter who the rulers are, Parsis will be where they had been. It suggests the assertion of their positive existence and flexibility of adjustment with the changing political scenario on the horizon of country's political movement.

Thus, *The Crow Eaters* reflects the ethnic anxieties of the Parsi-Zoroastrian community during colonial times and on the verge of transmission period to independent India.

*

II

Ice-Candy Man: Prufrockian Dilemma

This novel marks the second important phase of Bapsi Sidhwa's literary journey. The novel deals with the upheavals in undivided India on the verge of partition. It is the journey of a child narrator from innocence towards the realization of the hostile, cruel, cunning, calculated crookedness of the world whose manifestation of the universal truth, "One man's religion is other man's poison" (117) is the undercurrent of the subcontinent's traumatic, bloody partition story.

It is the story of Lame Lenny, who is a Parsi, member of minority community which is as lame as Lenny is. But as Lenny recovers from her physical impaired position, community too survives as a strong segment of the society. The novel also ends on other universal truth that love, compassion, and humanity can cure the disease of hatred, violence, and bloodshed. Jill Didur rightly describes the novel:

> **Conservative-nationalist discourse in Pakistan constructs Pakistani citizenship as normatively Muslim, elite, and feudal-patriarchal and pushes minorities, women, and subalterns, to the margins of the national imaginary. [Didur 1998:43-44]**

Sidhwa opens her novel with Iqbal's poem, "Complaint to God", in which poet complains:

> **Sometimes You favor our rivals then sometimes with us You are free, I am sorry to say it so boldly. You are no less fickle than we. (ICM: 01)**
> **(Iqbal: 'Complaint to God')**

It sets the tone of the novel. Hindu, Muslims, and Sikhs who claimed for their ancestor's land, were powerful at some point of time and oppressed at another. But the Parsi community is far away from this suffering, and trauma. The narrator Lenny, who is a child, dwells in the heaven of innocence and ultimately her loss of innocence with the knowledge of brutality of humankind is the crux of the novel. Jill Didur aptly comments:

> **As the narrative unfolds, it quickly becomes apparent that her subjectivity is mediated by a community identity undergoing a double-crisis. The shift in power from British to the Hindu and Muslim centric states of India and Pakistan respectively signals the end of the Parsis' privileged relation, despite their minority status, to the ruling class. [1998:46]**

In this sense, this novel offers the reader an imaginary peek into the location of the Parsi community of Lahore as a "...conjunctural site indetermination" [Sangari, 1993:872] where the discursive meaning of belonging is under revision. The novel engages with the implications of the end of British rule in India and the rise of competing conservative-nationalist forces and their intersections with the patriarchal relations that circulate in the "compressed" (01) world of Parsi community.

Madhu Jain in her review of the novel highlights the dilemma which the Parsi community faced at the dawn of Independence: "The Parsi dilemma is: whom do they cast their lot with?" [1989:47] This sets the tone of the novel. Sidhwa introduces the Parsi character Col. Bharucha, Lenny's doctor and head of the community. He scolds an ignorant Muslim father about his ignorance of his child's health and their demand for a separate nation. It shows that people were ignorant of the political upheavals in the country. Col. Bharucha blamed, British for bringing "polio in India" (16). Lenny was shocked by this revelation as being Parsi it was not expected from Col. Bharucha. Lenny thought it as an open declaration of war by her tiny community on the British Empire because "the Parsees have been careful to adopt a discreet and politically naive profile" (16). This tone of neutrality manifested in the narrator-character while describing the climactic incidents of Partition, is anticipated in the Parsi get-together for the Jashan prayer, to celebrate British victory at the Fire Temple in Lahore. While the Parsis have all along been loyal to the British government, they fear the Partition of India. Consequently they faced the dilemma to which community they should support. Col. Bharucha, the domineering Parsi doctor and the President of the 'Parsi Anjuman' cautioned his community as:

> **We must tread carefully... We have served the English faithfully, and earned their trust... So, we have prospered! But we are the smallest minority in India... Only one hundred and twenty thousand in the whole world. We have to be extra wary, or we'll be neither here nor there... We must hunt with the hounds and run with the hare! (16)**

This Parsi meeting presents the humorous nature of Parsis and their concern with politics and inclination to support the freedom movement. It is at this moment of Prufrockian dilemma that Col. Bharucha spoke on the mike about the severity of the freedom fighting. He has seen the future tug-o-war play for power among the majorities of India i.e. Hindu, Muslim and Sikh. In this power-play Parsis would "be mangled into chuttney!'(36), if they did not "...'stay at home - and out of trouble'" (37). Dr. Mody expressed his doubt about remaining "uninvolved" (37) and "siding with the English" (37). He considered it a betrayal towards fellow-Indians. It is important that with which community Parsi should remain loyal to as the possibility of two-nations based on religions was about to become a fact. At the same time, it was also problematic that to which neighbor they should be loyal to whether Hindu, Muslim or Sikh. Col. Bharucha feared the possibility of "two or even three-new nations" (37). He cautioned the Parsi audience to be very careful at this juncture of time as "the Parsees might find themselves championing the wrong side if they don't look before they leap!" (37)

The next problem this community faces is of consequent possibility of subjugation under Hindu, Muslim or Sikh majority. Parsis have suffered during Hindu as well as Muslim rulers as they were categorized as minority. Obviously, the anxieties of subjugation were renewed. It is aptly expressed as:

> **'...If we're stuck with the Hindus they'll swipe our business under our noses and sell our grandfathers in the bargain: if we stuck with the Muslims they'll convert us by the sword! And God help us if we're stuck with the Sikhs!' (37)**

Col. Bharucha narrated the story of their uprooting from Persia, and settling in India. It underscores the reasons of the Parsi passivity towards the politics. Parsis were given refuge on certain conditions like not to enter into politics, accept the rulers' culture completely without any distinct identity. It is this moment of Prufrockian dilemma that Col. Bharucha dismissed the fears of his community by advising them to cast their lot with whoever rules Lahore. It was their ageold strategy of passivity towards politics and loyalty to the rulers:

> **'Let whoever wishes rule! Hindu, Muslim, Sikh, Christian! We will abide by the rules of their land!' '...As long as we do not interfere we have nothing to fear! As long as we respect the customs of our rulers - as we always have - we'll be all right! Ahura Mazda has looked after us for thirteen hundred years: he will look after us for another thirteen hundred!' '...We will cast our lot with whoever rules Lahore!' (39)**

The memory of forceful conversion by the Arabs before thirteen-hundred-years gave way to another possibility of migration to Bombay where majority of the Parsis live. Col. Bharucha assured security of their distinct religious identity as a Zoroastrian Parsi community. He recollected another story from Parsi history:

> **'We prospered under the Muslim Moguls, didn't we?'... 'Emperor Akbar invited Zarathusti scholars to his *darbar* :he said he'd become a Parsee if he could... but we gave our oath to the Hindu Prince that we wouldn't proselytise - and the Parsee don't break faith!' (40)**

Thus he denied the possibility of the subjugation under any rule if community maintains its low profile and passivity towards the politics. Sidhwa ironically comments on her community who migrated to the West after independence as Parsis thought themselves as "English king's subjects" (40) and acknowledged themselves as "English!"(40). Col. Bharucha assured conditional security: "As long as we conduct our lives quietly, as long as we present no threat to anybody, we will prosper right here" (40). The banker cautioned not "to exercise real power" (40). Sidhwa with her bitter Parsi humor comments upon the historical facts of her community. She highlights the anxieties of the present existence and consistent future. This meeting highlights the Parsi attitude towards the Indian Freedom struggle. The Parsis were going to be neutral in the tug of war among the three major communities of India. The neutral attitude of the narrator character, Lenny, has its roots in this racial psychology of the Parsis. In a way, the attitude of the Parsi community revealed here is the externalized collective sub-consciousness of Lenny. Meher Pestonji's story titled "Dilemma" depicts that neutrality is the best policy adopted by the community to maintain safe distance for the survival, "There's no reason for a Parsi to poke his nose into something that doesn't concern him" [1999:82].

Though the novel has partition and subsequent ethnic anxieties as a dominant theme, Sidhwa mentioned some Parsi ceremonies, beliefs and prayers. Lenny informs the religious tolerance towards all other religions in her mother's words: "'I've to buy the children's clothes for Christmas and New Year.'(Christmas, Easter, Eid, Divali. We celebrate them all)" (69). Sidhwa narrates the ceremony of birthday celebration. Ayah poured a cup of milk with rose petals on her head. Imam Din was instructed to make sweet vermicelli with fried currants and almonds for her birthday.

Lenny doubted that her mother and aunty were rationing the petrol to set Lahore on fire. Lenny prayed to banish this evil from their mind to bring them on the virtuous path of Asha. She describes her prayers:

> **I cover my head with a scarf and in secluded corners join my hands to take the 101 names of God. The Bountiful. The Innocent. The Forgiver of Sin. The Fulfiller of Desire. He who can turn Air into Ashes: Fire into Water: Dust into Gems! The angle of the walls deflects the ancient words of dead Avastan language and the prayer resounds soothingly in my ears. (173-74)**

As Lenny was about to confront her mother in this regard, mother was preparing for the Friday prayers "to invoke the Great Trouble Easers, the angels

Mushkail Assan and Behram Yazd. (In troubled times they are frequently evoked by the Parsees.)" (241).

Clean and tidy surrounding is a highly recommended value of the Parsis. Sidhwa focuses on the purity of language of the Parsis who resent abusive language. Imam Din explains Hamida this decency of the Parsis, "'These are decent folk, mind you! They're not the kind that let fly dog-and-cat abuses…'" (191)

Subcontinent people are highly attracted by the complexion of the Europeans. Parsis desired to be like them and this fascination of the British is aptly reflected in the novel. Lenny's brother Adi is highly adored and loved by all for his fair complexion and Eurocentric beauty. Ayah loved her "little English baba!"(25). She was often enquired about his English parentage. Ayah readily denied by saying, "'Of course not!'… 'Can any dough-faced English's son match his spice? Their looks lack salt!'" (25) Here Sidhwa subverts the importance of being English and asserts nativism. Ayah was proud of Adi's paucity of pigment. Adi's fair complexion allowed him to merge in *white center:*

> **Sometimes she takes us to Lawerence Gardens and encourages him to run across the space separating native babies and English babies. The ayahs of the English babies hug him and fuss over him and permit him to romp with their privileged charges. Adi undoes the bows of little girls with blue-eyes in scratchy organdie dresses and wrestles with tallow-haired boys in the grass. (25)**

Simultaneously the anti-English discussions were in progress asserting the pride in national customs, culture, language, and dressing. Ice-candy-man quotes Subhash Chandra Bose, "'If we want India back we must take pride in our customs, our clothes, our languages... And not go mouthing the got-pit sot- pit of the English!'" (28-29) This is an assertion of national aspect of ethnicity to get separate identity instead of merging itself with the central or powerful and dominant ethnic group by adopting its norms. Here Sidhwa gives importance to 'swadeshi' rather than 'videshi'. But she also highlights how Ayah instead of wearing Punjabi attire, only for getting good salary wears sari like Christian-Goan ayah.

Sidhwa discussed the final rites of Parsis in details. Sidhwa shows differences among Parsis about their *dokhma*. Orthodox Parsis prefer tradition of dokhma or what is also called as sky-burial whereas modern Parsis are showing flexibility on various grounds like lack of Tower of Silences in remote or hill areas, decline in vultures etc. Lenny asked the Godmother about the 'Tower of Silence'. Godmother describes it as "*Dungarwadi*: not Tower of Silence" (193). She blames British for its funny name of Tower of Silence. It is just a big round of wall without any roof where the dead bodies are put inside and "'The vultures pick it clean and the sun dries out the bones'"(113). This traditional dokhma is considered as environment-friendly and final act of charity of the Parsis. Godmother favored dokhma on ecological as well as religious assumptions: "Instead of polluting the earth by burying it, or wasting fuel by burning it, we feed God's creatures" (114). Lenny wishes to see the Tower of Silence. Godmother explains the absence of *dungarwadi* in Lahore as ther number of Parsis is very few. In Bombay and Karachi Lenny could see the Tower of Silence from outside because only pall bearers are allowed to go inside it.

There is a constant controversy over the issue of *dokhma* on various grounds. This conflict of final rites is prevalent in Parsis today as lack of vultures also. Mini aunty expressed her opposition for it. For her it is outdated and somewhat horrifying: "'I prefer to be buried…You know why! It gives me the creeps…The thought of vultures smacking their beaks over my eyeballs!'" (114). Godmother stands for the traditional method of *dokhma.* She denounced Slave-sister for her anti-dokhma stand as, "'I'd be ashamed to call myself a Zoroastrian if I were you'" (114). Slave-sister (Mini aunty) ridiculed such religious stands and retorted satirically: "…Being devoured by vultures has nothing to do with the religion... Surely Zarathustra had more important messages to deliver…" (114). Such attitude seems against the norms of Parsi ethnicity, but at the same time it asserts the changes in the norms. Godmother explained *dokhma* as the last act of charity of Parsis. She remembered Sir Eduljee Adenwalla whose leg was amputated in Bombay. His leg was deposited in the *Dungarwadi* to feed vultures. In this way, Sidhwa very seriously contests the various opinions about traditional dokhma.

Lenny is exposed to various ethnic groups of India like Sikh, Muslim, and Hindu through ayah. Lenny being Parsi is identified as a member of harmless ethnic group and is appreciated by all of them. The synthesis of different cultures and unity of undivided India can be seen in the character of *Ayah.* She stands for unique culture of India. Her friends, who are from various ethnic groups, admire her. Ayah has great fan-following from all strata of the society irrespective of religion, caste and creed. The characters of Ayah and Lenny represent two different cultural, socio-economic classes but their strong bond harmonizes these differences in the colonial situation of subcontinent's partition. The Ayah is undiscriminating towards all and due to this she is turned into a symbol of diverse culture of India. Lenny's close association with Ayah takes her out of the margins of the bourgeois Parsi community and illustrates her to the heterogeneity of socio-cultural prospects of Lahore at the time of partition. Jill Didur aptly comments on:

> **Lenny's intimate relationship with her *ayah* and her visits to the Sikh/Muslim village of Pir Pindo take her outside the bourgeois circle of the Parsi community and make her aware of the heterogeneous cultural context of her society at large. Sidhwa's text figures Lenny exercising agency by questioning the hegemonic structures of meaning that infuse her "everyday" experiences. Her decentered view of the end of British rule within her local community helps to defamiliarize the dominant interpretation of history and nationalism at the time of Partition and disclose its patriarchal and majoritarian underpinnings. [1998:47]**

Jill Didur's reference to "the bourgeois circle" [Ibid, 47] can be seen as the urban elite class who estranges itself from rural crowd. It is obvious when Lenny saw the religious harmony and social synthesis in rural India (Pir Pindo). The village *Choudhary* defied the rumors of ethnic riots: "'But all that is in the cities...'It won't affect our lives'" (55-56). It suggests that he has believed "the issue for some time" (56). Imam Din painfully expressed the possibility of "Sikh-Muslim trouble" as a result of "Ugly trouble" of "Hindu-Muslim" riots (56). Sikh granthis talked about the racial unity and denied the possibility of riots in the village: "...our villages come from the same racial stock. Muslim or Sikh, we are basically Jats" (56).

Chaudhary's remarks on the strong bond among village ethnic groups and his observation of the contrasting communal attitudes of townsman and country-folk suggest the different attitudes. Here he asserts the division based on rural and urban settings. He describes it as:

> **'But our relationships with the Hindus are bound by strong ties. The city folk can afford to fight... we can't. We are dependent on each other: bound by our toil; by Mandi prices set by the Banyas - they're our common enemy—those city Hindus. To us villagers, what does it matter if a peasant is a Hindu, or a Muslim, or a Sikh?... the madness will not infect our villages.' (56)**

The remarks of the village Chaudhary have historical authenticity. A renowned sociologist, M.L. Darling, echoes Chaudhary's remarks when he says: "A class of Hindu money-lenders had arisen in the Punjab which had enriched itself by exploiting the helpless peasantry." [1925:116]

Lenny witnessed hot debate over partition in her home at dinner party. Inspector General Rogers, Mr. & Mrs. Singh discussed current situation of partition and subsequent ethnic angst. Mr. Rogers as a representative of the empire considered the worse possibility of riots after independence. Mr. Singh accused him: "'You always set one up against the other... You just give Home Rule and see. We will settle our differences and everything!'"(63) Same echo can be seen in E.M. Forster's novel *A Passage to India*. This view of Mr. Singh is highlighted by an Indian historian, M. Mujeeb: "[these] considerations made the Congress hold that the minority problem could wait till the country became independent" [1967:7]. Thus, Sidhwa portrays the changing scenario and gradual upcoming of the communal enmity in urban India as Jagdev Singh aptly writes:

> **As the setting sun of the British Empire gathers its parting rays before sinking into oblivion, the lumpen element around Ayah meet less frequently at the Queen's Park and more at the 'Wrestler's Restaurant'. The geographical shift in the get-together is a premonition of the emergence of the pattern of communal discord. The British Queen whose statue stands abandoned in the Park, is soon going to relinquish her suzerainty over India and the Wrestler's Restaurant to which all flock now is a symbol of the wrestling ring that Partition is going to raise on the joint borders of India and Pakistan. [1996:170-71]**

Butcher comments that initially Gandhijee politically favored Muslims over Sikhs and then sympathized with Sikhs which resulted into confusions among common people. The Gardener concluded it as "the English mischief" (92). Butcher explained that the Hindus too manipulated one or two Muslims against the interest of larger community. Sikhs were deceived in politics. In the heat of argument, Lenny became aware of the religious differences. She noticed:

> **It is sudden. One day everybody is themselves - and the next day they are Hindu, Muslim, Sikh, Christian. People shrink, dwindling into symbols. Ayah is no longer just all-encompassing Ayah - she is also a token. A Hindu. Carried away by a renewed devotional fervor she expends a small fortune in joss-sticks, flowers and sweets on the gods and goddesses in the temples.**
>
> **Imam Din and Yousaf, turning into religious zealots, warn Mother they will take Friday afternoons off for the Jumha prayers. Crammed into a narrow religious slot they too are diminished: as are Jinnah and Iqbal, Ice-candy-man and Masseur.**
>
> **Hari and Moti-the-sweeper and his wife Muccho, and untouchable daughter Papoo, become ever more untouchable as they are entrenched deeper in their low Hindu caste. While the Sharmas and the Daulatrams, Brahmins like Nehru, are dehumanized by their lofty caste and caste-marks.**
>
> **The Rogers of Birdwood Barracks, Queen Victoria and King George are English Christians: they look down their noses upon the Pens who are Anglo-Indian, who look down theirs on the Phailbuses who are Indian-Christians, who look down up on all non-Christians.**
>
> **Godmother, Slavesister, Electric-aunt and my nuclear family are reduced to irrelevant nomenclatures- we are Parsee.**

What is God? (93-94)

Here Sidhwa comments how society, friends, neighbours, lovers, admirers, servants, masters were categorized under the category of religion and God the supreme power has lost it hold on the human beings. But being the member of a minuscule community, her community fellows were not even worth of nomenclatures. Sidhwa also describes that not only people but even jokes were categorized on the basis of religion and ethnic groups: "Cousin erupts with a fresh crops of Sikh jokes. And there are Hindu, Muslim, Parsee, and Christian jokes" (95). Lenny noticed changes in the Queen's Garden. She noticed that people from all religion were sitting apart, separately. But the only group around Ayah remained unchanged. Hindu, Muslim, Sikh, Parsee, were as always unified around her. Here one could make observation that Ayah stands for the unity, harmony, beauty of people's heart and mind. But in due course partition has corrupted everything which evident with Ayah's kidnapping and brutal gang rape.

Sidhwa also highlighted the minority status of the Parsis and even it was unknown religion to the most of the people in India of those days as she writes:

> **The Sikh women pull me in their laps and ask my name and the name of my religion.**
>
> **'I'm Parsee.' I say.**
>
> **'O *kee*? What's that?' they ask: scandalised to discover a religion they've never heard of. (96)**

But the revelation of Lenny's religion caused fun for some of Hindu children who yelled at Lenny: "'Parsee Parsee, crow eaters! Crow eaters! Crow eaters!'"(100). Lenny asked Ayah the reason. Ayah replied: "**...** because y'll do "kaan! kaan!" at the top of your voices like a rowdy flock of crows" (100). Perin Bharucha comments on this matter that "It isn't the Parsis who eat crows but the other way round. And anyway, they're not crows but vultures to whom the dead are fed" [1986:37]. To divert the attention and soothe Lenny Ice-candy-man acted like Banya.

> **'We were only seventeen; they were a gang of four!**
> **How we ran; how we ran; as we'd never run before!' (100)**

Sidhwa further explains the meaning of couplet as Lenny remembered: "A glimpse of four Sikhs, Muslims or Parsees is supposed to send a mob of Banyas scurrying" (101). This underlines the strong sense of ethnic identity and characteristics of specific ethnic group.

The fear of partition and the violence made common man to think about his safety. On Lenny's second visit to Pir Pindo on the occasion of Baisakhi, Lenny went along with the members of Imam Din's family to Dera Take Singh. As they reached the village, the festivals were already in full swing. It was in the midst of these gay activities that Ranna sensed the suspicion and fear of ethnic enmity. Sidhwa captures this feeling thus:

> **And despite the gaiety and distractions, Ranna senses the chill spread by the presence of strangers: their unexpected faces harsh and cold. A Sikh youth whom Ranna has met a few times, and who has always been kind, pretends not to notice Ranna. Other men, who would normally smile at Ranna, slide their eyes past. Little by little, without his being aware of it, his smile becomes strained and his laughter strident. (106)**

The village people came to know the vivacious and sinister designs of an attack on the village by Granthi Jagjeet Singh. He fears about the plans of Akalis to wipe out or drive out Muslims out of East Punjab "if there is to be a Pakistan" (107). British lost their grip on Indians as their tricks (split-and-rule policy) were known to everybody. Sidhwa aptly reflects it by quoting Iqbal:

> **The times have changed; the world has changed its mind.**
> **The European's mystery is erased.**
>
> **The secret of his conjuring tricks is known:**
>
> **The Frankish wizard stands and looks amazed. (111) (Iqbal)**

Parsis, who are charged aptly with Anglomania, too became aware of the British rule and its effect when they saw the turmoil and Hindu-Muslim-Sikh riots. Their neighbours became their worst enemies. Lenny and Yousaf happened to come across a Brahmin pandit. The incident shows Lenny the clear hints of their ethnic status as the *other* when the Pandit, a Hindu-Brahmin did the *othering of* Lenny, a Parsi and Yousaf, a Muslim. She pointed out:

> **Our shadow glides over a Brahmin Pandit. Sitting crosslegged on the grass he is eating out of a leaf-bowl. He looks at Yousaf- and at me- and his face expresses the full range of terror, passion, and pain expected of a violated virgin. Our shadow has violated his virtue. The Pandit cringes. His features shrivel into arid little shrimps and his body retracts. The vermillion caste-mark on his forehead glows like an accusing eye. He looks at his food as if it is infected with maggots. Squeamishly picking up the leaf, he tips its contents behind a bush and throws away the leaf. (116-117)**

Lenny thought herself as a contaminated maggot and Yousaf as composed of shit, crawling with maggots. Here Lenny learnt the greatest lesson ever that "*One man's religion is another man's poison*" (emphasis added) (117).

Sidhwa through the changing behavioral pattern of Ice-Candy Man towards Sher Singh showed the fundamental nature of ethnic behavior irrespective of emotions of shared friendship, love and longing. Ice-candy-man helped Sher Singh to evacuate his Muslim tenants preaching the lesson of friendship. Later on Ice-Candy-Man in the frenzy of ethnic riots raped and brutally killed the relatives of Sher Singh. He displayed his wrath:

> **'I lose my senses when I think of the mutilated bodies on that train from Gurdaspur… that night I went mad, I tell you! I lobbed grenades through the windows of Hindus and Sikhs I'd known all my life! I hated their guts... I want to kill someone for each of the breasts they cut off the Muslim women ...The penises!' (156)**

This was the worst possibility of the revenge from someone like Ice-candy-man, who had never thought of insulting the women of his friends who shared joys and sorrows. This extreme fundamentalism destroyed the harmonious relations which were preserved, nurtured, and grown. He contradicted himself. It shows how his psyche is destroyed by the ethnic riots on the eve of the partition. Sidhwa asserts that ethnic identity is so strong and so violent that with slight anxiety, it can make its presence felt and is able to destroy the other ethnic group.

Lenny witnessed the processions. Even Lenny and Adi too, walk their own processions calling "'*Jai Hind*'" or "'*Pakistan Zindabad*'" (127). All the friends gave their opinions based on majority, money, lands etc. Sikh attendant of the zoo shouted: "'The Sikhs hold more farm land in the Punjab than the Hindus and Muslims put together!'" (129). Masseur pinchingly advised him:

> **'The only way to keep your holdings, Sardarjee, is to arrive at a settlement with the Muslim League,'...'If you don't, the Punjab will be divided... That will mean trouble for us all.'...'You're what? Only four million or so? ... And if half of you are in Pakistan, and the other half in India, you won't have much clout in either place.' (129)**

Whereas Butcher added to Masseur's advice: "'The British have advised Jinnah to keep clear of you bastards!'... 'The *Angrez* call you a "bloody nuisance"!'" (129). Here othering of ethnic groups is guided by the white ethnic group. Sher Singh too, denied the presence of Muslim as necessary by calling them "bastards" (130). Masseur's comments showing the othering of the Sikhs highlights the clear indication of the religious superiority and an effort to erase the majoritarian presence of Sikhs by denying it. Further, he underestimates the racial bravery and muscle power of the Sikh and tried to portray it's origin as 'a hybrid' from the religions of Hindus and Muslims:

> **'Shut up, *yaar,*' says Masseur, his face unusually dark with a rush of blood. 'It's all *buckwas!* The Holy Koran lies next to the Granth Sahib in the Golden Temple. The shift Guru Nanik wore carried inscriptions from the Koran... In fact the Sikh faith came about to create Hindu-Muslim harmony!' (130-131)**

But he soothes the atmosphere with humanistic pleading: "'In any case,'... 'there are no differences among friends...We will stand by each other'" (131). Though he said so, he had shown his true color in the heat of discussion. He proved that when it comes to religion and existence human beings are bound to be brutal and vicious.

Sidhwa gave the glimpses of the paradoxes of the ethnic behaviors in the state of religious anxiety. She sketches the Sikh processions and Muslim procession complementary to it:

> **'We will see how the Muslim swine get Pakistan! We will fight to the last man! We will show them *who* will leave Lahore! *Raj karega Khalsa, aki rahi na koi!*'...'*Pakistan Murdabad!* Death to Pakistan! *Sat Siri Akaal! Bolay se nihaal!*' And the Muslims shouting: 'So? We'll play Holi- with-their-blood! Ho-o-o-li with their blo-o-o-d!' (133-134)**

In Lahore humanity, love, caring, and human values were sacrificed in the fire. British government gave Pakistan to Jinnah and India to Nehru. Lenny was categorized as Pakistani: "I am Pakistani. In a snap. Just like that" (140). Jinnah declared his secular attitude of the Muslim state of Pakistan:

> **'You are free. You are free to go to your temples. You are free to go to your mosques or any other place of worship in the State of Pakistan. You may belong to any religion or caste or creed, that has nothing to do with the business of State... etc., etc., etc. *Pakistan Zindabad!*' (144)**

Sidhwa portrayed Jinnah as a secular leader of the Muslim State of Pakistan, where he proclaimed that all religions can live and prosper peacefully and harmoniously. It is the irony of the later day Pakistan which is hailed as the 'terrorist camp' in the world, that they are misguided under the name of Jinnah and his concept of Muslim State. The subjugation of the *other* nation or community is repeatedly associated with the feminization of the men and the violation of the women. Ice-candy-man reported breathlessly about the train carrying "all Muslim" containing "two gunny-bags full of women's breasts!"(149) Ice-Candy Man too had his vengeance by raping and killing Hindu women and openly declaring the plan to kill Hindus to quench his hatred. The gardener provided information that he had sent his family to Delhi because "'When our friends confess they want to kill us, we have to go...'" (157).

Moti decided to get converted as Christian. Ice-candy-man suggested restlessly the change of name also. It suggests how he hated Hindus and Sikhs that he just wanted to erase their total identity. All the loving friends, neighbours left their homes in search of safe places. Here Sidhwa has used brilliantly the movie song that aptly had shown the feelings of parting, the agony, anxiety of going away from their homes, their friends, completely erasing their past, booting themselves to root in an alien land they had never been:

> ***Mere bachpan ke sathi mujhe bhool na jana—***
> ***Dekho, dekho hanse na zamana, hanse na zamana.***
>
> **Friends from our childhood, don't forget us -**
> **See that a changed world does not mock us. (159)**

Lenny understood the meaning of the song as Rosy-Peter left Lahore for India. At the same time floods of Muslim refugees entered Lahore and the Punjab west of the Lahore. Within three months seven million Muslims and five million Hindus and Sikhs were uprooted in the largest and most terrible exchange of population known to history. Lenny and Adi were confused after knowing their mother and aunt's rationing of the petrol as it was an offence. They doubted their mothers were setting fire to Lahore. Lenny accused her mother of rationing petrol. Surprised by this revelation, mother explained that they rationed the petrol to help their Hindu, Sikh friends to run away as well as to send kidnapped women, like ayah, to their families across the border.

This "across the border" (242) help claims Parsis as the synthesizer of Hindu – Muslim harmony in times of trouble. Sidhwa portrayed her community as one which had maintained a safe distance from the communal conflagration, acted as the Messiah of Hindus and Sikhs trapped in the burning city. They, as Lenny learned later on, helped them in their transportation to India. Even Ayah was rescued by Lenny's Godmother and was sent to her parents in Amritsar. Thus, inspired by a feeling of humanism, the Parsis shed off their passive neutrality and became the active agents of a healing process. Lenny after partition noticed the erasure of cultural diversity for the cultural homogeneity of one ethnic group:

> **Lahore is suddenly emptied of yet another hoary dimension: there are no Brahmins with caste-marks - or**

> **Hindus in dhotis with *bodhis*. Only hordes of Muslim refugees. (175)**

Later on, Lenny noticed that Queen had disappeared from the garden. Now the Muslim families monopolized the garden. There were fewer women and more men as Pakistan was based on Islam which demands women to remain behind the veils. Gangs of fanatics looted and destroyed everything which was Hindu or Sikh, or belonged to Hindus and Sikhs. The *goondas* arrived in Lenny's house looking for Hindus. They mistook 'Sethis' for Hindus. They wanted to ensure the conversion of Hari to Himat Ali. The Barber, "nai" (181) assured them of his conversion to Islam. To ensure the conversion gang demanded recitation of the Kalma. Himat Ali recited it for them in the tone of chanting Hindu Mantra:

> **'*La Ilaha Illallah, Mohammad ur Rasulluah.*'(Italics original) (There is no God but God, and Mohammad is His Prophet.) Astonishingly, *Himat Ali injects into the Arabic verse the cadence and intonation of Hindu chants.* (*Emphasis added*) (181)**

This suggests that one can't shed off the originality or past identity of oneself when the new identity is imposed and opposed to the new one. One can't erase one's past totally: "that the former and present lives do not match, they quarrel, even contradict, cancel each other out" [Kuortti 1998:62]. Imam Din told them that Ayah had gone. Here Imam Din seems as the true follower of Islam who survives the humanity and compassion over hatred and communal anxiety. On the other hand, Ice-Candy-Man not only kidnapped Ayah and raped her and threw her to the wolves of the passion in the Kotha but also killed his co-religionist Masseur out of jealousy. Ice-Candy-Man very cunningly made Lenny to reveal Ayah's hideout. Lenny witnessed Ayah's humiliation. Sidhwa narrates the incidents of partition violence and subjugation of the Muslims by Sikhs from Rana's reconstruction of his memory of wounded past:

> **He began inching forward, prepared to dash across the yard to where the women were, when a man yawned and sighed, '*Wah guru!*'**

> **'*Wah guru! Wah guru!*' responded three or four male voices, sounding drowsy and replete. Ranna realized that the men in the mosque were Sikhs. A wave of rage and loathing swept his small body. He knew it was wrong of the Sikhs to be in the Mosque with the village women.**
>
> **'Stop whimpering, you bitch, or I'll bugger you again!' a man said irritably.**
>
> **Other men laughed. There was much movement. Stifled exclamations and moans. A woman screamed, and swore in Punjabi. There was a loud cracking noise and the rattle of breath from the lungs. Then a moment of horrible stillness. (203)**

It is horrible that people committed such heinous and sinful act in the house of God though in rage of communal and ethnic anxiety. they did not feel the presence of God . Sidhwa presents the heart rendering, traumatic and nauseating picture of the partition objectively. She has not favored any religion. She has portrayed the suffering and victimization of the people from all religions whether Hindu, Muslim, or Sikh. She has humanitarian approach while sketching the bloodshed and uprooting of the people.

Sidhwa also shows that 'forgetting' the cruelties and adjusting to new atmosphere is the only way to overcome the grudges, whether personal or communal. Godmother said to Ayah after her recovery from red-light area:

> **'That was fated, daughter. It can't be undone. But it can be forgiven... Worse things are forgiven. Life goes on and the business of living buries the debris of our pasts. Hurt, happiness... all fade impartially... to make way for fresh joy and new sorrow. That's the way of life.' (262)**

On Lenny's insistence, Godmother boarded Ranna into the Convent of Jesus and Mary as a boarder. It surprised Lenny how easily Rana had accepted his loss; and adjusted to his new environment. The flexible nature made Parsis survive in any hostile condition as expressed in Lenny's words:

> **It surprises me how easily Ranna has accepted his loss; and adjusted to his new environment. So...one gets used to anything... If one must. The small bitterness and grudges I tend to nurse make me feel ashamed of myself. Rana's ready ability to forgive a past none of us could control keeps him whole. (211)**

Thus, Sidhwa very brilliantly portrayed the changing scenario of ethnic anxieties in this novel. She portrays Parsis as synthesizer of humanity, love and compassion among the ethnic hatred and bloodshed on the eve of Partition.

*

III

An American Brat: A Cultural Shock

This novel deals with Sidhwa's new experiences of being a migrant to Canada. It is set in Lahore, Pakistan of 1970s and in USA. As people move from one part of the world to another, seeming to dissolve national boundaries, Sidhwa highlights the formation and maintenance of the community talk on new dimensions. It is a quest that preoccupies the immigrant caught between the world left behind and the new one he or she faces. In the novel, Sidhwa explores the complexities of being a Parsi, of being a Pakistani, and of migrant to the West while carrying the other two identities together. Various reasons are given for the migration of the Parsis to the West, as Nilufer Bharucha reveals with reference to India which can be co-related with Pakistan:

> **It is this distance between the Parsis' elite consciousness and their downgraded position in postcolonial India that the migrant Parsi is trying to escape. This end-of-Empire unease in the Indian Diaspora is a reason for the Westward movement by many Parsis in the 1950s, 60s, and 70s. However, there is a certain degree of guilt connected with this Western Diaspora, which is a voluntary one, unlike**

> **the feeling of self-esteem generated by the forced diaspora from Iran. [Wasafiri 1995:34-35]**

The novel reflects the typical dilemmas of the Parsis today and their multiple alienations. It also reflects fractured images of their glorious past, their reduced present and insecure future. It talks of marginalization through ethnicity and gender discourse. In a comment on the novel, Sidhwa writes in the Indian Review of Books:

> **Not that the book lacks a darker side. You cannot comment on politics anywhere in the world, or on the politics within the community itself, without presenting a fairly grim picture. [1993:24]**

The novel is a socio-political critique of a bleak society which suffered under political instability, military suppression and increased Islamic fundamentalism. It talks in detail of the increasing uneasiness that the Parsi community feels in Pakistan. Sidhwa discusses how there is a general descent into authoritarianism in the name of religion and how even the non-Islamic communities like the Parsis were affected by the increasing fundamentalism. She centralizes the Parsi community and examines several themes of vital importance to the Parsis in the last decade of the 20th century. Issues like colonial mentality in Parsis is one of the undercurrents of the novel. It also underlines the identity crisis and quest for security in the Parsi psyche and influence of a patriarchal society. Above all, this novel examines a very controversial issue amongst Parsis, the taboo of insular marriage. In making this theme the central concern of the narrative, Sidhwa reveals her ongoing preoccupation with an issue that has very serious ramifications and implications for the Parsi community. In an interview with Naila Hussain, Bapsi Sidhwa says:

> **...the book deals with the subject of the 'culture shock' young people from the subcontinent have to contend with when they choose to study abroad. It also delineates the clashes the divergent cultures generate between the families 'back home' and their transformed and transgressing progeny bravely groping their way in the New World. [1993:19]**

The novel deals with the Americanization of a young Parsi girl and reflects the new American theme. Parsi values and beliefs are discussed in the novel. Sidhwa comments that most of the young generation Parsis don't know much about religious beliefs and prayers. Feroza was not much aware of her religion but had a comfortable relationship with her faith. She used to visit the fire-temple four to five times a year, mostly on New Year or on impending voyage. Feroza visited "to the trendy new *agyari* in the Parsee colony" (40). Zareen could not go along with her because she has her menses and "her presence would pollute the temple" (40). Feroza said tandarosti prayer- the happy little Jasa-me-avanghe Mazda prayer in Avastan language of the Gathas. She knew its meaning from the English translation in her prayer book, "Come to my help, O Ahura-Mazda! Give me victory, power, and the joy of life"(42).

This is another problem of the Parsi community that Avastan language is no more understood and they have to rely on English translations of their religious prayers and gathas. All the members of the family prayed for Feroza and her safe journey. Sidhwa describes the effect of the prayers and the power on Feroza:

> **Even though she had not understood a word of the extinct language of the Sacred Book, Feroza had blind faith in the power of its verses and imbued them with whatever exalted concepts and spiritual longing her soul and emotions periodically required. (47-48)**

In America, after rescuing herself from stairwell darkness, Feroza surrendered herself to the God by reciting the "***Kemna Mazda*** prayer" (90). In the process of Americanization Feroza once committed the cardinal sin of smoking. This pollution of sacred fire underlined her guilt. Feroza hunted out her Kusti and Sudra and said the "***Hormazd Khoda-ay prayer***" (165) to plead "divine forgiveness for desecrating the holy fire- the symbol of Ahura Mazda- by permitting it such intimate contact with unclean mouth" (165).

Parsi community has a strong belief in religious tolerance. They respect and pay homage to the saints and visit their tombs and sacred places. Zareen pays visit to the Muslim saint "Data Gunj Baksh's shrine" (18). Sidhwa also comments how fundamentalism has overshadowed the communal harmony and tolerance. The novel being concerned with the politics of religion, Sidhwa significantly talks of how fundamentalism damaged peace in the subcontinent where all religious groups have co-existed over several generations. Zareen, despite being a faithful Zoroastrian, worshipped at the shrine of the Muslim saint Data Gunj Baksh, a sacred place of religious harmony and tolerance:

> **Given the medley of religions that exists check-by-jowl in the subcontinent and the spiritual impulse that sustains them, people of all faiths flock to each other's shrines and cathedrals. They came to the fifteenth-century *sufi's* shrine from all over the Pakistan, and before Partition they came from all over northern India. When Sikh and Hindu pilgrims from across the border in India visit the temples and *gurudwaras* in Pakistan, they never fail to "pay their respects" to the Muslim mystic known for his miraculous power to grant wishes. (18-19)**

This act of Zareen can be seen as the desperate effort to conform to the religion of the nation she lives in. The variance in a language determines the ethnic identity. Manek had sold the Bible to maintain his financial status in his early days in the USA. "The moment Manek opened his mouth and spoke, the Atlanta Patel could tell from his distinctive accent that he was a Parsee." (200-201)

Sidhwa has also mentioned the Parsi ceremonies like farewell, welcome, good luck etc, where all the elders bless the younger or particular person for his betterment and security. Feroza was given the farewell which was an almost ceremonial occasion and an essentially Parsi affair:

> **She (Soonamai) stood before her granddaughter while Zareen stood at hand, holding the prayer-tray. Khutlibai put her thumb into the red paste in a silver container and left her imprint on Feroza's forehead. Feroza leaned forward accommodatingly, and Khutlibai pressed the rice she held in her palm on Feroza's forehead. Quite a few grains stuck to the drying paste, and Khutlibai was pleased. It meant as many blessings on the child. She next popped a lump of crystallized sugar into Feroza's mouth, handed her a coconut, and bestowed a long list of specific blessings… God-blessed… Aa-meen! (46)**

Parsi ceremonies, like this one, clearly show the cultural and religious hybridity. The first part displays the Hindu ceremony and the last word "Aameen"(46) is from Christianity and close to 'Amin' in Islam. Feroza came back to Pakistan to spend her holidays with her family. Feroza received a grand welcome. Parsi community too believes in the good omen of a married woman, and the presence of a widow is considered inauspicious on certain religious or auspicious occasions. Being a widow, Khutlibai remained behind when good-luck ceremony was about to be performed for Feroza.

Parsi community does not allow the insular marriage. Sidhwa focuses on this aspect too in her novels. In *An American Brat,* this issue is prominent. Zareen insisted on Feroza's visit to America. It made Feroza's father anxious as he thought over the situation as forthcoming problem of insular-marriage:

> **Zareen might be complacent about Feroza's taking part in a play, believing their daughter would come out of the experience unscathed to marry a suitable Parsee boy at the proper time.... Zareen's complacence stemmed from her confidence in Feroza's upbringing. Every Parsee girl grew up warned of the catastrophe that could take the shape of a good-looking non-Parsee man. Marrying outside her community could exclude the girl from community matters and certainly bar her from her faith. (17)**

Manek planned Feroza's education in the USA that was opposed by Khutlibai on the note of insular marriage and the USA's exposure, broadmindedness and freedom pushed Feroza in the arms of a non-Parsi. It created the dilemma in Khutlibai's mind. This dilemma of Khutlibai synchronizes the predicament of the Parsi community which is on the verge of extinction and the Parsis who are tradition bound and refuse to change. Khutlibai expressed her doubts about Feroza's marriage:

> **Good Parsee boys are scarce, and you know how quickly they are snapped up. The right time will come and go, and mark my words, the child will be lost to us! God knows what kind of people she'll mix with. Drunks, seducers, drug addicts... (121)**

Khutlibai's doubts have aptly reflected the generation gap and changing times. At the same time she brings out the differences between the upbringing of male and female child:

> **We don't know what kind of friends Manek has. All I can do is pray he won't marry some white tart. But he's a man; he can get away with a lot. But who'll marry a girl who's been up to God knows what? Our elders used to say, keep the girls buried at home. (121)**

Khutlibai's comments precisely reflect the orthodox attitude towards the upbringing of a female child and the restriction on female members of the family. Manek came to see Parsi bride for him. Khutlibai received him laughing with relief. She also revealed the fact that "in the end one is comfortable with one's own kind!" (196). So "one's own kind" (196) is very important for the post-married life which is full of compromises and responsibilities. Khutlibai highly believed in the philosophy of "ours are ours!" (196). Manek expressed his desire to get married with "a Parsee girl" (203). Everyone appreciated his respect for the religion and the elders. Sidhwa also highlights the duality towards issues like marriage, as Jeroo says:

> **I've told my Dara... When he goes for foreign education he can have whatever fun he wants. But when he wants to marry, it must be to a Zarathusti. He will be happy only with a Parsee. Isn't that so? (203)**

Jeroo's advice to her son connotes some other implications related with the moral ethos. Dara can have "whatever fun" (203) implies the sexual extravagances "but when wants to marry... a Zarathusti" (203) is compulsory. Everyone adored Manek's sentiments and took the racial pride. Thus Manek proved himself a champion of their community's future by setting an example before the younger generation of the Parsis. Manek married Aban in traditional way following all the ceremonies.

Feroza revealed Manek her plan to marry David. Manek responded maturely and tried to persuade her on the basis that "*our cultures are very different*" (263) (Emphasis added). Feroza wrote a letter to her parents about David and his parents. They were Jews. She also highlighted that the religious differences are irrelevant in America. They decided to solve the problem by becoming "Unitarians" (266). Zareen gave Feroza's letter to Cyrus and told him about her desire to marry "a non" (266) Parsi. Feroza's informal tone in the letter appeared more dangerous to her parents. The letter caused uproar in the family where the argument among elders and younger clearly shows the generation differences and the changes that time has brought. Young generation expects from their elders to move ahead with the time if their tiny community has to survive. Sidhwa writes:

> **Mixed marriages concerned the entire Parsee community and affected its very survival. God knew, they were few enough. Only a hundred and twenty thousand in the whole world. And considering the low birth rate and the rate at which the youngsters were marrying outside the community-- and given their rigid non-conversion laws and the zealous guardians of those laws-- Parsees were a gravely endangered species...the youngsters... urged their uncles and aunts to enlarge their narrow minds and do the community a favor by pressing the stuffy old trustees in the Zoroastrian *Anjuman* in Karachi and Bombay to move with the times; times that were already sending them to study in the New World, to mingle with strangers in strange lands where mixed marriages were inevitable. (268)**

This conflict between the generations was the result of changing times whereas the elders denied any change. Perin Bharucha in her novel *Fire Worshippers* has discussed this conflict when Nariman wants to marry a non-Parsi girl. His father Pestonji Kanchwalla resists disintegration of his community. Rhoda, Nariman's sister explains and interprets the change and new times to her parents:

> **And that isn't your fault or Mama's or any one's, it's the fault of the times we are living in. Everything is changing. The age of miracles is gone. There is no mystery left- no heaven and no hell, not even your Chinvad Pul. Zoroastrianism is**

no longer a faith to be believed, it's just a unique cultural heritage. [1968:194]

It is a paradox that Parsis who take pride for being Westernized and liberated community are in fact not so liberal. Sidhwa here portrays the Parsi community's traditional dictum of double standards - one for man and another for woman. Man's inter-faith marriage is acceptable and his wife of other faith and their children are accepted into the Parsi fold. But if a woman marries a non-Parsi, she is an outcast and debarred from the community and even from the Fire Temple. The Parsis are fundamentalists to the core and the priests prove to be resistant to the change even when the community is dwindling. Freny in a very cajoling voice told tearful Bunny: "Parsee girls are not allowed into the fire temple once they marry out" (269). Elders gave the example of women who suffered due to their marriage with non-Parsis among them Perin Powri, who married a Muslim, was the prime example of victim of orthodox patriarchal Parsi community who denied her "accommodation in the Karachi *dokhma*, and the priests refused to perform the last rites"(270). Perin Powri's body was eventually buried in a Muslim graveyard. The names of other transgressors were rehearsed, with each offense illuminating a new and catastrophic feature of the ill-considered alliance. Roda Kapadia, who married a Christian, was not permitted into the room with her grandmother's body. She is called as a "misguided woman" (270). She was compelled to sit outside on a bench "like a leper!" (270). At this juncture, Sidhwa also highlights another aspect of this problem related with Parsi males. The problem of Parsi males marrying outside the community caused the serious question regarding the future of Parsi girls. It is question to whom Parsi girls should marry or remain virigin for whole life.

Sidhwa points out that since Parsi men marry non-Parsi women, Parsi women are also compelled to marry out of their faith due to lack of fellow Parsi men. Soonamai requested her thirteen year old grandson not to marry a "*parjat*" (271). In America Zareen enquired about David's ancestry, "*khandaan*" (277). It made Feroza laugh. But Zareen considered it to be a very serious issue of her community. She expressed the fear of expulsion from community as well as becoming more religious once debarred from community:

You'll be thrown out of the community! Do you know what happens to girls who marry out? They become ten times

> **more religious! ...Take Perin Powri. Like most of you girls, she never wore her *sudra* or *kusti*. After her marriage to a non, she wore her sari Parsee-style, and her *sudra* covered her hips! Her *kusti* ends dangled at the back! Till the day of her death, she missed her connection with community. She would have given anything to be allowed into the *agyari*.... They won't allow you into any of our places of worship, *agyari* or *Atash Behram*. (277-278)**

This passion for racial purity caused great problems for Zoroastrians as younger generation Parsis are marrying outside the community. For them, these are not important issues. Such "Nazi or Afrikaaner" way of thinking is outdated for them as "This is the age of democracy" and "The racial superiority humbug went bust long ago." [Pestonji 1999:63]. Feroza intended to have "a civil marriage" (278) to keep their religion as they were "Unitarians" (278). Zareen was shocked as if Feroza was already converted. She was very anxious over her daughter's "outcaste status" (278). She persuaded Feroza:

> **It is not just a matter of your marrying a non-Parsee boy.... your life -- it will be so dry. Just husband, wife and maybe a child rattling like loose stones in this huge America!"... "It's a different culture...you'll have to look at it our way. It's not your culture! You can't just toss your heritage away like that. It's in your bones! ...You'll disgrace the family!"..."Love? Love comes after marriage. And only if you marry the right man. Don't think you can be happy by making us all unhappy. (278-279)**

In the course of her interaction with David she began to change the orthodox views and seriously thought over the reformation in Parsi Anjuman's laws about the marriage. At such moments, Zareen yearned for David's Parsee status or at least Zoroastrians would allow "selective conversion" (287) to their faith. For the first time, Zareen seriously questioned the prohibition on insular marriage. She had often thought that it was unjust that a Parsee man can marry a non-Parsi woman and can preserve his faith as well as brought up his children as Zoroastrians. But a Parsee woman couldn't do so. Sidhwa describes this inner turmoil of Zareen :

> ***But she argued this from a purely feminist and academic point of view....*** **How could a religion whose prophet urged his followers to spread the Truth of his message in the holy *Gathas* -- the songs of Zarathustra -- prohibit conversion and throw her daughter out of the faith? (287) (Emphasis added)**

Zareen realized that insular-marriage is now a global phenomenon. But she lived in a fundamentalist country like Pakistan. Zareen was aware of the controversy raging surrounding these concerns in Bombay, Britain, Canada, and America "where the Parsees had migrated in droves in the past few years" (287). Sixty thousand Parsees, fifty percent of the total world population of Parsi community, resided in Bombay. Zareen believed that the Bombay Parsee Panchayat was the hub of influence on community matters. She was aware of its inclination "to be conservative" (287). She was vaguely sure that "the controversy would be resolved in an enlightenment manner *(after all, her community was educated and progressive*) and that she could live with its decisions whichever way they went" (Emphasis added) (287). Thus, Zareen felt herself suddenly aligned with the thinking of the liberals and reformists. She came to know that changes are unavoidable. Zareen understood the teenagers in Lahore. She too focused the need for "minor reforms if they wished their tiny-community to survive" (288). Zareen discussed the matter with Manek who advised to leave things alone so the romance would "die a natural death" (290). He also predicted the possibility of the opposite. She retorted angrily on Manek's suggestion because Manek married a Parsi woman. Zareen declared her departure and pleaded Feroza to get married properly. Zareen offered an invitation to David with all his relatives for the marriage at Lahore. Later on Zareen started to narrate all the ceremonies in such a way which startled and frightened him. Thus Zareen took on cultural onslaught and humiliated David with his religion and its tradition in a comic way. She felt she was seeing him in his true colors:

> **...we break a coconut on your head,"... David blinked his bewildered eyes and looked profoundly hurt. "She's only kidding," Feroza said. "Then we have the *adarnee* and engagement. Your family will fill Feroza's lap with five sari sets, sari, petticoat, blouse, underwear. Whatever**

> **jewelry they plan to give her must be given then. We give our daughters-in-law at least one diamond set. I will give her the diamond-and-emerald necklace my mother gave me at my wedding… We'll give your family clothes-- suit-lengths and shirts for the men, sari sets for the women. A gold chain for your mother, a pocket watch for your father. Look here, if your parents don't want to do the same, we'll understand. But we'll fulfill our traditional obligations. (Emphasis added) (297-98)**

David controlled his anger as he realized that Zareen's offence was not personal but communal. He knew that a Jewish wedding would be similarly a grand affair, and though he did not want to go through that either, he felt compelled to defend his position:

> **"My parents aren't happy about the marriage, either. It's lucky they're Reform Jews, otherwise they'd go into mourning and pretend I was dead. We have Jewish customs, you know. My family will miss my getting married under a canopy by our rabbi. We have a great dinner and there's a table with twenty or thirty different kinds of desserts, cake and fruit. Then there's dancing until late at night." David stopped to catch his breath and looked angrily at Zareen. "I belong to an old tradition, too." "All the better," Zareen said promptly, "We will honor your traditions." (298)**

This stance taken by both Zareen and David suggests that modernity is a fragile veil which can be easily unveiled by the cultural abuses and underestimating other culture. Such kind of ethnocentric attitude is aptly defined by CHAMBERS 21st century Dictionary as: "relating to or holding the belief that one's own cultural tradition or racial group is superior to all other." This cultural 'othering' and differences surely resulted into the breakup of Feroza and David's love affair who decided that all these cultural, religious differences would never come in between their relationship. Zareen's humiliations were so powerfully affected that she was sure of the break up:

> **"Next, we come to the wedding. *If there is a wedding*," Zareen said solemnly.... "I thought you said the priests refused to perform such marriages." David was sarcastic, a canny prosecutor out to nail a slippery opponent. "I know of cases where such marriages have been performed," Zareen said, as if confessing to knowledge better left concealed. "Feroza's grandmother has ways of getting around things -- she's president of the *Anjuman*. The ceremony won't make you a Parsee, or solve Feroza's problems with the community, but we'll feel better for it; so will Feroza." (Emphasis added)(298-299)**

Feroza explained David about grandmother's status as "a tribal chief" (299). Zareen's shock was natural because it attacked her racial superiority and modernity because:

> **As far as she was aware, tribesmen inhabited jungles and mountain wilderness, observed primitive codes of honor, and carried out vendettas. A far cry from the Westernized and urban behavior of her sophisticated community. (299)**

This underestimating of David's culture left him hurt. The meeting ended in great emotional theatrics with silence and changing attitudes of all three towards each other. Zareen's performance was unbelievable and magically guided by the idea, "If you can't knock him out with sugar, slug him with honey" (302). David ridiculed Feroza as ZAP on the basis of her cultural heritage. But Zareen could not understand it. Feroza laughed and explained it to Zareen that "ZAP stood for Zoroastrian-American Princess, an innovative spin-off on JAP, Jewish-American Princess" (302). After the fiasco, Zareen boarded the plane for the return journey. Once she was airborne, she removed the notices, papers and started reading.

The message was typed in capitals:

NOTICE

PLEASE NOTE THAT ACCORDING TO THE PARSEE, ZOROASTRIAN RELIGIOUS BELIEFS, PERCEPTS, TENETS, DOCTRINES, HOLY SCRIPTURES, CUSTOMS AND TRADITIONS, ONCE A PARSEE-ZOROASTRIAN MARRIES A NON-ZOROASTRIAN, HE OR SHE IS DEEMED TO HAVE RENOUNCED THE FAITH AND CEASES TO BE A PARSEE-ZOROASTRIAN. THE LAWS OF PURITY OF THE ZOROASTRIAN FAITH FORBID INTERMARRIAGES, AS MIXING PHYSICAL AND SPIRITUAL GENES IS CONSID- ERED A CARDINAL CRIME AGAINST NATURE. HENCE, HE OR SHE DOES NOT HAVE ANY COMMUNAL OR RELIGIOUS RIGHTS OR PRIVILEGES. (305)

The notice from the religious institution compelled Zareen to realize that however her community boasts to be westernized, educated and modernized, it is still a fundamentalist to the issues like race and purity. These educated guardians of the Zoroastrian canon were as rigid and ignorant as the fanatic Muslims in Pakistan. She felt sorry as "This mindless current of fundamentalism sweeping the world like a plague had spared no religion, not even their microscopic community of 120 thousand" (305). After the great fiasco of David-Feroza love-affair, Zareen had convinced David that "the differences mattered" (309). Zareen had made David feel that they had been arrogant and immature in dismissing the dissimilarities in their backgrounds. He felt whether he could manage with some of the Parsi rituals. Zareen made the details horrible. He knew she was just teasing but "her attitude had distressed and humiliated him" (309). Thus Zareen dexterously championed the cause of racial purity.

Parsi community also suffers from identity crisis. Sidhwa opens her novel with the discussion of Zareen and her husband Cyrus about their daughter Feroza. Feroza's unParsi outlook and orthodox behavior in the fundamentalist Pakistan worried Zareen. She complains of Feroza's "becoming more and more backward every day" (09) because of the Islamic conservatism in one way or the other and forgets her own Parsi tradition:

> **I went to bring Feroza from school today. I was chatting with Mother Superior on the veranda- she was out enjoying the sun- and I had removed my cardigan. Feroza pretended she didn't know me. In the car she said: 'Mummy, please don't come to school dressed like that.' She objected to my sleeveless sari-blouse! Really, this narrow-minded attitude touted by General Zia is infecting her, too. I told her, 'Look, we're Parsee, everybody knows we dress differently.' Instead of moving forward, we are moving backward. What I could do in '59 and '60, my daughter can't do in 1978! Our Parsee children in Lahore won't know how to mix with Parsee kids in Karachi or Bombay. (10-11)**

Cyrus provided the possibility of her attitude towards Zareen as Feroza probably felt "to conform, be like her Muslim friends. There are hardly any Parsee girls of her age. She wants you to be like her friend's mothers, that's all."(12) Here, Cyrus's remarks suggest that minority takes efforts to merge in the majority by confirming the majority traits. This effort to shift this marginal people to center leads to the identity struggle .i.e. cultural identity. To save her daughter from this fundamentalism of Pakistan, Zareen suggested sending Feroza to America to her brother Manek. This made Cyrus anxious about another kind of loss of identity. He fears that his vulnerable young daughter would fall in love and marry a non-Parsi. So the solution to send the girl for a holiday to USA is doubtful though later he thinks, "Travel will broaden her outlook, get this puritanical rubbish out of her head" (14). The paradox is described by Novy Kapadia as:

> **The paradox, here is self evident. It adds to the irony that exists throughout the novel. The Ginnawallas fail to realize that the journey to the USA (the New World) will broaden her thinking and open up further avenues for her. She will become 'modern' in the truest sense of the word. By thinking for herself she will challenge traditional views, static orthodoxy and grow beyond the confines of**

> **communality and the norms of a patriarchal society... the journey to the USA was supposedly a learning process but instead it makes her 'too modern' for her patriarchal and seemingly liberal family. So in this novel of self-realization, the self-awareness that Feroza Ginnawalla acquires, ironically isolates her from her Parsi heritage. [1996:188]**

Zareen explained at length how upsettingly "timid and narrow-minded Feroza was becoming" (31). Khutlibai abused Zareen about her carelessness towards the upbringing of her child. She also charged her about the political nonsense fired up in their house and religious carelessness. She expressed her concern for religion: "If I hadn't been around, God knows who'd have taught my granddaughter to pray" (31).

Away from Pakistan, Feroza wanted to know all the affairs of Pakistan during and after the death of Bhutto. Her argument highlights her longing for homeland and struggle for national identity. Feroza's reminder of her nationality shocked Zareen:

> **"After all, it's my country!" Zareen did not mention the innuendo, the odd barb, that had suddenly begun to fester at the back of her consciousness. The insinuation that her patriotism was questionable, or that she was not a proper Pakistani because she was not Muslim. What was she then? And where did she belong, if not in the city where her ancestors were buried? She was in the land of the seven rivers, the Septe Sindhu, the land that Prophet Zarathustra had declared as favored most by Ahura Mazda. What if, on the strength of this, the 120 thousand Parsees in the world were to lay claim to Punjab and Sindh? ((237-238)**

Zareen found Feroza fussy over national issues in relation to her micro community. She thought it as "absurdity" (238). Sidhwa captures this alienation from national concerns. Zareen thought that such remarks were a passing thing. She blamed the fanatical Islamization encouraged by General Zia. It has supported "religious chauvinism" (238) and harassed "the marginalized people like her - the minorities" (238). The paradox of the situation is that

Feroza denies marrying any Pakistani or Parsi and return to Pakistan, after her break up with David. For her Pakistan is not the country where she could explore the possibilities of her individual existence and development. Sidhwa ends her novel on such a note that Feroza could not regain her former identity after gaining new American identity of universal citizen sans boundaries of religion or nation. It suggests her complete assimilation into American melting pot.

Sidhwa also commented on the attraction of sub-continent people (here Parsis) for white-skin which is called as gora complex. Feroza in excitement of her visit to America talked loudly on telephone. Manek calls her "Third World Pakis" (26) and warns her to stay away from "*gora* complex" (26) and to get rid of "'white man complex'" (26) before coming to America. In USA, Manek stopped her from offering a dollar bill to an American young man to make her aware of their status as "ignorant and dirty... bastards" (84). In college, Jo mistook Manek and Feroza as "Mexican" (147). But Manek's revelation of their Pakistani identity changed Jo's attitude. She answered only with more than a monosyllable. Here the racial prejudice is evident, brown races are not accepted in the sphere of white circle which often lead immigrants to keep to their own communities. Neil Bisoondath also highlights such a problem. In the story "Dancing", Shiela James, on her arrival in Toronto, is cautioned by her sister Annie: "You must stick with your own, don't think that any honky ever going to accept you as one of them. If you want friends, they going to have to be West Indian" [1985:198]. Though it is paradoxical here that Manek was pleased with the reactions from Jo as it helped Feroza to realize "the dimensions of the *gora* complex that constantly challenged his brown Pakistani psyche. And he'd been so prompt to accuse Feroza of her awe of the whites!" (147).

Sidhwa deals with the cultural encounter of Third World and First world. Sidhwa cleverly pictures the conflicts and differences between these two worlds. She analyzed how an individual from Third World aspire for the First World to develop himself/herself by merging their Third World identity in First World for the survival. Feroza was extremely happy and started dreaming about "the land of glossy magazines, of "Bewitched", and "Star Trek," of rock stars and jeans..." (27). She asked her parents innocently, "Why am I a Paki Third Worlder?" (27) The creation of third world is western capitalist product. So Feroza's question that why she is a third world Paki can be answered when this structure is noticed:

> **The capitalist West as the First World, the socialist block as the Second World, and the non-aligned, the underdeveloped (the former colonies) countries as the Third World have been posited as enemies one against the other. [Purushotham K. and N.S. Rahul. 2003:45-46]**

This innocence was shattered on the airport where authority abused her and Manek as lovers. This innocence is like an identity trait of the girls from the Third-world. Manek discussed about the backwardness of Pakistan and Feroza guessed the probabilities of being backward as once colonized nation, fundamentalism, or not developed in technology and failure to make nuclear bomb.

Manek denied and explained her reasons of the backwardness, i.e. waste of time. Feroza's consciousness of surrounding compelled Manek to say: "Only illiterate natives like you, from Third World countries, waste time..." (77). It occurred to her that Manek might not want to return to Pakistan. She felt a surprising and "almost tragic sense of loss" (78). She was trapped in the cubicle of YMCA building. After rescuing from it she heard Japanese man's irritable voice. She found: "*His rage was protective, fussy, Asian*" (emphasis added) (94). Feroza's observations about Manek clarified Feroza how Manek had encountered the hazards and humiliations while adjusting with the First World:

> **She could only guess at how he had been taught American ways, American manners. He must have endured countless humiliations. And his experiences- the positive and the humiliating- had affected him, changed him not on the surface but fundamentally... Manek was humbler and, paradoxically, more assured and quietly conceited, more considerate, yet she sensed that at an essential level he had become tougher, even ruthless.... Feroza vaguely sensed that America had tested Manek. Challenged him, honed him, extended his personality and the horizon of his potential in a way that had made him hers. (102-103)**

Manek taught Feroza the importance of hard work in America. Manek revealed the secret of America's richness in its free economy and a true democracy. Feroza got offended by the mentioning of "Third World" (124). Further he added, "You and your Bhutto, with his socialist ideas, are like those lazy Communists" (124). Feroza warned him not to say anything abusive about the "voice of the masses" (124). Manek called him "Third World crook" (124). Sidhwa attacks the paternalism that marks all Western communication with the economically weaker Asian nations. Zareen complains about the behavior of an American who tried to establish the complexity of western countries showing it as the sign of the progressed and developed nations:

> **The man did not think me as a person, as somebody. I was not Zareen, just some third-rate Third Worlder, too contemptible to be of the same species… He was so cynical. He asked the most simplistic questions, as if the complexity that makes up our world doesn't exist. I've never felt the way he made me feel… valueless… genderless.** (177)

Thus, Sidhwa very minutely discussed the vivid problems and conflicts between the First World and Third World countries focusing on various aspects.

Sidhwa highlights the problems of immigration and related issues of assimilations and changing patterns of one's identity after adopting the culture and the language of one's host country. She focuses on the dark as well as bright aspects of one's host country (here USA) and how it helps the immigrant to develop the personality after due explorations of one's individual talents and possibilities of progress. Feroza's visit to USA was fixed under the guidance of her uncle Manek. Khutlibai opposed it because of his quarrelsome relations with Feroza in childhood. Zareen assured her mother about his responsible dependable personality and maturity to look after Feroza in an alien country. Sidhwa talks about the outlook of Parsis towards the Parsis who had migrated abroad. She also highlights the double standards concerning male and female migrants. All Parsee boys as the future of the community were accepted as geniuses until they turned out to be "nincompoops" (39). This is calculated in terms of money, business and social reputation. This community stands up with financial, business, engineering, doctoring, accounting, stockbrokering, computing, and researching masterminds. Girls are not considered worthy to indulge in these jobs. They are confined to home. If they insist to go abroad to study, they were allowed to do so "either to prepare them for or divert them from marriage" (39).

Landing in New York, it was the new world for a girl like Feroza. When she asked for the help to a young man, he stared at her. Sidhwa exposes Feroza to the cruel and harsh realities of life when she lands in America. On the airport she was harassed by an immigrant officer. Immigration officer exceeded his bounds and abused Manek, as her lover. Feroza being a typical oriental (Pakistani) girl, where the respects for the elders is observed, was not able to put up with the way immigrant officer handled her mother's nightgown. Manek advised her that she had to learn to stand so many things in this world. Feroza reacted violently. She scolded Manek: "Look. You didn't stand up for your sister's honor. So don't shout at me for defencing her *izzat*" (66). But Manek being in America has changed his notions of these all thing and in a very casual way suggested to forget such "honor-shonor business" in America (66).

Sidhwa describes vividly the impressions a new arrival has about modern America. Adam L. Penenberg rightly calls the novel, "a sensitive portrait of how America appears to a new arrival" [1994]. This was the first step towards the Americanization of Third World Paki girl, Feroza. For the first time in her life Feroza saw the glamour in the world such as advanced, lighted cities, skyscrapers, traffic and roads. She was fascinated by all these. America had mesmerizing effects on her mind. Feroza witnessed "a rich slice of the life and experience she had come to America to explore" (83) as well as "the callous heart of the rich country" (81). Manek planned for Feroza's education in USA. He chose completely puritanical environmental university of Salt Lake City for her to protect her virtues and values to assure her granny and parents. Even Coke and beer were forbidden in the state governed by Mormon values. Even Khutlibai would appreciate the sobriety of Mormon principles. Manek felt that the junior college and the size of the city would ease her assimilation into the American way of life. Manek described Khutlibai, Zareen, and Cyrus about the Mormon faith through a letter. Idaho State did not allow the liquor, striptease, prostitution, discos and all forms of provocative dancing. Even tea or coffee was not served in most restaurants as it contains caffeine. He left it to them to assume that "a community that forbade even coffee was not likely to permit promiscuous sex" (139).

Manek promised her to treat with free dinner in McDonald. But both of them were badly humiliated. Feroza was ashamed of what had happened. On the other hand Manek told her to be humble and not to be proud to feel the humiliation. He taught her "to get over culture shock" (144) and to "learn humility" (144). He showed her American way of life. Manek observed her licking rice off her fingers in an Indian restaurant. He cautioned her not to do it because following one's cultural habit in USA is hailed as inferior and coarse:

> **"You've got to stop eating with fingers," he said. "It makes them sick."... "It's very nice and cozy to be 'ethnic' when we're together, but those people won't find it 'ethnic', they'll just puke."(145)**

Here, Manek's remembering of his home atmosphere and its irrelevance in America can be described what Irwing Howe has identified nostalgia as "the real reason for the expatriate's need to evolve ethnic origins" [1978:174].

Sidhwa points out that the loss of mother-tongue is inherent in diasporic experiences. Rushdie too, talked about the 'loss of language' as one of the undercurrent in diasporic discourse:

> **Manek had not spoken Gujarati in so long. He relished each word and enjoyed the sound of his voice uttering the funny little phrases that have crept into the language since the Parsees adopted it almost fourteen hundred years ago, when they fled to India as religious refugees after the Arab invasion of Persia. (68-69)**

Here Sidhwa talks about the 'Farsi' which Parsis lost when given refuge in India and adopted Gujarati as mother tongue. So a migrant can suffer again and again while moving from one place to another.

Manek was happy that Feroza was living with Jo because Feroza could learn more from her about the American ways. Sidhwa describes the conditions of Jo and Feroza when they were trying to talk in a normal tone. Jo was surprised when Feroza talked in a very humble manner and typical British accent. Sidhwa comments that extreme politeness in speaking with Americans is suspected as the appeal for charity. This difference in outlook towards the public interaction is the outcome of oriental and occidental mind-set. Feroza asked very politely to see some items from the store and the woman replied: "You'll have to pay for it. This isn't the Salvation Army, y'know; it's a drugstore"

(150). Jo scolded Feroza, "Y'goota learn! You don't have to take shit from trash like her!"(151) Within few days, Feroza adopted the American pronounciation: "Hey, you goin' to the laundry? Gitme a Coke!"(154). Feroza also learned the coarse and abusive language like, "motha-fuka" (154).

A Parsi girl like Feroza had never shown any part of her anatomy. But in USA she is highly impressed by the American life. When Jo undressed, Feroza would change direction. When Jo talked to her in a state of semi-or entire nakedness, Feroza avoided her or gazed fixedly into Jo's eyes. But Feroza could not avoid all these natural passions, though strictly supervised in Parsi families by the hordes of elders specially, mother, grandmother, aunts etc. Feroza soon realized that all these things are natural in other cultural atmosphere i.e. American. Sidhwa portrays Feroza's realization of sexual desires. She relished the thought of copulation with pink, soft bodies as well as dreamed the close physical relationship with the "fully clothed, hard, brown bodies of the men she had crushes on in Lahore" (152). Such thinking would be considered as the sign of ill or vulgar mind in her own country. Though Feroza changed her attitude and outlook towards American life style, she never got over her feelings of guilt. Jo instigated Feroza into American life i.e. she flirted modestly with young men, began to drink the wine. Feroza wondered and enjoyed the freedom that American has offered to "independent and unsupervised lives of young people in America" (164). In their company Feroza thought "she had taken a phenomenal leap in perceiving the world from a wider, bolder, and happier angle" (164). In this way Feroza was Americanized. In the process of Americanization, she even committed the cardinal sin of smoking. Feroza started living with David. In course of time, their physical intimacies grew. They indulged in sexual intercourse. It was kind of exploration of Western life and culture. These close physical intimacies between Feroza and David show that Feroza was not comfortable with Shashi because they shared the "common culture" (256) whereas David has released her from the "baffling sexual limbo" (256). Both of them were captivated by "the otherness of the other-- the trepidation, the reticence imposed on them by their differing cultures" (256).

When Feroza returned Pakistan for a few days she found herself alienated from her motherland. This alienation was the direct result of her assimilation into the melting pot of USA. Feroza completely sheds off her Parsi Pakistani cultural identity. She is completely absorbed by American multicultural mosaic society. Her understanding of America's immense possibilities of progress compelled her to defend America. Sidhwa writes:

> **Feroza, who had been scathingly critical of America, of its bullying foreign policy and ruthless meddling in the affairs of vulnerable countries, in her discussions with her roommates and the new friends she had met through Shashi, found herself defending it in unexpected ways. Which other country opened its arms to the destitute and discarded of the world the way America did? Of course, it had its faults-- terrifying shortcomings-- but it had God's blessings, too. Feroza was disconcerted to discover that she was a misfit in a country in which she had once fitted so well. (239)**

This division of her identity raised the questions of her belonging. She no more identified herself with fundamentalist and patriarchic communities of Pakistan. Feroza in her due stay in USA witnessed the racism, poverty among American people. She also found gender, ethnic bias in American society. In a way, she witnessed miniature Pakistan in USA. This experience is aptly pointed out:

> **Coming to the First world, it is not altogether free from the characteristics of the Third World. The backwardness and the race and the gender-based exploitation in the First World is as predominant as it is in the Third World. Similarly, within the Third World, there are the ruling classes that are at one with the First World in their typology. In other words, some of the characteristics of the Third World can be seen in the First World, and *vice versa*. It can be argued that the Third World features, namely the backwardness and the exploitation based on caste, class, race, gender and religion- within the Third World get submerged in the tripartite division. [Purushotham, K. and N.S. Rahul, 2003:46]**

Thus Sidhwa reveals another feature of the American experience. Sidhwa also dealt with the problems of changing identity in migrated country by changing the names according to the host country. Manek handed his business card to Feroza with his new name as it was difficult for the people at work. For them it is "too foreign" (260) making them uneasy. But being "Mike" (260) is like "one of the guys" (260). This urge to assimilate completely into the American ethos can be traced in Margaret Atwood's *Surfacing* where narrator says: "If you look like them and talk like them and think like them then you are them" [Atwood 1983:113]. Sidhwa suggests that in a foreign country, assimilation and adaptation is very necessary. But here Manek had completely changed his identity to become "one of the guys" (260). It also connotes his loss of identity i.e. ethnic, cultural, religious, national and individual too. Here, Manek in his obstinate enthusiasm to disguise himself as *them* renounces all that is his – his inherited culture, beliefs, language and sensibility, he risks being a "free floating… citizen of the world" [Atwood 1983:113].

Another problem which immigrants suffer from is the sense of loss of one's people. But in the host country immigrants too always communicate through formal organizations of the ethnic groups where they celebrate every occasion and try to relive the homeland. Aban complained about her loneliness in America. They talked about four hundred Parsis spread over suburbs and community organized functions every month for fellow Parsis to strengthen bonding in alien land.

When Feroza visited David's parents, Feroza observed their culture and noticed some of the cultural similarities in it like breaking bread, sharing salt: "-- these concepts curled in her thoughts with comforting familiarity-- they belonged also to the Parsee, Christian, and Muslim traditions in Pakistan." (257)

During her visit to USA, Zareen realized that one night Feroza was not in her cot. For the first time, Zareen suspected that her daughter probably slept with David. Zareen feared the ultimate loss and accused Feroza of losing her virginity. Feroza shouted, "I'm perhaps the only twenty-year-old virgin in all America… Examine me if you want!" (292). This incident made Zareen nervous and she regretted sending Feroza to USA. Zareen complemented Laura and Shirley as "decent girls" (299) without boyfriends focusing on studies alone. But it caused great shock to Zareen when she came to know Feroza's explanation of their being "lesbians" (299) and Laura's detailed explanation of their relationship. Zareen came to know Feroza's loss of innocence and acquisition of "worldly wisdom" (300). Zareen was shocked to witness this transformation in Feroza because she had been properly brought up into "respectful, sexually innocent, and modest" (300) Parsi family.

Feroza noticed the changes within her as well as her point of view of the world after her break up with David. She knew that the way her life bloomed and fallen apart in America would be put together in America itself. Feroza suffered "the sense of dislocation, of not belonging" (312), which was more intense in America, but at the same time she too came to know: "it would be more tolerable because it was shared by thousands of newcomers like herself" (312). Feroza realized that her experiences in America have transformed her immensely: "She was dislocated, perhaps forever, like the clock in Strasbourh Cathedral" [Gallant 1981:204]. Feroza's attitude completely changed towards life since she became flexible and more optimistic, self-asserting, and self-confident:

> **There would never be another David, but there would be other men, and who knew, perhaps someday she might like someone enough to marry him. It wouldn't matter if he was a Parsee or of another faith.... It really wouldn't matter; weren't they all children of the same Adam and Eve? As for her religion, no one could take it away from her; she carried its fire in her heart. If the priests in Lahore and Karachi did not let her enter the fire temple, she would go to one in Bombay where there were so many Parsees that no one would know if she was married to *a Parsee or a non* (emphasis added). There would be no going back for her, but she could go back at will. (317)**

In this connection Novy Kapadia writes aptly: "The novel ends ambivalently, the mature Feroza, despite an estranged love affair and general feeling of depression prefers the struggle for freedom and self-fulfillment at the USA instead of the settled life, family and every contentment at Lahore." [1996:191]

Most Parsis identified themselves with British, and considered themselves different from Indians during the Raj. Both the Parsis who migrated to West faced severe identity confusion. In the West, they found themselves being grouped together with other sub-continental Asians- an identity they were trying to escape. In India and Pakistan too they came up against the hegemonic community.

Thus Sidhwa highlights the predicament of a Parsi girl in a brave new world of America from fundamentalist Pakistan. She cleverly underscores the dilemma interfaith marriage and sudden cultural shock Feroza and her family undergoes in America.

*

Thus, Bapsi Sidhwa meticulously portrays the Parsi predicament in the her fictional world. *The Crow Eaters* portrays the Parsi community as prosperous during colonial period. Parsi ceremonies, customs and rites are vividly described in this novel. In *Ice Candy Man*, Sidhwa portrays the effect of the partition of India on Parsi community. It shows the loyalty of the Parsis towards the British. *An American Brat* depicts Pakistani girl's new experiences in USA as well as her Americanization. The novel also deals with the insular marriage that is forbidden in Parsi community. Sidhwa, thereby, suggests reforms in Parsi laws.

Sidhwa very minutely highlighted various themes, issues, problems and dilemmas of her Parsi community. She has focused on insular marriage, dokhma problems, conversion, minority, subaltern status, political passivity, post-colonial crisis of identity etc. which caused the ethnic angst for her community. All her novels show variety of ethnic anxieties Parsi community suffers due to internal and external factors.

*

V

Rohinton Mistry: Sailing In the Times of Crisis

Rohinton Mistry was born in Mumbai on 3rd July 1952 to Behram Mistry and Freny Jhaveri Mistry. Cyrus Mistry, wellkown playwright and short-story writer, is his younger brother. He did his schooling from Villa Theresa Primary School and then St. Xavier's High School. He graduated from St. Xavier's College in Bombay. He completed his degree in Mathematics in 1974. His craze for music was such that Polydor released an EP, ***Ronnie Mistry***, on which he sang his own compositions and traditional folk songs. Later on, he migrated to Canada and there he married to Freny Elavia in 1975. In Canada, at Toronto, he worked as clerk in the Canadian Imperial Bank of Commerce. In 1978, Rohinton Mistry and his wife enrolled for evening courses at the University of Toronto. He completed his second degree in English Literature and Philosophy in 1982. He wrote his first short story ***One Sunday*** in 1983 and won Hart House Prize for it. Next year he won it second time for ***Lend Me Your Light***. In 1985 ***Auspicious Occasion*** won the contributor's award of *Canadian Fiction*. Thus, in 1987 Penguin Canada published his collection of stories entitled ***Tales from Firozsha Baag*** and later in Britain and USA under the title ***Swimming Lessons and other stories from Firozsha Baag***. It was short-listed for the Canadian Governor General's Award. Mistry published his first novel ***Such a Long Journey*** in 1991. It was short-listed for the Booker Prize and The Trillium Award. It won the Governor General's Award, the

Smith Books/Books in Canada First Novel Award and the Commonwealth Writer's Prize for the Best book. His second novel ***A Fine Balance*** appeared in 1995. It was shortlisted for the Booker Prize. It won the Governor General's Award and the Giller's Prize. It also received the Royal Society of Literature's Winfred Holtby Prize and the 1996 Los Angeles Times Award for fiction. ***Family Matters*** was published in 2002 and won several awards including the seventh annual Kiriyama Prize for literature of the Pacific Rim and the South Asia Subcontinent. It was also shortlisted for the Booker Prize and IMPAC award.

Mistry's fictional world deals with his home metro-polis Bombay. His brother Cyrus is great influence on his literary career, who advised him to write about his home city as "Bombay is as viable a city for fiction" [Saraiya, *The Independent*]. His books are re-fashioned from memory. Mistry himself said:

> **Writers write best about what they know. In the broad sense, as a processing of everything one hears or witnesses, all fiction is autobiographical- imagination ground through the mill of memory. It's impossible to separate the two ingredients. [Lambart, The Guardian]**

In 1996, Mistry was awarded an honorary doctorate of the Faculty of Arts at Ottawa University. His main concern in his fictional world is the representation of his microscopic community under the various political phases in India and its subjugation by majority. He portrays the various problems faced by his community in the present times.

*

I

Tales from Firozsha Baag: Parsi Microcosm

Rohinton Mistry's collection of short stories *Tales from Firozsha Baag* marks the beginning of his literary career. The locale of these short stories is a Parsi housing complex. It describes the daily life of the Parsi residents in a Bombay apartment. The stories are concerned with the troubles and the idiosyncrasies of Bombayite Parsis. Mistry explores the relationships at the heart of this community, their cultural identity and the uniqueness of their community. At the same time Mistry seeks to shed light and fully embrace the syncretic nature of the diasporic Parsi experience whether in North America or in India. Some of the stories focus on the journeys undertaken by some of the Firozsha Baag's Parsis, those who dared to leave for North America, leaving behind their imaginary homeland. However, Parsis have felt guilty after their flight and subsequent world-wide resettlement, particularly their movement towards the west. This diaspora, contrary to the Iranian diaspora, has been fulfilled in a positive way by the Parsis. Western diaspora results into guilt-consciousness as it is reflected in the story entitled as *Lend Me your Light.* Mistry has aptly reflected the *psychological diaspora* of the Parsis after their loss of elite consciousness in post-colonial India. Parsis found themselves toeing *the line of discontent* between two regions. This situation provoked many departures to England and to America, marking the Western diaspora of the Parsis. Mistry's fictional world is guided by this experience of double displacement. As a Parsi, Mistry aligns himself to the margins of Indian society and so his writing challenges and resists absorption by the dominating and Hindu-glorifying culture in India. Mistry used the memory and remembering as narrative techniques in *Tales from Firozsha Baag.* Mistry through his recollection of Parsi past in Mumbai tried to reconstruct the Parsi identity, as Craig Tapping aptly said: "Mistry is engaged in identity construction through the location of the present in the past" [1992:39]. The space, locale or its inhabitants are not sentimentalizing on a large scale. They are presented to us as unveiling the layers of memories of the Baag, what could be said as remembering the past and constructing it for the readers. Nilufer Bharucha while talking about '*On white hairs and Cricket*' gives the recurrent themes in this volume of short stories. It weaves within itself various persistent themes in the collection.

> **First of all... the leit motif of the Parsis as an ageing and dying race;... the motif of cricket stands for notions of honor, valour, and manliness as it is the game of the rulers and also called as gentleman's game... that had been inculcated into the Parsis by the British during the colonial period; the remembered past leads to alienation from postcolonial India; this in turn leads to immigration**

> **to the West; this immigration mainly by the young leaves behind old parents; loneliness and age is thus the other motif; related to this loneliness of the old Parsis in India, is the loneliness and lack of acceptance of the Parsis in the West; such alienation and loneliness often leads to dysfunctional and aberrant behavior both within the Indian as well as the Western contexts. [Bharucha 2003:92]**

The First story in the collection *Auspicious Occasion* is typical in its Parsipanu, which can be said as identity construction. It highlights various issues regarding Parsi community like Ethnic mores, Zoroastrian religious rituals, Parsi customs, costumes, and cuisine, we-consciousness among the Parsis, estrangement from the center, dominant community and decline in status in postcolonial India. It has made it "'Shadow-window' discourse for… the *Parsipanu*" [Bharucha 2003:74]. It represents the Parsis as warts without any glorification. It is in a real sense "a myth-buster" [Bharucha 2003:74] sentimentalizing the daily confrontations to so many havocs of the common life. Thus the Parsis in Firozsha Baag are portrayed as middle class. Being middle class in Bombay, they have "to engage in daily battle with intermittent water-supply, dilapidated homes, peeling paint, falling plaster and leaking WCs." [Bharucha 2003:74]

The story *Auspicious Occasion* opens with the male protagonist Rustomji's complaint about leaking WC. It sets the tone of the story. Rustomji's language is salted with Gujarati phrases and slang abuses. Mistry shows the age difference between Rustomji and Mehroo which is the result of the rarity of a 'Parsi Suitable' boy in the community. Mehroo was married to thirty-six year old Rustomji when she was just a girl of sixteen. He was "a fine catch" (03) by her parents. The story covers the action of a religious festival day of Behram roje, an auspicious occasion. Mehroo belonged to "an orthodox" (03) Parsi family which celebrated all important days on the Parsi calendar with prayers and ceremonies performed at the fire-temple. Her family had "a room with an iron-frame bed and an iron stool for the women during their unclean time of the month" (04).

Mehroo had practiced "all the orthodoxy of her parents" (04). Mistry highlights the duality of modern Parsis, who pretend to be modern but at the same time enjoy the age old traditions. Mehroo is permitted everything during her "unclean" (04) phase once a month as Rustomji insisted not to follow religious mores. Here Mistry shows the paradox in Rustomji's character that "secretly enjoyed most of the age-old traditions while pretending indifference" (04). He cherished going to the fire-temple clothed in his "sparkling white *dugli*, starched white trousers, the carefully brushed *pheytoe* on his head…" (04). Mistry portrays the poor and unhygienic conditions of Parsis living in the Baag. It is the result of lost glory of the Parsis of the Post-Raj India where they became minority suffereing from many problems. As Rustomji complains about WC:

> **That stinking lavatory upstairs is leaking again! God only knows what they do to make it leak. There I was, squatting - barely started- when some one pulled the flush. Then on my head I felt- pchuk- all wet! On my head! (04)**

It is this inauspicious beginning of the day so auspicious to both of them. She peeked into the WC and experienced "fearing a deluge of ordure and filth" (04). Mehroo suggests hiring a good plumber themselves instead of complaining to the Baag trustees. She doubts of "shoddy work" (05) by Baag trustees. Mehroo's remark suggests the corruption in the Parsi trustees and misuse of the funds. Rushomji abuses Baag trustees as "scoundrels" (05), who have "piles of trust money hidden under their arses" (05), suggesting the fraud and corruption in Parsi trusts. Mistry highlights the policy adopted by the trustees as: "…to stop all maintenance work not essential to keep the building from being condemned" (6). It results into Rustomji's anxiety when he planned to take a bath but water was covered by "plaster from the ceiling" (05). Mistry highlights the reasons why the Firozsha Baag building, like other Parsi Trust properties in Bombay, were in worse condition. Mistry gives the reason of dilapidated plaster of flats in the Baag as:

> **The… flats had been erected in an incredibly short time and with very little money. Cheap materials had been used, and sand carted from nearby Chaupatty beach had been mixed in abundance with substandard cement. Now during the monsoon season beads of moisture trickled**

> **down the walls...which considerably hastened the crumbling of paint and plaster. (07)**

Mistry gives the details of Parsi ceremonies. He describes the preparations of Behram roje:

> **Her (Mehroo) morning had started early:... cooked *dhandar -paatyo* and *sali-boti* for dinner; ...decorate the entrance with coloured chalk designs, hang up the tohrun... and spread the fragrance of *loban* through the flat - it was considered unlucky to omit or change the prescribed sequence of these things. (07)**

But for Rustomji customs were "dead and meaningless" (07-08). Mistry states the way Parsis have the perceptions of other Non-Parsis specially the servants. Mistry comments on the colonial attitude of the Parsis to see Indians as the source of pleasure. As a young boy, Rustomji had heard that most house-maids, "gungas, had no use for underwear- neither brassiere or knickers" (09). Gajara has provided this proof, "proof which popped out from beneath her short blouse during the exertion of sweeping or washing" (09). Parsis have inherited such notions of racial superiority from British during coloinal period, as the rights of the 'Master Race' [Bharucha 2003:76].

Mistry focuses on the changing attitude of young Parsis and their approach to the religious rituals. Mehroo remembered how her brothers and sisters and she used to enjoy all the rituals but expressed sorrow on her children's indifference towards Parsi ceremonies and rituals. She had to persuade them to finish "the *chasni* or it would sit for days, unnoticed and untouched" (12). Mistry underscores how old generation Parsis respected and adored the religious cult. Mehroo even as a child adored visiting the Fire Temple. It is described as:

> **She loved its smells, its tranquillity, its priests in white performing their elegant, mystical rituals. Best of all she loved the inner sanctuary, the sanctum sancotrum, dark and mysterious, with marble floor and marble walls, which only the officiating priest could enter, to tend to the sacred fire burning in the huge, shinning silver *afargaan* on its marble pedestal. (12-13)**

Here, Mistry highlights the fact that common Parsi people can not enter into the "inner sanctuary" (12). Only "the officiating priest" (13) who has undergone the state of complete purity can enter. Mistry captures the changing attitude of modernized Parsis towards the priests and their morality as a religious person:

> **Under the priestly garb of Dhunjisha… lurked a salacious old man taking advantage of his venerable image: "Loves to touch and feel women, the old goat- the younger and fleshier, the more fun he has hugging and squeezing them." (13)**

On Mehroo's protest Rustomji explains Dhunjisha's manners to exchange vulgar remarks between lines of prayer, "especially on days of ceremony when sleek nubile women in their colourful finery attended in large numbers" (14).

It was a famous joke among "the less religious" (14) Parsis. Rustomji calls all dustoors as "masked bandits" (14). Rustomji's remarks on WC of Fire Temple suggest the superiority complex among Parsis: "To look at it, it was not Parsis who used the WC, he felt, but uneducated, filthy, ignorant barbarians" (15). It suggests the mentality of the Parsis and we-consciousness which is inherited from the Raj era. Everything which is neat, tidy, beautiful, ordered, organized, systematic is Parsi and exact opposite is non-Parsi. This is the colonial mentality, which is permanently imprinted on their psyche. They are still unhappy over the departure of British-Raj that's why they are called as "reluctant Indians" [Kanga 1991: 27]. The sadness was the unavailability of Johnnie Walker Scotch in the Indian market which was easily available in British Empire. Rustomji mourned over the British departure.

This Anglomania Parsis suffer from what is described as "the Parsee disease" [Kanga 1991:161]. The reasons of this grief of loss of colonial elite status are aptly reflected by Tanya Luhrmann:

> **They [Parsis] were remarkably successful during the Raj. But their success came at the cost of jettisoning their adopted Indian identity in favour of western one. As a native colonial elite, Parsis were more westernized than most other Indian elites, and as displaced Persians, they committed themselves thoroughly to a non Indian**

> **sensibility. Now they feel marginalized in a postcolonial world, with an aching sense of loss of status, of cultural genius, of their historical moment. [1996:81]**

Rustomji left home for the Fire Temple. While stepping down at Marine Lines someone spat "a surfeit of juice ... of sticky, viscous, dark red ... stuff" (16-17) on his complete stark white dress from the upper deck. Rustomji yelled cursed the crowd who made fun of him. The crowd started to harass him and Rustomji played a clown to escape from the situation. Mistry picturizes the traumatized effect of the situation: "Tears of shame and rage welled in his eyes, and through the mist he saw the blood-red blotch" (18). Bharucha aptly writes on this:

> **Behind Rustomji's self-directed joke lies the trauma of the realization that in spite of the Parsis' continued belief in their superior status, in postcolonial India they have been downgraded to the unenviable status of a has-been community of eccentric old men and women. [Bharucha, 2003:78]**

Rustomji anxiously remarked on Dhunjisha's murder: "What is happening in the world I don't know. Parsi killing Parsi...*chasniwalla* and *dustoor*..." (20). It is an allegorical incident of Dustoor Dhunjisha's murder in the Fire temple which refers to the legend of Zarathustra's death in the temple while he was praying.

The second story in the collection *'One Sunday'* deals with Najamai - the only Fridge owner in the Baag. Boyces and Tehmina enjoy the facility of the Fridge. Tehmina used the fridge as an equipped resource of ice cubes for her midday drinks of ice-cold lemonade and evening scotch. The Boyce family made abundant use of it to store the weekly supply of beef. As beef is cheaper than mutton, poor Parsis like Boyces use it, though cow is sacred and venerated in Parsis. The eating of beef aligns Parsis with Muslims to some extent though their customs and habits were different from Muslims which is another subaltern group in India. Drinking wine by female members of the community suggests the freedom and liberty in Parsis; it aligns them with Christians, another subaltern group in India.

On a Sunday, in Najamai's absence Tehmina forgets to lock the door properly. Kersi and Percy ran through the Tar-gully to trace Francis, Najamai's servant who presumed him as a thief with their bats. In Tar-gully, they were disliked as representing the race that measured itself superior to them. The boys were teased as "Parsi *bawaji*! Cricket at night? Parsi *bawaji*! What will you hit, boundary or sixer?"(35) Both of them retorted them as "bloody *ghatis*" (35). The term is used for people from Western Ghats, but here it connotes as uncouth, barbaric person. The story ends with the brutal beating of Francis by the Boyces and other residence of the Baag. Kersi broke his bat in the frenzy of guilt as he had beaten Francis, one of their friends. It reflects the post-colonial status of the Parsis in India. Kersi has shown empathy with the more subaltern group. Kersi's destroying the bat "can also be seen as the ultimate inability of the 'elite' group to align with the truer subalterns" [Bharucha 2003:81].

The third story in the volume *'The Ghost of the Firozsha Baag'* has non-Parsi narrator and sees the Parsi colony and Parsis with a different way. Here it is the shift from internal to external perspective of the Firozsha Baag. The narrator is a Goan ayah Jacqueline - hailed as Jaakalee by the Parsis of the Baag. For Parsis ghaati women were good enough for the rough work, but children could not be given in their custody. For this purpose the English-speaking Goan ayah was imported by Mr. Karani. This was the part of the heritage of being colonial elite. Jaakalee herself tells in the story that, "They thought they were like British only, ruling India side by side" (46).

Mistry highlights the hybridity of language used by Parsis: '*Jaakalee*' (44) for Jacqueline, '*iggeechur*' (44) for easy chair and '*ferach beech*' (44) for French beans. This was done by all old Parsis as though, they have created their "own private language" (44). Mistry notes down the influence of Parsi atmosphere on Jaakalee: "I talk Parsi-Gujarati all the time instead of Konkani, even with other ayahs" (44). It suggests that Parsis adopted what was forced on them. Indianization of the English by the Parsis in such a way has created the comic situation and confusion too. Once again the *gora* or white complex is reflected by the Tar-gully people who hailed Jaakalee as "Blackie, blackie" (46). Mistry highlights how Parsis liked "light skin" (46). A child born with light-skin is praised as: "O how nice light skin just like parents" (46). But a baby with dark skin is considered as "*ayah no chhokro*" (46) or the child of a nurse.

The next story in the collection deals with *'Condolence Visit'*. The story has serious, ethno-religious and black-humor overtones. Mistry very brilliantly has used the *tape recorder* to take reader to the past and back to present with the buttons *Rewind* and *Forward* to narrate all the incidents surrounding the death of Minocher Mirza. After *charam* -fourth day- ceremony, the lamp should be extinguished as per the Parsi custom. This would help the soul to break the ties with this world and go "quickly-quickly to the Next World" (64). But Daulat ignores it. In Najamai's opinion, burning lamp would confuse the soul between two worlds. Daulat has decided to keep it going until the proper time to extinguish it. As per the Parsi charity, all the clothes of the dead are donated to the destitute, poor and needy Parsis. She sorted all the items of Minocher. Among these items, she found his Parsi pugree, which is rare in the vastly changing Parsi outlook where all the Parsis prefer to clothe like the Westerners even at wedding ceremonies. The pugree is worn on ceremonial occasions by Parsi men. Minocher's pugree was an antique, valuable piece, as these typical ethnic dresses are also vanishing with the Parsi traditions in the whirl of westernization. Daulat decided to give it to someone who would value it more. She gave an advertisement in Jam-e-Jamshed, in the hope that Minocher's pugree would find a suitable home. The visit by the approaching buyer of the pugree gives Daulat as relief from her oversympathetic first 'condolence visitor' i.e Moti. In a melodramatic and almost mock-tragic manner Moti falls upon Daulat's neck reeking of eau de cologne, uttering loud cries of distress. This cologne is normally associated with the sick room and death in the Parsi psyche. A Parsi patient is often made comfortable by the careful use of a little eau de cologne on his/her forehead. A Parsi dead body is kept smelling fragrant by moderate sprinklings of this scented water.

Hence it is the most appropriate perfume to be worn on a condolence visit. As the young man came for the pugree, both Najamai and Moti were horrified as: "Minocher's pugree being sold and the man barely digested by vultures at the Tower Of Silence!" (74). Daulat was firm and she not only made him try on the *pugree* but also denied to accept the payment for it and then she extinguished the lamp. She gave him as a souvenir of Minocher to continue the cultural heritage to new generations to preserve it for future generations.

'*Of White Hairs and Cricket*' highlights the gluttony of the Parsis and other Parsi issues. The story opens with Kersi's unwillingly pulling out the gray hair of his unemployed father who dreamt of bright future prospect while searching for job opportunities in news-paper. Mistry comments on the poor condition of the Parsis. Kersi and his father have had the toast smelling of kerosene due to unavailability of microovens and toasters. This reference to kerosene suggests the poverty and financial troubles so many poor families suffer from. Kersi's maternal grandmother used to purchase the edible items from the hawkers. But Kersi's disability to digest the food always revealed the truth. On such occassions Mamaiji in rage shouted at him. It was fun to listen to her scatological reproaches:

> **"*Mua ugheerparoo!* Eating my food, then shitting and tattling all over the place. Next time I'll cork you up with a big *bootch* before feeding you." (112)**

Pulling out the gray hair from father's head is considered to be illusion of the youth (past glory) and truth of coming of old age (dying community). These hair-pulling activities resulted in the conflict between his father and grandmother. Like most orthodox Parsis, she was sure that hair was a thing of evil and could be used for the black magic. That's why Parsis always covered their heads with white clothes by women and cap by men. She thought by compelling Kersi to pull hair, his father was committing a sin: "Sunday dawns and he makes the child do that *duleendar* thing again. It will only bring bad luck" (109). She is not only superstitious but also a devout Parsi woman who spun wool for the kustis.

The next story*'The Paying Guests'* deals with the problems of tenants and their evacuation from the rented house. The Baag has all the Parsi inhabitants, except one Muslim sub-paying-guest. An old Parsi couple had become the paying guest in the flat of the young couple Kashmira and Boman. This is typical situation in space-trapped Mumbai where an outdated rent act in cooperation with extremely high real estate prices, makes it unfeasible for the average person to either rent or own a flat. Neighbours sympathized with Boman and Kashmira but no one wanted to go to court as witness. Boman was desperate and knew that the only person who would speak up in court was the Muslim who lived in the next flat. Though he was very desperate to get rid of these tenants, he was not ready to request him "to testify against a fellow Parsi" (138). At this juncture, Nilufar Bharucha aptly comments:

> **There are two interesting things happening in this refusal to approach, one is the fact that the Parsis like most minority communities have a 'closing-of-rank' approach**

> **to their problems. A minority does not invite attention to one's self or expose one's internal weakness, to the communal other. [Bharucha 2003:98]**

Here it is understandable that most Parsis still brood over the inherited distrust towards the Muslim as inherited enemies because they caused their expulsion from their ancestral land of Persia. Parsis still blame Muslims for their booting out from Persia. It was the outcome of the feelings of nostalgia of their homeland: "It's [Persia is] the land of our ancestors… of great Zoroastrian empires… under Cyrus…. Darius. If it weren't for the bloody Mussalmans, Zoroastrians would be ruling the world" [Pestonji 1999:43]. But here is another reason. Baag is firmly a residence for the Parsis and supervised by the Parsi Trust. So it is scandalous that Parsi Baag has a Muslim resident.

'The Exercisers' highlights the issues related with better future prospects, love-marriages and religious beliefs. The story opens with Mr. and Mrs. Bulsara in quest of the aid of their family guru, Bhagwan Baba, to induce Jehangir of how unsuitable the girl was for him. Here, Hindu element of the personal guru is unfamiliar to Zoroastrianism which does not believe in the negotiator between believer and God. However, centuries of living in India and co-existence has apparently meant that some of the beliefs of the dominant community have been absorbed by the Parsis. After two years at college, Jehangir succeeds in the love affair with a girl from his choir group. His parents resented her as too modern. Moreover his mother charged her with her interest in Jehangir just because, "she knows you will go to study in America one day and settle there" (207). Parsi children are brought up with the purpose of studying abroad as Pestonji points out : "Young men and women grew up with the idea of emigrating to Velaat-which could mean England, America, Canada or Australia- as soon as they were qualified enough to seek higher qualifications abroad" [Pestonji 1999:5-6].

The three stories *'Squatter', 'Lend me Your Light',* and *'Swimming Lessons'* belong to the group of Mistry's Canadian stories. They deal with the diasporic experience of the writer in Canada and vying for the homeland, searching for existence in both locations. These are the stories which are concerned with Rushdie's *Periscopic vision* of both India and Canada.

Nariman Hansotia begins the story of *Squatter* by shaping it within the story of the courageous Savukshaw, the cricketer and hunter. Savukshaw changed his professions at will. The disgrace of and mortification of the contemporary Parsi immigrant to the West is thus off-set by the boasting Parsi. Savukshaw had single-handedly salvaged the prestige of the touring Indian cricket team by hitting whatever the English bowlers sent him, all round the field with complete freedom. Savukshaw would have escorted the Indian team to victory. But due to the rain, it had resulted in a draw. This reflects the pride of the Parsis and their contribution to modern India, as Bharucha rightly says:

> **This tale of derring-do filled Hansotia's young listeners-all male- with pride in thier lineage. This has for long been one of the reasons for story-telling, magnifying the self-esteem of the tribe. [Bharucha 2003:104]**

Mistry describes the Parsiness in eating habits while giving the description of Mrs. Savukshaw's mastery in the cooking of the favourite Parsi dish - dhansak. Mrs. Savukshaw' dhansak is described with details of ingredients of spices and one can almost smell "the aroma" (151) that wafted around Mr. Savukshaw's camp-fire as he heated up his chicken dhansak dinner. Nariman begins the story of '*Squatter*' whose hero is Sarosh - Sid. He figures in the backdrop of *'Condolence Visit'*. Mistry highlights Sarosh's immigration and his problem to cope with Canada and compares it with Vera and Dolly's successful immigration. Unlike them, he did not "find happiness there" (153). The glorious opening of the Savukshaw's story is contrasted with the pathetic stance of Sid- as he climbs up onto the toilet seat in his Canadian home every morning to clear his bowels. This scatological opening is an ironic comment on the immigrant's identity-construction and identity-confusion that at the front level imitate the Western mores. It depicts him in the mirror of the White world. But the personal self is often unwilling to keep rhythm with outward, cosmetic changes.

Before flying to Canada, at the farewell gathering he promised his friends and family to return to India if he does not become "completely Canadian" (155) within ten years from the time he lands there. This promise resulted into the traumatized and pathetic condition which however led to great humiliation as Sid was unable to assimilate in the American atmosphere:

> **The absence of feet below the stall door, the smell of faeces, the rustle of paper, glimpses caught through the**

> **narrow crack between the stall door and jamb -- all these added up to only one thing: a foreign presence in the stall, not doing things in the conventional way. And if the one outside could receive the fetor of Sarosh's business wafting through the door, poor unhappy Sarosh too could detect something malodorus in the air; the presence of xenophobia and hostility. (156)**

Excessive visits to toilets and late comings were marked by the supervisor who advised him to visit for "an immigration-related problem" (157) to his Immigrant Aid Society: "They should be able to help you. Every ethnic group has one: Vietnamese, Chinese- I'm certain that one exists for Indians" (157). Here the concept of ethnic group can be said to be an American term for the non-Europeans or one from outside the USA. It also suggests the national aspect of ethnicity. Nariman Hansotia explained the "Multicultural Department" (160) to his audience:

> **The Multicultural Department is a Canadian invention. It is supposed to ensure that ethnic cultures are able to flourish, so that Canadian society will consist of a mosaic of cultures - that's their favourite word, mosaic - instead of one uniform mix, like the American melting pot. If you ask me, mosaic and melting pot are both nonsense, and *ethnic is a polite way of saying bloody foreigner.* (Emphasis added) (160)**

P.A.Abraham has highlighted the various connotations of the term 'ethnic'. He says: "Personally, I consider 'ethnic' to be a derogatory term. The expressions 'mainstream' and 'ethnic minority' should be replaced by 'ethnic majority' and 'ethnic minority', as these terms imply a more balanced and comprehensive framework for Canadian life and which can be meaningfully related to the historical and social reality of Canadian society" [Ed. Jasbir Jain 2003:51].

Sarosh instead of CNI and Multicultural Department opted for the travel agent's office for his departure from Canada. Just as the plane began to move down the runway, Sarosh labored in the washroom. Sarosh for the first time in ten years was able to perform without squatting. He was not sure when he succeeded. Sarosh was once again uprooted, this time from Canada. He was searching his roots in India but was unsuccessful in his attempt. Sarosh desparetly searched for lost tracks in the pattern of his life.

Everything was strange and unknown. He was unable to identify himself with the home: "The old pattern was never found by Sarosh; he searched in vain. Patterns of life are selfish and unforgiving"(167). Ashish Gupta highlights such predicament of the immigrant suffering the double dislocation from hostland and homeland. He describes it as "...seem to be living with ghosts from... past. They are like hyenas ripping apart the carcass of... personality... little consolation in the fact that cultural dislocation is not restricted to... alone, but is a phenomenon affecting many in Indian society as well" [Ed. Jasbir Jain 2003:45]. This is exactly what Edward Said has said: "Exile is punishing... Once you have lost your homeland, it cannot be recovered as Paradise." [Nikhil Padgaonkar 1998]

Then Nariman Hansotia talks to the protagonist of his story directly. Sarosh denies to be called as 'Sid' as "that name reminds...of all troubles" (167). This reflects that changing names to adopt new identity is troublesome, because they remind people the troubles and suffering after shedding that identity. Protagonist himself speaks to preach the moral of the story by his own example:

> **Tell them... 'that the world can be a bewildering place, and dreams and ambitions are often paths to the most pernicious of traps'... "When you shall these unlucky deeds relate, speak of me as I am; nothing extenuate, nor set down aught in malice: tell them that in Toronto once lived a Parsi boy as best as he could. Set you down this, and say, besides, that for some it was good and for some it was bad, but for me life in the land of milk and honey was just a pain in the posterior." (168)**

Here, Mistry has adopted self-mocking tone, suggesting the failure in adopting and adapting the host country.

In the next story, *Lend me Your Light*, Mistry expressed his guilt-consciousness that comes with immigration. The story begins with Tagor's line from Gitanjali: "Your lights are all lit- Lend me your Light". These words of Tagore obtain a critical poignancy in the context of the story. It interprets "the need for Indians to remain rooted to their soil, help their fellow brethren who are oppressed, deprived and exploited, but are completely helpless and at the mercy of the powerful" [Chandra 2002:69]. The story focuses on complex issues related with Parsi diaspora, identity crisis, and assimilation. The three protagonists of the story highlight different dimensions of above problems. Jamshed's character portrays the alienated Parsi in the Indian context, who in the postcolonial period pants for the elite status that colonialism bestowed on his forefathers. Like many westernized rich Parsis, his life as a boy had circled round imported model-airplane kits, records of Mantovani and Broadway musicals and later classical music "from Bach to Poulenc"(175). Jamshed is a completely westernized Parsi who sees India as nothing but heat and dust, poor, hungry and hell like place to live. It suggests the reluctance of the post-colonial Parsis to merge with Indian masses. Percy deep-rooted in Indian soil works for the upliftment of the oppressed in the villages. He is an idealistic social worker working for villagers at the stake of his life for farmers to free them from the yoke of the landlords and moneylenders whereas Kersi because of his English education migrates to west for better future prospects. Kersi, a migrant, is confused with his new space and identity. At the same time, he does not want to lose the roots and wanted to be connected with his country. He appreciates the efforts of his brother, thinks himself guilty of running away from the home-reality and hates the ways of Jamshed and tries to assimiliate in the new environment. It is rather contradictory to convey that even though he might have abondoned India, he did not share Jamshed's anti-Indian sentiments, as India is the land which had given the refuge to his ancestors.

Kersi's brother Percy and Jamshed were friends at school, but later their ways become different, as Jamshed's obssession with all western things led him to migrate to the USA, while Percy had different vocation having greater assimiliation within Indian diasporic situation through work in the Indian villages. Jamshed's anger is concerned with instability and no future in postcolonial India. He lamented over the inability to see a decent English movie. This suggests that Parsis are "reluctant Indians" [Kanga 1991:27] and Anglophilia is "the Parsi disease" [Kanga 1991:161]. The same hint of migration was echoed in Kersi's preparation to immigrate to the USA. It is fully supported by his parents as foretold, his "education and ...westernized background, and... fluency in the English language" (178). The night before departure Kersi suffered from a searing pain in his eyes and wondered if he was being punished for the sin of immigration:

> **...the sin of hubris for seeking emigration out of the land of my birth, and paying the price in burnt-out eyes: I Tiresias, blind and throbbing between two lives, the one in Bombay and the one to come in Toronto... (180)**

This use of classical European myth is the direct result of English education that the British colonisers had imposed on their Indian subjects. The irony here is the immigrant acquired the status of blind prophet unable to see either the past (Bombay) or the future (Toronto). It is the beginning of the conflict between Indian roots (soul) and Canadian space (dream). In Toronto Kersi became a member of the Toronto Zoroastrian Society. Percy's letters from India about his work in the Indian village show the brutal reality of poverty and exploitation that Parsis like Kersi are trying to leave behind them, when they migrate to the West. Mistry gives the difference of lives Kercy and Percy were leading: Percy "waging battles against corruption and evil" whereas Kersi was watching sitcoms on... rented Granada TV.... attending dinner parties at Parsi homes" (184). Percy's letters revealed that the gulf between him and Jamshed was unbridgeable. When Kersi made his first visit back home, he bought gifts for everybody and wondered why he was doing that:

> **I felt like one of those soldiers who, in wartime, accumulates strange things to use as currency for barter. What was I hoping to barter them for? Attention? Gratitude? Balm to soothe guilt or some other malady of conscience? (186)**

A wellknown writer and critic Ashis Gupta points out that guilt of immigration is not escapable, "I was trying to expiate a nagging sense of guilt, but knew in my heart that I didn't really deserve forgiveness. This is the guilt of expatriate Indian, the cornerstone of the immigrant personality" [Ed. Jasbir Jain 2003:40]. Like most immigrants, Kersi, too, encountered the culture-shock after reaching Bombay. He felt a contrast between the lush greenery of the West and "the parched land: brown, weary, and unhappy" (186) of India. Indian soil was strikingly different. The city also appeared dirtier and more crowded. Mistry used the device of the morality play to describe scenario of the city: "All the players were there: Fate and Reality, and the latter's offspring, the New Reality, and also Poverty and Hunger, Virtue and Vice, Apathy, and Corruption" (187). Dom Moares too has similar feelings of alienation from

India. Standing at Kanheri, he feels, "a kind of vacancy of hollowness waitng to be inhabited... in Eurpoe I had positive emotions, in India I sank into the dream in which the whole country was sunk." [Moraes 1990:162]

This distancing from India is evident when he gives up the option of boarding a running bus and the realisation hits him: "I was a tourist here, and not committed to life in the combat zone" (188). This is the debatable point where immigrant visits his imaginary homeland and lives in the present of his past, but is no longer member of the combat zone, i.e. life in India. But Mistry's picturization of *comfort zone* i.e. life in Canada is not that glorious as expected by the immigrants.

The last story in the collection *'Swimming Lesson'* has autobiographical overtones. It highlights the various issues what Bharucha says:

> **...the trauma of finding an identity and location in a Western space is linked to sexuality, in a trajectory that is a deliberate or inadvertent mirroring of the manner in which imperialism itself saw in sexual terms - the male West and the female East and also in the way in which current postcolonial theorists image colonisation as a rape of the non-West by the West. [Bharucha 2003:115]**

It also highlights that in the white-western space of Canada, the elitist status of the Parsi-immigrant and the Parsi self-esteem is in even greater danger than it is in Post-colonial India. Mistry exposes the racism and growing influence of the majoratarian culture. Yet, even this lowered status is to be preferred to the real or perceived threat and pressure on Parsis of post-Shiv Sena Bombay:

> ***The postman rang the doorbell the way he always did, long and continuous; Mother went to open it, wanting to give him a piece of her mind but thought better of it, she did not want to risk the vengance of postman, it was so easy for them to destroy letters; workers nowadays thought no end of themselves, strutting around like peacocks, ever since all this Shiv Sena agitation about Maharashtra for Maharashtrians, threatening strikes and Bombay*** **bundh** ***all the time.*** **(231)**

Mistry highlights the attraction of white- pink bodies for the Indians, here the Parsis. He also comments on the disillusion Kersy witnesses. The women, he saw sunbathing from his upper floor window, were rather unattractive with "wrinkled skin, aging hands, sagging bottoms, varicose veins" (233). Kersi compared the clean swimming pool with dirty beach of Bombay Chowpatty. He was unable to swim in the sea at Bombay as well as in the pool in Canada too. These failures could be seen as the failure of Kersi and through him most Parsis, to assimilate in either Indian or Canadaian (Western) Diasporas. However by the end of the story, Kersi was able to open his eyes underwater in his bath-tub and see life in a double-perspective i.e. Indian and Canadian. But before the successful assimilitation Kersi went through horrible problems faced by any immigrant - the racism, the bitter winter etc. Kersi's first encounter with racism and xenophobia were when he enrolled himself in swimming class where he found three boys singing: "Paki Paki, smell like curry.... pretty soon all the water's going to taste of curry" (238). His final comments bring out the inner fear of immigrants evocatively:

> **Maybe the swimming pool is the hangout of some racist group, bent on eliminating all non-white swimmers, to keep their waters pure and their white sisters unogled. (239)**

The next problem he suffered was the bitter winter in Toronto. He saw the old man staring outside watching the snowfall. Kercy imagined the old man's thoughts of childhood days, snowmen with hats and pipes, and snowball fights and white Christmas, and Christmas tree. He imagines his condition when he would grow old in this alien country:

> **What will I think of, old in this country, when I sit and watch the snow come down? For me, it is already too late for snowmen and snowball fights, and all I will have is thoughts about childhood thoughts and dreams, built around snowscapes and winter- wonderlands on the Christmas cards so popular in Bombay; my snowmen and snowball fights and Christmas trees are in the pages of Enid Blyton's books, dispersed amidst the adventures of the Famous Five, and the Five Find-Outers, and the Secret**

> **Seven. My snowflakes are even less forgettable than the old man's, for they never melt. (244)**

This reflects the problem of memory and aging. At the same time it suggests that one can't become the native unless born in that particular land. The contrasts between the memory of the old man and Kersi as would be-old man is that old man has experienced those all snow-games and related adventures in his childhood whereas Kersi has just read and seen all those things in the books alone. In this reference George Steiner describes the expatriate writer as "the contemporary everyman". It is also described as "a state of mind and emotion which includes a wistful longing for past. It is often symbolized by the pain of exile and homelessness. There is a complex view of the double vision of the expatriates-both a looking forward and a yearning backward. It is, in fact, part of every person's life, it is part of the human condition. No matter where you lived, even if you lived in the same place all your life, you would look at the past, at lost moments, at lost opportunities, lost loves. [Ed. Jasbir Jain 2003:51]. Kersi gave the glimpses of the Canadian experiences directly to the reader. There are other readers also within the story who experience and comment on it. His parents, especially his father evaluate his son's work mainly the last one, i.e. *'Swimming lessons'* which dealt with Canada:

> ***...if he continues to write about such things he will become popular because I am sure they are interested there in reading about life through the eyes of an immigrant, it provides a different viewpoint; the only danger is if he changes and becomes so much like them that he will write like one of them and lose the important difference.*** **(248)**

Here, the need of the diasporic writer to write about the homeland and about the host-land is important. The writer has to maintain the distance with the host-country as well as enjoy the previlege of being one of them. It also relates the problem of assimilitation of mental set-up. All these diasporic writers dealt with such problems. While reading the stories one by one, Kersi's father remarked on the portrayal of Parsi families in the Firozsha Baag. He expected the positive aspect of Parsis and Parsiness:

> ***... all the Parsi families were poor or middle-class.... but there should also have been something positive about Parsis, there was so much to be proud of.... he should have found some way to bring some of these wonderful facts into his stories, what would people reading these stories think, those who did not know about Parsis- that the whole community was full of cranky, bigoted people; and in reality it was the richest, most advanced and philanthropic community in India and he did not tell his own son that Parsis had a reputation for being generous and family-oriented.*** **(245)**

Thus, it is obvious that Mistry's Canadain stories draw dark and gloomy picture of Canada and even warn reader against the act of immigration. Thus Tales from Ferozsha Baag has proved the land mark in the history of Indian Writing in Literature for its appeal to portray anxieties of Parsi community in Indian cultural milieu in post independent India. It has become the spirtius mundi for Mistry's journey as a sensitive artist.

*

II

Such a Long Journey: From Innocence to Wisdom

In this novel, Mistry has brilliantly used three epigraghs from well-known poets to initiate readers into the leit-motives of the narration. The first epigraph is cited from famous Iranian (Persian) epic *Shah Nama* that recalls both the glorious Iranian heritage of a mighty empire: "...the kings who had once possessed the world. ...hold the world in the beginning," as well as marks the downgraded condition of the present-day Parsis, even in Iran: "and why is it that it has been left to us in such a sorry state". It also hints the post-colonaial predicament of the Parsis as they are always worried of their minuscule community and its existence: "... they were able to live free of care during the days of their heroic labours?" The second epigraph is from T.S. Eliot's *Journey of the Magi* that reminds the three wise ancient Zoroastrian priests who were present at the nativity of the Christ. This epigraph not only provides the title of the text but also highlights the central motif of *journey* as a metaphor:

> **A cold coming we had of it,**
> **Just the worst time of the year,**
> **For a journey, and such a long journey...**

This most difficult journey is undertaken by the protagonist of the novel. The final epigraph from Tagore's *Gitanjali* concludes the way in which the Parsis have moved from one country to another and how they had adapted themselves to new realities by forgetting the old thing: "where the old tracks are lost, new country is revealed with its wonders".

Mistry has reviewed major phases of the Indian political history of 70s and 80s where there are references of Indo-China war (1962) and humiliation of defeat that resulted into the end of Nehruvian era of dream of a secular India, Indo-Pakistan war (1965), death of Shastri at Tashkant, Indo-Pakistan (East) war (1971) which led to the liberation of Bangladesh from the ruins of East-Pakistan. It reflects how contemporary politics has severally affected Mistry's miniature community under the uprising of fundamentalist right-wing parties like Shiv-Sena. The nationalization of the banks was the terrible shock to the Parsis, who were the Kings of the Banks. There is mutual hatred for Indira Gandhi who troubled Sohrab Nagarwala, the cashier of State Bank of India, and a Parsi agent from RAW. In the novel Mistry has used the story with the fictional name of Major Jimmy Bilimoria.

This is the betrayal of marginal Parsi community by central ruling government which Mistry portrays in the novel. It is precisely what Bharucha said:

> **As a Parsi he is on the periphery even in India, so his discourse also challenges and resists the totalization of dominant culture within India itself. [Bharucha 1995:59]**

Mistry has provided the vision of Bombay that was falling victim to the fundamentalism where all the religions, communities were at peace in idealistic *utopian* world. During partition, whole of north India was set on the fire of ethnic hatred because of Hindu-Muslim riots. It was the direct result of increasing fundamentalism of right wing parties like Shiv Sena whose cry for the *son of the soil* shattered this frame that entrapped Bombay in the clutches of the fundamentalist, mafia dons and all other criminal activities in 1960s.

Mistry opens this novel against the backdrop of portraying the lives of the *Khodadadad* building, a Parsi housing complex where Gustad Noble and his family lives. In the war time (1962) Gustad had put the black-out paper on the window panes and ventilaters that he never removed then. Gustad's family grumbled but then "grew accustomed to living in less light" (11). This adjustment suggests the submission of marginal cultures to the mainstream cultures. In 1965 the same blackout papers needed to go up again, as Pakistan waged war against India. Years after it was trouble in East-Pakistan that attracted the attention of Gustad to read from the daily newspaper. It reminded him and his family his neighbour Major Bilimoria through whom Gustad's Parsi world got extended to the wider experience of Indian world. Mistry has created the dynamic character of the Wall which is used as the open lavatory "like a wholesale public latrine" (16). All the passersby urinated there which resulted in the great stinky smell and caused mosquito nuisance to the residents of Khodadad building. It also marks the boundary which stands for the inclusion and exclusion. It is protective as well as reductive. It protects the Parsi minority from the outer world but at the same time reduces their world within it and isolates them from the Indian millieu.

Mistry highlights pathetic conditions of Gustad's family after his interaction with Jimmy Bilimoria's plan to deposit ten lakh rupees in his bank. This captures the happiness of Gustad and his family into a vortex of political turmoil of India and subaltern status of his community fellow. Mistry's use of irony underlines the growing corruption in Indian politics and society as Sohrab expresses his views:

> **Jimmy Uncle says this is government money, right? So let's spend it on all the things government is supposed to do. Wouldn't it be nice to fix the sewers in this area, install water tanks for everyone... (121)**

Gustad's delay in depositing the money in bank earned rage and danger for his family as he found one morning "A headless bandicoot" (134) and "the dead cat" (137). At last he received a paper scrap with rhyming couplet, *"Bilimoria chaaval chorya/ Daando lai nay marva dorya"* (140). Such threats to his family enraged Gustad and raised a sense of betrayal from a fellow Parsi, a dear brother to him:

> **Damn Jimmy, the bastard. Once like a brother... and now? Those Bible stories, that Malcolm used to tell me. One about Cain and Abel..... Fairy Tales, I used to think. ...Jimmy, another kind of Cain. Killed the trust, love, respect, everything. And that other story, about Absalom, son of David. (178)**

The use of biblical story is the effect of Gustad's Christian friend Malcom and the English education of Parsis. Dinshawaji showed Gustad a newspaper Colum entitled, "CORRUPTION RIPE IN RAW" (194) which made Gustad angry. It described the details of Mr. Bilimoria's arrest on the charges of impersonating the Prime Minsiter's voice on telephone and ordered Bank's Chief Cashier to hand over sixty lakh rupees to Bangladeshi Babu. Mr. Bilimoria received the money in the persona of Bangladeshi Babu. The report read that Mr. Bilimoria took the whole responsibility of this plan as he wanted to help "The Mukti Bahini" (195). Mistry very brilliantly focused the gap-holes of the real incident. The crime is described as "highly imaginative" (195) and the circumstances as "unusual" (195). It put forth the question of faith in the banks as well as great political leaders. The news was a great blow to the Parsi community as it caused the decline in their honour and respect:

> **It was not very often that a Parsi made the newspapers for a crime. The last sensation had been more than a decade ago, when a naval commander had shot and killed his wife's lover. (207)**

Major Bilimoria requested Gustad to come and see him in the prison at Delhi. Ghulam brought the news from the newspaper which said: "SENTENCING SOON IN RUPEES-FOR-RAW CASE" (233). Ghulam added more information and confirmed the corruption in the government and its system as "the courts" (233) were managed. The "chief investigator" (234) suddenly died in a car accident. Ghulam's bitter comments and rage hints at the corruption rate and indulgence of influencial leaders in the fraud scam as well as the common public cry against such ill-activities. Gustad read the signs in the hotel: *"Don't Discuss God & Politics"* (174). It shows the corrupted politics of contemporary India. Sohrab's comments are apt in this context, as he says:

> **But what about the leaders who do wrong? Like the car manufacturing licence going to Indira's son? He said Mummy, I want to make motorcars. And right away he got the licence. He has already made a fortune from it, without producing a single Maruti. Hidden in Swiss bank accounts. (68)**

Dr. Paymaster explained corruption as "gangrene at an advanced stage" (313). While discussing the East-Pakistan problem, Pakistan is called as "Bloody butchers" (76), America as *"maader chod"* (76), Nixon as *"chootia"* (76) licking his way up into Pakistan's arsehole. This description of Pakistan and America suggests the anger among the common people of India. Mistry shows the paradox of the American attitude which they are famous for the roles and identities worked out for a long on all the essential international stages: "that Americans were a kind and friendly people, champions of justice and liberty, supporters of freedom struggles and democracies everywhere" (299). Gustad left for Delhi to meet Jimmy. Jimmy narrated all the events of his present condition. Jimmy described the Prime Minister as "Spy", "blackmail"(er), "control"(er), "very strong woman... very intelligent"(270), "calm", "crooked"(271), "Very clever woman"(277). Jimmy provides the information of her cabinet suggesting the corruption rate on moral as well as economic level: "One of them... prefers little boys. Another takes pictures of himself... doing it with women" (270). He further describes the attitude of the Prime Minister who keeps control over friends and foes by black-mailing as "Blackmail is the only way she can keep control" (270). The Prime Minister took the written confession from Jimmy Bilimoria about the telephone and sixty lakh rupees:

> **She said, yes, but he did not see me speaking... we can always say someone imitated my voice... all you have to say is.... you imitated my voice. ...under proper conditions, people will believe anything. She promised... nothing would happen to me. (277)**

But the money was rerouted to "a private account" (278). Jimmy thought to tell this corruption to the press and opposition parties. But Prime Minister controlled everything like "RAW, the courts, broadcasting..." (278). Jimmy thought if Prime Minister used money for her personal causes, then he and his friends can also use it. For this he put ten lakh rupees aside. This changing behavioural pattern of Jimmy, an honest Parsi, suggests the adverse effect of dictatorial political rule of majoritorians on honest and tiny community like Parsi.

After Major Jimmy Bilimoria's death, Ghulam planned to take revenge. His plan displays the growing hatred among marginalized subaltern groups against the central majoratrian rule. Ghulam is ready to wait for the right time:

> **From whoever is responsible. If it's the car manufacturer, he will have to pay. Lots of possibilities - his car might explode, for instance. He also likes to fly aeroplanes, so: bhoom, crash, the end. As I said, whatever is necessary to get the job done. (323)**

Ghulam revealed the dictatorship and dirty politics of the Prime Minister who made enemies "from Punjab to Tamil Nadu." (323)

Mistry has portrayed the caricaturesque character like Dinshawaji who used to flirt with the young woman Laurie Coutino. Here his remarks on Laurie Coutino expressed the moral superiority of Parsis with racial pride:

> **'*Arre*, Gustad, these Catholic girls are all hot-hot things. Listen, my school was in Dhobitalao area, almost hundred per cent *ma-ka-pao*. The things I would see, my eyeballs would fall out. Not like our Parsi girls with all their don't touch-here and don't-feel-there fussiness. Everything they would open up. In every gully-gootchy, *yaar,* in the dark, or under the stairs, what-what went on.' (99)**

Mistry focuses on the religious tolerance of the Parsis. Gustad agreed to visit the Mount Mary on Malcolm's suggestion. Before this time, Gustad would have promptly dismissed such an invitation because: "Dabbling in religions was distasteful and irreverent, an affront to the other faith and his own" (222). The pavement artist had described him the miracle of Mount Mary. Malcolm, too, said the same thing:

> **Gustad learned more about the Church, how it had a tradition of welcoming Parsis, Muslims, Hindus, regardless of caste and creed. Mother Mary helped everyone, She made no religious distinctions... Like divine intervention. Maybe Dada Ormuzd is telling me something. (222)**

Gustad visited Mount Mary. Prayer brought him peace of mind.

Another important character standing for religious tolerance is the *wall* which encompassed all the religions of the world. Pavement artist made heaven out of hell by painting the portrayals of the saints, religious places of different religions:

> **Gautama Buddha in Lotus Position under the Bodhi Tree; Christ with Disciples at the Last Supper; Karttikeya, God of Valour; Haji Ali Dargah, the beautiful mosque in the sea; Church of Mount Mary; Daniel in the Lions' Den; Sai Baba; Manasa, the Serpent-Goddess; Saint Francis Talking to the Birds; Krishna with Flute and Radha Holding Flowers; the Ascension; and finally, Dustoor Kookadaru and Dustoor Meherji Rana. (212)**

Inspector Bamji congratulated Gustad to make the wall "pisser-proof" (213). But some of the tenants from Khodadad building complained in private about presence of "*parjaat* gods on a Parsi Zarathosti building's wall" (213). The wall became the sacred place of all religions, "a shrine for all races and religions" (286).

Mistry focuses on religious beliefs, ceremonies and customs of the Parsis. The novel begins with Gustad Noble turning Eastward to rising sun to "offer his orisons to Ahura Mazda" (01). Ghulam has arragnged the funeral of Jimmy Bilimoria. Dilnavaz read about it in *Jam-E-Jamshed*. Thus, Mistry very aptly highlights that humanity, emotion and love are very essential things to live and die happily which are sans-religion, caste and any ethnic group. Contradictorily, Mistry also highlights the rigidity of Parsi community as Ghulam, being a non-Parsi, was denied entrance into The Tower of Silence: "Your Parsi priest's don't allow outsider like me to go inside" (322). Slaughtering in the house brings bad luck. Dilnavaz opposed Gustad for his "mad and wholly impractical scheme" (18) of cooking chicken by bringing it alive in kitchen and then killing it in the house. In Dilnavaz's family "a chicken was always brought home slaughtered" (18). Parsis believe in good and bad omens. Mistry gives the details of such omens. Miss Kutpitia excused Dilnavaz for her dinner invitation, as she faced the bad omen in the morning and decided not "to step outside her home for the next twenty-four hours" (35). Raining is considered as "good luck if it rains when something new is beginning" (57).

Parsis perform some religious rituals before the start of some work. Mistry gives the details of such a ceremony:

> **Before leaving, he had been adorned with a vermilion dot on the forehead, and a garland of roses and lilies. Dilnavaz did the *overnaa* and sprinkled rice, presenting him with a coconut, betel leaves, a dry date, one areca nut, and seven rupees, all for good luck. She popped a lump of sugar in his mouth… They said more or less the same things as on a birthday, but the emphasis was on school and studies. (57)**

Mistry gave the details of final rites of Dinshawji. The news of Funeral and Uthmna Ceremony was published in the *Jam-E-Jamshed* to convey all the people about Dinshawji's final rites. Parsis pray for one day or four days. The corpse is washed before dokhma for "purity" (246). Alamai argued with the men who came to perform Dinshawaji's *suchkaar* and sponging the corpse with *Gomez*, "'All this nonsense with bull's urine is not for us… 'We are modern people. Use water only, nothing else'" (246). Mistry gives details of Kusti prayer for Dinshawji:

> **Two men entered with the body, white-clad now, and laid it on the low marble platform. The face and ears were left uncovered by the white sheet. A priest arrived and lit an oil lamp next to Dinshawji's head… The priest picked up a sliver of sandalwood, dipped it in oil and held it to the flame. He transferred it to the thurible and sprinkled *loban* upon it. The fragrance of frankincense filled the room. The priest started to pray. (247)**

Gustad felt the serene and powerful impact of prayers on the listeners. Mistry highlights the extinction of the Avestan language as Parsis adopted Gujarati and English. He points out the Parsi attitude of following the prayers without understanding the language:

> **...Gustad was under its gentle spell. He listened to the music, the song in a language which he did not understand, but which was wondrously soothing. All his life he had uttered by rote the words of this dead language, comprehending not one of them while mouthing his prayers. But tonight, in the *dustoorji's* soft and gentle music, the words were alive; tonight he came closer than he ever had to understanding the ancient meanings. The *dustoorji* cantillated the verses of the ancient Avesta. (247-248)**

Dog is considered as the life-detector in Parsis. Parsis use it to know whether the person is really dead or not. When the *char-chassam* dog walked round the bier, sniffed and left in silence, Alamai wailed: "'O dog! Make some little sound at least! O Parvar Daegar! No barking? Now it is certain! O my Dinshaw, now you have really left me!'" (251). Gustad observed the contrasts between her "modernistic ideas and her orthodox confusions" (251). After due time, the *nassasalers* carried the bier to the Tower, to the well of vultures. Gustad wished to carry Dinshawji, but in Zoroastrianism only nassasalers could carry the dead body. Gustad points out the contrast between belief and reality: "Silly custom, to have professional pall-bearers. And on top of that, poor fellows treated like outcasts and untouchables" (252).

Women are not allowed to approach "the well of vultures" (252). So, women lined up on the "*bungalee's* verandah" (252). The procession had arrived at the Tower. The common Parsis are not allowed to enter the well. So, only *nassasalers* entered inside the Tower closing the door behind them. But they knew what would happen inside:

> **...the *nassasalers* would place the body on a *pavi,* on the outermost of three concentric stone circles. Then, without touching Dinshawji's flesh, using their special hooked rods they would tear off the white cloth. Every stitch, till**

> **he was exposed to the creatures of the air, naked as the day he had entered the world. (254)**

Mistry presents some of the problems related with Dokhma and suggests the reforms to improve on it by giving some paradoxical and comic details. Gustad at the Tower of Silence heard from the man at counter that two women last week requested him:

> **'We forgot to remove a diamond ring from Grandmama's finger,' they said. 'Can you please shoo off the vultures for a few minutes? So we can go inside the Tower and get it back?' (316)**

Mistry shows the dual nature of such Parsis with practical purposes:

> **But the women told him to hurry before the priceless diamond ring wound up in a vulture's belly. Money was not the question, it was the sentimental value. 'We have no faith in the work of illiterate cretins like *nassasalers,'* they said, ignoring his reminders that laity were forbidden inside the Tower. (316)**

The most important problem related with the Dokhma is the littering of the flesh by the vultures which troubled the clerk a lot as tenants from costly luxurious flats around *Doongerwadi* had often complained against vultures:

> **'Control your vultures! Throwing rubbish on our balconies!' They claimed that the sated birds, flying out from the Tower after gorging themselves, invariably snatched a final bite to savour later. And if the tidbits were lost in mid-flight, they launched on the exclusive balconies. This, said the indignant tenants, was absolutely intolerable, considering the sky-high prices they had been charged for their de luxe flats. (316-317)**

On the other hand, relatives of dead read about the skyscraper scandal and protested:

> **...they were not paying funeral fees to have their dear departed ones anatomized and strewn piecemeal on posh balconies. The bereaved insisted that the Punchayet do something about it. 'Train the vultures properly,' they said, 'or import more vultures, so all flesh can be consumed in the well. We don't want a surplus which can be carried off and lost in impure, profane places.' (317)**

Mistry highlights the continuous battle between the reformists and the orthodox Parsis. They fought over any topic with community interest like "the chemical analysis of *nirang*", "the vibration theory of Avesta prayers" (317). On the vultures' controversy, both the orthodox and reformists joined the battle. The orthodox defended it as "a pure method, defiling none of God's good creations: earth, water, air, and fire" (317) and on the basis of "modern hygienic standards" (317). Here, the stance taken by orthodox can be seen in what Kanga said: "That we are burned to ashes like the Hindus? Or chewed by worms like the English men? I, for one, prefer to be eaten by vultures" [Kanga 1991:73]. The reformists, who favoured cremation, rejected it on suitability ground and changing of the time:

> **...the way of the ancients was unsuitable for the twentieth century. Such a ghoulish system, they said, ill became a community with a progressive reputation and a forward-thinking attitude. (317)**

Mistry provides very funny as well as intelligent reasons for the battle between Orthodox and Reformist on the issue of traditional dokhma. The reformists called orthodox "vulturists" (317). Orthodox Parsis put charge on reformists as their relatives in foreign has no access to Tower of silence or some of them own "shares in crematoria" (317). That's why these reformists are not interested in traditional dokhma. The orthodox provided the proofs from well-known ornithologists that "vultures, as a species, were unable to fly after a heavy meal or if their talons and beaks were loaded" (318). In the bank, there was passionate argument over "the Tower of Silence controversy" (71). Whenever matter grew worse Dinshawaji would manage to end matters on a light note, saying things like:

> **'Better that my dear domestic vulture eats me up than the feathered ones. With her I have a guarantee- she at least won't scatter pieces of my meat all over Bombay.' (72)**

Mistry deals with religious issues and other values which resulted into ethnic anxiety. Parsis held the cow in the highest regard as promised to the king, Jadav Rana. But for the economical reasons some Parsis started eating beef. Malcolm taught Gustad to eat beef. Malcolm thought to be blessed as:

> **'Lucky for us,'...'that we are minorities in a nation of Hindus. Let them eat pulses and grams and beans, spiced with their stinky asafoetida - what they call *hing*. Let them fart their lives away. The modernized Hindus eat mutton. Or chicken, if they want to be more fashionable. But we will get our protein from their sacred cow.' At other times he would say mimicking their economics professor, 'Law of supply and demand, always remember. That's the key. Keeps down the price of beef. And it is healthier because it is holier.' (23)**

Here, one can understand that the prices of mutton and chicken are raised as the majority of Hindus eat mutton and chicken as the sign of "modernized" (23) or for being "fashionable" (23). But they never ate beef. So the prices of the beef are always down. Minority like Christian and Muslim eat beef because it is cheap as well as "healthier because it is holier" (23). They have an interesting notion about vegetarians that vegetarians do not have physical stamina. It is reflected aptly as: "Vegetarianism is the reason for India never winning medals at the Olympics" [Pestonji 1999:10]. Gustad experienced an embarrassing incident in the bus while carrying beef in the basket. He dexteriously carried the beef in the multi-layerd paper bag. But to his misfortune was disclosed to the woman. She covered her nose and mouth with a sari corner. Gustad says, "Smells my fear, like a dog. Eyes of a Doberman. These bloody vegetarians. A sixth sense for meat"(223). Gustad and Malcolm used to go Crawford Market for the beef. But Gustad gave up to go there for "his fear of riots and bloodshed" (220). He was afraid because he had witnessed such riots which began with rallies. Rally had brought "a herd of cows" as per the "modern trends in political campaiging and public relations" (221).

Gustad observed the Church rituals and found them just opposite to the rituals in the Fire Temple:

> **Gustad went in with him, dipping his fingers in the font of holy water and crossing himself, imitating his friend closely, to fit in and not give offence to anyone. The first time, Gustad was quite intrigued by the church and its rituals, so different from what went on in the Fire Temple. (23-24)**

But Gustad knew that he should respect all religions. For him all religions were equal but at the same time one should be faithful to one's own religion as "religions were not like garment styles that could be changed at whim or to follow fashion" (24). His parents always opposed the "conversion and apostasy being as rife as it was, and rooted in the very history of the land" (24).

Gustad preferred the Fire Temple to Church for its "sense of peaceful mystery and individual serenity" (24). Sometimes he doubted whether Malcolm was making "an amateurish, half-hearted attempt at proselytism" (24). Malcolm provided the information regarding the arrival of Christianity in India. He tried to impress Gustad with his knowledge and superiority over the Parsis. But Gustad too, answered with the same zeal:

> **'Long before you Parsis came in the seventh century from Parsia,' he teased, 'running away from the Muslims.' 'That may be,' rejoined Gustad, 'but our prophet Zarathustra lived more than fifteen hundred years before your Son of God was even born; a thousand hundred years before the Buddha; two hundred years before Moses. And do you know how much Zoroastrianism influenced Judaism, Christianity, and Islam?' (24)**

Gustad and his friends used to tell jokes from various ethnic groups like Sikh, Madrasi, and Gujarati etc. "No linguistic or ethnic group was spared; perfect equality prevailed in the canteen when it came to jokes" (71).

The widening of the roads caused great violence as the *religious wall* was about to be demolished by Bombay Municipal Co-operation. Malcolm was the project supervisior. The *morcha* against the corruption in muncipality was proceeding ahead and stopped before the wall. The leader called it "sacred wall of miracles" (326). He appealed to all the religions and its followers:

> **The wall of Hindu and Muslim, Sikh and Christian, Parsi and Buddhist! A holy wall, a wall suitable for worship and devotion, whatever your faith! So let us give thanks for the past success! Let us ask blessings for future endeavours! (326)**

Mistry highlights the diversity of Indian culture with multi-religious, multi-ethnic, multi-culture attitude. It can be noticed from the members in queue, the decline in Parsi demography as "At the painting of Zarathustra there was only one person: Dr.Paymaster" (326). There was public uproar after learning the destruction of the wall:

> **Disbelief turned into indignation, then to outrage, that surged through the congregation and swelled into a tidal wave, making the ground tremble as it galloped for the shore… The wall of gods and goddesses cannot be broken! We will see that not one finger is raised against the deities! We will protect them with our blood if need be! (326)**

Mistry shows minoritorian trend to learn the tactics of majority group for the assimilation. Inspector Bamji explained Gustad about the indifference toward the incident to be occurred. He learned from "Maratha buggers" (330) to say "*umacha* section *nai*" (330) shamelessly. It shows hatred for *the center* and inherited indifference of minority from majority as well as following rules of the majority. Tehmul's reiteration of the Bamji's abuses and grinning at the crowd resulted into the violence which took his life. Thus in violence the wall, a place of worship for all religions, was destroyed by the authorities causing the ethnic anxiety among the people. Pavement artist leaves the place. Gustad asks him where to go. His reply shows the Indian cultural sceanario as, "In a world where roadside latrines become temples and shrines, and temples and shrines become dust and ruin, does it matter where?" (338)

Mistry gives the post-colonial predicament of the Parsis in India. Dinshawaji expresesed sorrow for present conditions of the Parsis and remembered the glorious past of his community which used to enjoy the "respect" (38). In those days Parsis were "the kings of banking" (38). But the present is full of frustration because "Indira Gandhi nationalized the banks" (38). Dinshawji, as the representative of his tiny community, disrespects the Prime Minister. He abuses her as "a shrewd woman", *"Saali"* (38). He also highlights the mischievious attitude of the Prime Minister who encouraged the demands for "a separate Maharashtra"(39) which caused bloodshed and the parties like Shiv Sena raised the questions of religious-other, lingual-other, favoring the sons of the soil. This move of the Prime Minister caused the downgraded condition of the Parsis:

> **'How much bloodshed, how much rioting she caused. And today we have that bloody Shiv Sena, wanting to make the rest of us into second-class citizens. Don't forget, she started it all by supporting the racist buggers.' (39)**

Shiv Sena harassed the minorities like Parsis with the processions and hooliganism resulting into the violence: "They were shouting "Parsi crow-eaters, we'll show you who is the boss" (39). He calls Marathas as "...all those Sakarams and Dattarams and Tukarams only stood outside, screaming like fishwives" (40). These rioteers were pushed back by the Pathan guards and "the Maratha brigade ran like cockroaches" (40). Dinshawji's word-selection for the Maratha majority clearly suggests his anger for them just because of making their lives hell. Dinshawji calls Shiv Sena leader as the worshiper of "Hitler and Mussolini" (73). He blames Shiv Sena for the arrogant attitudes of the "low-class" (73) people like "*dubbawalla*" (73) who hijacked his seat in the bus. Dinshawji talks of Shiv Sena and its agenda:

> **'He and his "Maharashtra for Maharashtrians" nonsense. They won't stop till they have complete Maratha Raj.'... 'Wait till the Marathas take over, then we will have real Gandoo Raj,' said Dinshawaji. 'All they know is to have rallies at Shivaji Park, shout slogans, make threats, and change road names.' (73)**

He describes them as "*Saala* sisterfuckers!" (73). He talks about sheer nonsense of changing the road name from English to Marathi. It is a genuine grief of the Parsis as they lead western life with all that is English. To change these things was like an attack on their existence and identity as an ethnic group. He expressed it in a rage:

> **'Hutatma Chowk!'... He spat out the words disgustedly. 'What is wrong with Flora Fountain?'.... Names are so important. I grew up on Lamington Road. But it has disappeared, in its place is Dadasaheb Bhadkhamkar Marg. My school was on Carnac Road. Now suddenly it's on Lokmanya Tilak Marg. I live at Sleater Road. Soon that will also disappear. My whole life I have come to work at Flora Fountain. And one fine day the name changes. So what happens to the life I have lived? Was I living the wrong life, with all the wrong names? Will I get a second chance to live it all again, with these new names? Tell me what happens to my life. Rubbed out, just like that?' (73-74)**

Tehmul was recruited by Shiv Sena to "distribute racist pamphlets aimed against minorities in Bombay" (86). He was about to be beaten up for being "a Shiv Sena agent" (86) by a group of enraged South Indians.

Mistry attracts the attention of his reader on the poverty of Parsis in post-independent India. Gustad's family can't afford costly rice of superfine quality like basmati. Dilnavaz prepared "fragrant *basmati* rice" (45) for Roshan's birthday obtained from the "black-market" (45) by exchanging tasteless rice worth one week's quota. When Gustad was trapped in the financial crisis, he sold his camera for "medicine bills" (209) and Dilnavaz sold her "two gold wedding bangles" (219).

Gustad planned IIT degree for his son, Sohrab to go abroad in future for better prospects. Gustad prayed to God:

> **What kind of life was Sohrab going to look forward to? No future for minorities, with all these fascist Shiv Sena politics and Marathi language nonsense. It was going to be like the black people in America -twice as good as the white man to get half as much. How could he make Sohrab understand this? (55)**

He thinks B.A. as a "useless degree" (69) because even peons and clerks too have such degrees. It suggests a western attitude towards education that gives weightage to the professional degrees and hires the Indian brain for their countries. Gustad had applied to many Parsi institutions for financial help for Sohrab's education. He visited "Parsi Punchayet Education Fund. R.D. Sethana Trust. Tata Scholarships. Wadia Charities For Higher Studies." (81)

Mistry highlights the ill-services given in the Parsi General hospital where financially sound Parsis avoid getting treatment. After Gustad's accident Major Billimoria told Dilnavaz:

> **'Take him to a regular hospital like Parsi General, and all you will get is regular treatment. Or regular ill-treatment, depending on Gustad's luck.'... 'They love to use their chisels and saws and hammers and nails in the hospitals. And after their carpentry is done, they give you a big fat bill because their tools are so expensive.' (60)**

Mistry has depicted pathetic conditions of the Parsi General hospital (only for the Parsis, now only for the poor Parsis). Dinshawaji describes:

> **O give me a home where the nurses' hands roam,**
> **Where they all have big beautiful tits;**
> **But where seldom is heard an encouraging word,**
> **And the patient is treated like shit. (209)**

Doctors and nurses harass patients in various ways like, "'When you ask for the bedpan, they make you wait and wait till you think you cannot hold it any more'" (209).

Mistry highlights economical conditions of the middle-class Parsis who are trapped in finanacial crisis. Gustad even could not afford "Odomos" (79) to prevent mosquito trouble. There were times when "the water supply was generous and the milk from Parsi Dairy Farm was both creamy and affordable" (82). Gustad denied to give English newspaper to Roshan and Sohrab as "... they used a newsprint quality superior to the regional ones, and fetched more by the kilo" (83) to pay the monthly paper bill. Darius wanted *Times of India* because his friends would make fun of "the Parsi *bawaji* newspapers" (83). Gustad encouraged and then warned: "You should be proud of your heritage.

Take the *Jam-E-Jamshed* or nothing at all" (83). The only person with luxurious life style was Miss. Kutpitia. She was the only "telephone" (85) owner in Khodadad Building. Other Parsis used to gossip about her:

> **There was no shortage of money, they said, that much was certain. How else could she afford Parsi Dairy Farm milk and custom-catered meals from the Ratan Tata Institute? (85).**

Mistry focuses on the vast economical gaps among the rich and poor Parsis. Through the character of Cawasji, Mistry depicted the economical problems of the middle class and poor Parsis.

> **'To the Tatas You give so much! And nothing for me? To the Wadias You give, You keep on giving! You cannot hear my prayers? The pockets of the Camas only You will fill! We others don't need it, You think?' (87)**

Cawasji complained God when he heard the cry of people fire. He blamed God to inflict suffering on poor people like the stink, the noise, the flood and the fire. He questioned God, "Have You ever burnt the homes of rich *sethiyas*? Have You ever, tell me!' (168). Caswasji gave ultimatum to God to take care of poor Parsis also and not only business tycoons like Tatas, Mafatlals, Birlas and Godrej. During the war nights Cavasji warned God to guard the poor Parsis:

> **I am warning You now only! If You let a bomb fall here, let one fall on Birlas and Mafatlals also! *Bas*! Too much injustice from You! Too much! If Khodadadad Building suffers, then Tata Palace also! Otherwise, not one more stick of sandalwood for You, not one silver!'(299-300)**

Thus, Mistry brilliantly portrays the long journey of Gustad Nobel and his family facing the political, financial, racial, problems in course of changing times.

Mistry addresses the issues of Parsi religious beliefs, final rits, and political conspiracies of majority groups, subjugation of minorities and ethnic anxieties of Parsi community in the novel Such a Long Journey. It gives the glimpses of corruption in personal and national life as the result of socio-political turmoil. Similarly, it underscores the dignity of pain and suffering in human life. It helps human beings to come together forgetting personal loss for a more sublime and supreme cause. Mistry has brilliantly portrayed the story of human relations, anxieties with kneat texture of socio-political, psychological, emotional as well as love, longing and perpetual struggle against destiny.

*

III

A Fine Balance: Between the Life & Death

A Fine Balance deals with the emergency period during 1977 in India and it focuses on the contemporary political scenario and its adverse effects on the middle class and poor people in India. It is "...a history of oppression, the cultures, of longings much suppressed" [Sunwani V.K. 1997:107].

The novel traces history from the perspective of people who were thrown on margins. Thus novel becomes the fictional history of emergency. Muriel Wasi briefly highlights this inter-relation of history and fiction:

> **It...can explore large areas of the world's history that have not yet been illuminated by the human memory, or its imagination. History is an abiding source, for the novelist of the future. It need not yield the unpopular historical novel; it could give rise to novels that use history as a parallel. [1993:1]**

It is the tragedy of four characters that accidentally crossed each other and became the important facets of each other's life who fought against all the odds of destiny to keep themselves on the surface from sinking down in the drastic famine of poverty, caste and politics during the emergency period. They share the common bond of humanity and emotional attachments. It made their life heaven, though for a very brief time. Later on they were scattered by the whirlwinds of corruption and destiny and yet they maintained their 'fine balance' except Maneck. After reading this cosmic tragedy, one can aptly think what Honore de Balzac, Le Pere Goriot says at the beginning of the novel:

> **'Holding this book in your hand, sinking back in your soft armchair, you will say to yourself: perhaps it will amuse me. And after you have read this story of great misfortunes, you will no doubt dine well, blaming the author for your own insensitivity, accusing him of wild exaggeration and flights of fancy. But rest assured: this tragedy is not a fiction. All is true.'**

The novel is a critique of internal emergency and contemporary Prime Minister of India. It is a bitter criticism of that particular political turmoil of a comman man and a minority groups who suffered in India during emergency. A. G. Khan aptly puts the reasons behind such portrayal:

> **Everything in India stinks-not only the place but also her leaders as well. Hence, a writer with a conscience cannot keep his tongue-tied. As soon as he is away from the Indian soil his conscience pricks him to be frank and fearless. As long as Indira was alive their courage was under control. Her death made them bold (and democratic honest). Away from Bombay, Mistry is bold enough to curse and abuse... [1995:16]**

Mistry portrays the contemporary political scenario. He satirically criticizes the Prime Minister's declaration of emergency as another "government tamasha" (06). Mistry comments on the linguistic fundamentalism in Maharashtra when Darab Uncle points out the banner: "'It's another silly morcha about language....The fools want to divide the state on linguistic lines'" (66).

Mrs. Gupta's complaint about the labour union suggests the harrassment of the factory owners by the labour unions, the leaders and their strikes. She criticized Jay Prakash Narayan for encouraging civil disobedience. She comments that he thinks of himself as **"Mahatma Gandhi the Second.' (80)**

Such reference to Mahatama Gandhi reminds the British rule in India and the subsequent colonization and imperialism Indians suffered during the period. Pradeep Trikha rightly comments in this connection:

> **'A Fine Balance' portrays the years of the Emergency in Bombay- a mini India. In this period, the functioning of the government revived the memories of colonial India under the British rule. It was the period when 'the nationlist imperialism' was challenged by people like Jaya Prakash Narayan. [2001:214-215]**

But Mrs. Gupta's attitude describes the variety of point of views regarding the emergency as it has blocked the freedom of common man. She was happy at declaration of Internal Emergency. She admires the actions of Prime Minister to crush the democratic values and putting students, leaders, opposition leaders into Jail for opposing her capitalist motives.

Such remarks suggest the alienation of the rich section of the society from the problems of common people who are trapped in poverty. Mrs. Gupta's tone reflects the capitalist tendency of loss and profit for money making:

> **'Union loafers want to work less and get more money. That's the curse of this country- laziness. And some idiot leaders encouraging them, telling police and army to disobey unlawful orders. Now you tell me, how can the law be unlawful? Ridiculous nonsense. Serves them right, being thrown in jail.' (90)**

Mrs. Gupta thinks Prime Minister must be "someone strong at a dangerous time like this" (90). Ishvar's question displays his innocence of politics and unawareness of national events like emergency. Dinabai sees emergency as "'Government problems -games played by people in the power. It doesn't affect ordinary people like us'" (92). In Emergency discipline is highly regarded. But this discipline is imposed on common people and not on government orgnization as the "train keeps coming late" (96). Ishvar's bitter comment shows the indifference of common people towards the government and worse conditions of contemporary politics: "If government kept their promises, the gods would come down to garland them" (96). Corruption, injustice crept into all walks of life which badly affected common man's life. The Goverment strategies about sterilization, temptations as well as threats given to officers suggest the tyrany and dictatorship of the government. Every officer has to persuade people "to get sterilized" (217). If he doesn't fill his quota, there is no promotion for him.

Mistry describes the suppression of "the Prime Minister's enemies- union workers, newspaper people, teachers, students" (221). Mistry's description of the statue highlights the paradox of freedom ransacked in emergency:

> **The plaque said he was a Guardian of Democracy. Om had studied about the man in his history class, in the story of Freedom Struggle. The photo in the history book was nicer than the statue... The sides of the pedestal were plastered with posters extolling the virtues of the Emergency. The obligatory Prime Ministerial visage was prominent. Small print explained why fundamental rights had been temporarily suspended. (232-233)**

Mistry portrays the corrupted political situation where political parties attract people to attend the public meeting. People did not fall prey to the promises. So Sergeant Kesar ordered his men to block the slum exits. They were threatened to "be arrested for trespassing on municipal property!" (320) Rajaram described the meeting as: "a day at the circus- we have clowns, monkeys, acrobats, everything" (324). Mistry also highlights how Shiv Sena harrassed common people during emergency. Even in the movie theatres common people were targeted and compelled to respect the National Anthem.

In the emergency, the poor people were harrased and thrown on the road as all the shacks were destroyed to clean the city.Thus Om and Ishvar became homeless. Om and Ishvar experienced that, "homelessness is always a curse" [Hartman 1984:07]. On the way to Dinabai's home they came across two hoardings of Prime Minister. The workers were unanimously working on the slogans:

> **THE CITY BELONGS TO YOU! KEEP IT BEAUTIFUL!... FOOD FOR THE HUNGRY! HOMES FOR THE HOMELESS!... THE NATION IS ON THE MOVE! (373)**

These slogans reflect contradictions and various aspects of emergency. Om and Ishvar, at the chemist shop, were loaded to the camp where all beggars and people from slums gathered together to clean the city. Instead of Garibi Hatao, they followed the Garib Hatao motto. The life in the camp was hell. Mistry presents a vivid picture of contemporary Bombay, a mini India:

> **... the poor struggling for their 'survival of the fittest' in the metropolitan city where 'a roof to cover the head' is a dream. [...] Thematically, the novel articulates the sagacity of the cultures which are very much suppressed.... the age old problems of caste and communalism, the burnt of which has been borne by the down trodden, has been duly focused. [Gajendrakumar 2001:76-77]**

The Emergency ruined every opponent like Avinash who struggled for the rights of the students. Mistry dexterously describes the ethnic anxiety right from emergency to Indira Gandhi's assassination. Ibrahim remembers the Partition riots in 1947 when he decided:

> **...with great reluctance, to leave behind his distinctive fez. It was like abandoning a dear friend. The only other time he had forsaken this fixture of daily wear was during Partition, back in 1947, when communal slaughter at the brand-new border had ignited riots everywhere, and sporting a fez in a Hindu neighbourhood was as fatal as possessing a foreskin in a Muslim one. In certain areas it was wisest to go bareheaded, for chossing incorrectly from among fez, white cap, and turban could mean losing one's head. (107)**

Here, Mistry aptly highlights that dress codes are considered as an authentic ethnic markers. It is easy to deceive by abandoning such ethnic markers for the survival. Novel has abundant occurrences of oppression and hatered against the oppressor as well as predicament of the oppressed. Bharucha, in an article published in *The Independent*, focuses on the tendencies of oppressor:

> **It is colonial ideology to consider the colonized as underdogs having "inferior" qualities like having primitive feminine qualities, thereby establishing doctrine**

> **of racial superiority and sexual inequity. The effects of colonialism do not end with the transfer of political power or first giving the right of self-dertermination for electing their representatives. As a result, postcolonial societies continue to image themselves in the mirror of colonialism. [Bharucha 1992]**

This novel also highlights the ethnic anxieties within Hinduism. India's caste system includes hierarchy and is often considered to be a feature of Hinduism. Individuals are believed to be born into a particular caste and continue to live in that caste throughout their lives. Such rigidities stuck to Hinduism that T. Kumar describes it as:

> **Broad caste categories (*varnas*) separate caste groups according to occupation (although mobility between occupations does not lead to change in caste identity). Outside these caste categories are the "untouchables", like sweepers, tanners, sanitation workers, etc were viewed as "polluting" the community. Untouchability of *dalits* continues to be practiced in India in many forms, reinforcing an iniquitious social hierarchy and allowing for the continuing disempowerment and humiliation of millions of people. [2005:1-2]**

The localities and housing colonies of lower caste people are often segregated from those housing non-dalits, a segregation which often extends to the provision of separate wells, eating places and temples and restrictions on the use of land to defecate. Dalits do not have proper access to schools which accounts for high illiteracy rates and serves as a basis for increased discrimination. Additionally, dalits are routinely subjected to beatings, mutilation, murder, rape, and destruction of property by members of the upper-caste and the police. A culture of impunity ensures that most of the criminals go unpunished. T. Kumar has enlisted the various abuses committed against dalits. Such abuses include variety of punishments like:

> **Socioeconomic discrimination. Beatings, slashings, and other forms of torture. Arson- the burning of *dalit***

> **communities. Violence against women - Rape, gang rape, and the parading of women through the streets naked**
> **As a form of punishment**
> **As the right of the upper-caste male**
> **To punish or embarrass the woman's family**
> **Beating and torture of women**
> **Summary execution, many times by burning alive**
> **Bonded labor**
> **Denial of rights, especially land rights**
> **Police abuses against *dalits*, custodial abuse.**
> **[2005:1-2]**

Mistry portrays the caste-system and inherent oppression of lower-caste by the upper-caste people. Mistry comments on punishments given to the lower-caste for their minor mistakes or mistakes not at all:

> **'...But where he (Bhola) was working, they accused him of stealing. - they chopped off his left-hand fingers today.' 'Last year Chhagan lost his hand at the wrist. Same reason.' 'Dasu got a whipping for getting too close to the well. Buddhu's wife... refused to go to the field with the zamindar's son, so they shaved her head and walked her naked through the square.' (117)**

Injustices were continuously done to lower-caste people with slight change in the name; otherwise the details were identical. For strolling on the upper-caste side of the street, Sita was stoned till she bleeded. Gambhir was found within hearing range of the temple when prayers were in progress so "he had molten lead poured into his ears" (132). Dayaram did not keep his promise of ploughing a landlord's field. He was forced "to eat the landlord's excrement in the village square" (132). Dhiraj requested to get few sticks in advance from Pandit Ghanshyam for the wages for chopping wood. But Pandit went distress and accused Dhiraj of poisoning his cows. Dhiraj was "hanged" (132). Dukhi's wife Roopa was raped by orange-grove guard as she stole oranges from the grove. He first allowed her to take oranges and then asked to sleep with him. He threatened her about the possibility of whipping and communal rape

("They would take turns doing shameful things to your lovely soft body" (119)) by the upper-caste land-lord. Then he raped her.

Ishwar and Narayan were punished cruelly for entering the class-room. Pundit Lullaram also appreciated the punishment who talked at length in favor of the caste system.

Dukhi sent Ishwar and Narayan to Ashraf the tailor to train them in tailoring. It was the decision taken with purpose to change the ethnic group, subaltern in the hierarchy of Hinduism. Though he chose another ethnic group, it was less harmful, and shameful. It produced great rage for Thakur Dharmasi who decided to punish Dukhi for his daring "to break asunder" (180). Dukhi had turned cobblers into tailors, "distorting society's timeless balance" (180). Thakur Dharmasi burnt Dukhi's home in the night when all the members were sleeping. All members died except Om and Ishwar as they were at Ashraf's home.

When Dukhi and Roopa begot two sons, it caused "envy in upper-caste homes" (121) where women were "still childless" (121) or waiting for "a male issue" (121). They lamented on the reversal of the Manu's law of hierarchy.

This typical Hindu belief of importance of male issue is criticized here. All Hindu families desperately wanted a male child to continue the family for the generations to come. Such kind of topsy-turvy of the hierarchy was considered as the result of Kaliyug, "…the Age of Darkness" (122).

Mistry highlights Hindu-Muslim conflicts during the turmoil of partition. The two-nation theory was based on the religion. Pakistan was purely based on Islam. It caused problems of belonging and partition exchanged largest population based on religion from Pakistan to India and vice versa. This caused hatred within these two religions.

This organization was making Hindus aware of the violent intention of Muslim community. They cautioned to be ready to defend all Hindus (including Shudras). If Muslims cause the blood-shed of Hindus, whole nation would "run red with rivers of Muslim blood" (150). It highlights Islamic invasions on Hindu India centuries ago as well as Islamic fundamentailism during Mogul Emperor like Aurengzeb which impinged Hindu psyche permanently. In Dukhi's village, the Muslim population was too small to cause a threat to anyone. But the landlords perceived an opportunity in the stranger's caution. They did their best to stimulate people against the imaginary danger from Muslims by recalling the history of Moguls and Muslim invaders and the destruction they caused to Hindu people and their "temples" (150), "wealth" (150). So it is "Better to drive out the Mussulman menace" (150).

Gandhi was "the chief traitor, Mohandas Karamchand Gandhi" (150) in the eyes of RSS. Dukhi and his friends discussed the RSS men and the stories they brought with them. They concluded not to believe the religious bias of upper-caste Hindus after their injustice and suffering:

> **....The lower castes were not impressed by the rhetoric. They had always lived peacefully with their Muslim neighbours. Besides, they were too exhausted keeping body and soul together... 'The Zamindars have always treated us like animals.' 'Worse than animals'. 'Mussulman... never bothered us before. Why would they do it now? Why should we hurt them because some outsiders come with stories?' 'Yes, it's strange that suddenly we have all become Hindu brothers.' 'The Muslims have behaved more like our brothers than the bastard Brahmins and Thakurs.' (150-151)**

Such situation focuses that the margin denies being hold by the center. These subaltern groups wanted to align together to stand against the center.

Rajaram shaved the long-hairs of women or men at crowded places. At the docks, mathadis unloading ships cheered the exploits of the mysterious hair-hunter, convinced that "it was the work of a lower-caste brother extracting revenge for centuries of upper-caste oppression, of stripping and rapes and head-shavings of their womenfolk" (588).

In the city, Ashraf Chacha, Om and Ishvar symbolized as the paragon of India's composite culture who stood by each other in the vast fire of ethnic angst. It is strongly admitted by Maya Pandit:

> **Dukhi's sons and Muslim Ashraf's family look after each other in times of uncertainty and communal discord, and so cement bonds of unity for all times to come in spite of the British strategy of dividing the country into India and Pakistan. [Pandit M.L. 1998:20]**

Mistry gives the details of the riots after Prime Minister's assassination by her Sikh guards. Her assassination was a protest against 'Golden Temple' action. It casued anti-Sikh riots:

> **Such terrible butchery for three days… 'They are pouring kerosene on Sikhs and setting them on fire. They catch men, tear the hair from their faces or hack it with swords, then kill them. Whole families burnt to death to their homes.' (711)**

The Driver was afraid of Maneck's beard as looters were killing every person having beard. Here one can understand that how the symbol of a particular ethnic group can be harmful in severe condition like riots. To survive, one has to shed the sacred, religious symbols of the faith to change identity for the security. But it is not possible, as an identity can be verified by the official documents:

> **'There will be no trouble because of my beard. If we are stopped, they'll at once know I'm a Parsi- I'll show them the sudra and kusti I am wearing.'**
> **'Yes, but they might want to check my license.'**
> **"So?"**
> **'You haven't guessed? I am a Sikh- I shaved off my beard and cut my hair two days ago. But I'm still wearing my kara.' He held up his hand, displaying the iron bangle round his wrist. (711-712)**

Mistry aptly describes the misguided people who became the puppets in the hands of politicians. Politicians would never be punished though they target any ethnic group for the sake of power and benefits:

> **'The real murderers will never be punished. For votes and power they play with human lives. Today it is Sikhs. Last year it was Muslims; before that, Harijans. One day, your sudra and Kusti might not be enough to protect you.'(712)**

After such terrific details of riots and insecure position of harmless community like Parsis, Mistry highlights lost glory of the Parsis. Mistry used the powerful medium of memory and nostalgia. Manek's parents and neighbors often "shifted gently to times gone by, to the stories of their lives" (253). Mr. Kohlah used to tell about the glorious days of his family, "not from self-pity or notions of false grandeur, nor to sing his own achievement in the present" (253). The purpose was to remember the great lesson of history:

> **...a lesson in living life on the borderline- modern maps could ruin him, but they could not displace his dreams for his family. (253)**

The Partition was recollected by remembering the chronology of events, and mourning the senseless slaughter. Brigadier Grewal imagined if only by magic "the sundered parts would some day be sewn together again" (254). All these neighbours consoled themselves by criticizing the colonizers for their lack of proper decision.

The novel contains various references regarding Parsi belief, values and rituals. After the death of Mr. Shroff, Mrs. Shroff attended her husband's prayers at the fire-temple. Mistry focuses on the contradictory behavioral pattern of Dustoor. He portrays the character of dustoor in complete contrast to their profession. Dustoor takes disadvantages of his much respected position as a religious person. He gave Dina "a prolonged hug of the sort he reserved for girls and young women" (23). His habit for squeezing and fondling had earned him the title of "Dustoor Daab-Chạab" (23). His colleagues feared that one day he would disgrace the fire-temple.

Nusswan and Dina used to visit the fire-temple once a week. While she bowed before the sanctum, he travelled along the outer wall hung with pictures of various dustoors and high priests. He applied the ash on his body – "a pinch on his forehead, another bit across the throat, and undid his top two shirt buttons to rub a fistful over his chest" (24). Cutting hairs in the house is considered as the bad omen in Zoroastrianism. So, when Dina cut her hair and entered into house with hair clippings, Nusswan yelled at her to take a bath because spreading hairs after cutting bring "misfortune upon" (28) family. After Rustom's death, Dina began with haricut for her earnings. But it was not successful as an indoor activity that "most people regarded hair clippings within their dwellings as extreme bad luck" (72). People used to make hue and cry about her hair cut within four walls. Some of them helplessly tried to appeal emotionally: "'Madam, you have no considerations? What have we done to you that you want to bring misfortune within our four walls?'" (72) Some people offered her their children's heads but only "outside" (72).

Mistry highlights the professional envy among the dustoors. Dustoor Dab-Chaab was very unhappy as ceremonies regarding Dina's wedding were performed by some other Dustoor in the Fire-temple. He complained that he is invited only for sad occasions.

Parsis are famous for their gluttony. Mistry comments on food loving nature of Parsis. Parsis performed all their religious ceremonies after sunset. In the evening Nusswan gave small reception party as "where Parsis were concerned, food was number one, conversation came second" (47).

Zorostorianism doesn't allow suicide as it is against Ahura Mazda's wish and belief. In the hot debate over suicide, Dina expressed her religious belief in Almighty's plan of life:

> **'…as a Parsi, my belief makes me say this: suicide is wrong, human beings are not meant to select their time of death. For then they would also be allowed to pick the moment of birth.' (582)**

Parsis felt alienated from the Indian freedom fighting which resulted in their indifference or neutrality towards it. Mistry does talk about Parsi attitude towards the Freedom movement. Nusswan cursed the Indians as "bloody uncultured savages" (29) because of his financial loss during the partition. Here the reasons are economical rather than political or racial pride. He expressed his anger at Indians and freedom struggle. Mistry described his anguish as:

> **Cooped up inside the flat, Nusswan lamented the country's calamity, grumbling endlessly. 'Every day I sit at home, I lose money. Those bloody uncultured savages don't deserve independence. If they must hack one another to death, I wish they would go somewhere else and do it quietly. In their villages, maybe. Without disturbing our lovely city by the sea. (29-30)**

Here, the reference "our loverly city by the sea" (30) is made to Bombay which was built and developed by Parsis. Bombay suffered a lot during the independence struggle. It has also created problems in the lives of Parsis as they reside in Bombay in large number.

Parsi community is hailed as the most westernized and modernized community in India. Mistry highlights the modern outlook of the Parsis. Nusswan tried to find out a good Parsi boy for Dina. He explained her about her fortunate position being a Zoroastrian:

> **'Do you know how fortunate you are in our community? Among the unenlightened, widows are thrown away like garbage. If you were a Hindu, in the old days you would have had to be a good little sati and leap onto you husband's funeral pyre, be roasted with him. (63-64)**

It was really a blessing for the young widows like Dina to remarry and lead a happy life which was just impossible in Hindu community at that time. This moder outlook was the outcome of English-associations. This association also gave Parsis elite-consciousness and a sense of superiority.

Parsis have distinct way of final rites. Mistry focuses on Parsi final rites. Maneck returned home to attend his father's funeral. Maneck's family lived on the mountain so the "nearest fire-temple" (715) was quite far. His mother arranged for the prayers. Dustoors were coming from the nearest fire-temple. Being on mountain, and as per Mr. Kolah's last wish, he was cremated. It created great problem for his family. Most of the Dustoor rejected to perform Zoroastrian ceremony on cremated soul:

> **It had been an effort to find two who were willing to perform the ceremony. Most had refused the assignment when they discovered the deceased was to be cremated, saying their services were available only to Zoroastrians bound for the Towers of Silence - never mind if it was a long trip by railway. (715)**

Such "narrow-minded" (715) attitude raised the debate in the community. Mrs. Kohlah questioned Maneck, "But what about the people who cannot afford to transport the body? Would these priests deny them the prayers?"

(715) Here, Mistry highlights the financial weakness of the Parsis residing on mountains or in remote areas who could not afford to transport the dead bodies to the cities like Bombay. So, the traditional dokhma was replaced by the "electric crematorium" (715) in Mr. Kolha's case instead of "an open-air pyre" (715).

Mistry highlights the poverty and adverse conditions in Mumbai to live a minimum common life. Maneck's early life in mountains made him uncomfortable to cope with the poverty and pollution of Mumbai. Om and Ishvar too, came for short span of time to make money. Both of them fade up of Bombay life: "Noise and crowds, no place to live, water scarce, garbage everywhere. Terrible.' (08).

Mistry focuses on the poverty of Parsi community. Nusswan planned the wedding of Dina and Rustom. He wanted to book a hall for reception and pay for everything out of the money he had been collecting for her. He afforded three hundred guests. His budget did not permit him liquor in the wedding.

Dina suffered from financial crisis time and again. She had to keep a paying guest and run a garment factory at home with the help of two tailors. She had to go back to get help from her brother against her wish.

The colonial attraction for the white skin is an important part of Parsi psyche. Mistry deals with this *gora complex* when Dina, Nusswan, Ruby, his wife went to visit their grandfather. When Ruby bagan to massage grandfather's foot, he yelled angrily and tore his foot from her hands: "Kya karta hai? Chalo, jao!" (33)

The grandfather pressumed Ruby as an ayah because of her dark skin and spoke in Hindi as a sub-standard medium to address servants especially non-Parsi or non-Christian:

> **Too startled at being addressed in Hindi, Ruby sat there gaping. 'Doesn't she understand? What language does your ayah speak? Tell her to get off my sofa, wait in the kitchen.' Grandfather turned to Nusswan. Ruby rose in a huff and stood by the door. 'Rude old man!' she hissed. 'Just because my skin is a little dark!' (33)**

Western education, westernization, modernization are the causes which led Parsis to appreciate everything western as a high standard. Mistry gives various references of western books and music. Dina knew very little about music – "a few names like Brahms, Mozart, Schumann, and Bach" (36). She was introduced to these habits by her father. This initiation into everything western made Parsis to think of themselves as superior to others. Rustom too was initiated into music. He practiced the violin: "Like all good Parsi parents, mine made me take violin lessons when I was little" (40).

Mistry highlights critically on the decline in eco-system. He deals with the *Coco-Colanization* perpetuated by foreign multi-national companies. Mr. Kohlah has created his own niche in his cold-drink business. He was unhappy about the sudden sprouting of foreign companies on the hills. His friends called it "a malevolent growth" (264). It reduced the business at the General Store. It had very adverse effect on his psyche as well as financial affairs. This wave of urbanization of mountain brought urban problems of poverty, unemployment, homeless beggars and mushroom growth of slum areas. It resulted into the decline in the Mr. Kohlah's Cola. Mistry expressed Mr. Kohlah's fears and strategies of multi-national companies:

> **But the giant corporation had targeted the hills; they had Kaycee in their sights. They infiltrated Mr. Kohlah's territory with their boardroom arrogrance and advertising campaigns and cut-throat techniques. Representatives approached him with a proposition: 'Pack up your machines, sign over all rights of Kohlah's Cola, and be an agent for our brand. Come grow with us, and prosper.'(268)**

Thus, Mistry has thrown light on the politics of the corporate world, where expansion, merging, destruction of the opponents are highly practical and practiced all tricks of the trade. The company applied various tactics to win the race and finally Kohlah's Cola didn't survive.

Mistry focuses on the Parsi virtue of flexibility of accepting the change as a survival tactis as they survived through all invasions and calamities. Proofreader explains Maneck:

> **Accept it, and go on. Please remember, the secret of survival is to embrace change, and to adapt... to quote "All things fall and are built again, and those that build them again are gay." (282)**

He explained Maneck to maintain "a fine balance between hope and despair" (282) because "In the end, it's all a question of balance" (282). But unfortunately Maneck failed to maintain *a fine balance* and committed suicide on the railway track. On the other hand Om, Ishvar and Dina accepted the change and reality of the life and by maintaining the fine balance in their life continued to live.

Thus, Mistry underscores the importance to identify the necessity of the change and urgency to adapt it for maintaining the fine balance in human life.

*

IV

Family Matters: All About Bonding

Family Matters is the story of a modern day Parsi King Lear in Bombay (now Mumbai) especially Bombay of post-Ayodhya issue where minorities were threatened by the increasing Hindu fundamentalism. Mistry tells the story "of familial love and affection, of personal and political corruption, the religious complexity, the power of memory to keep truth alive, and the ultimate peril memory denied" [Daruwalla 2002]. It is the story of Nariman Vakil, 79 year old Parsi patriarch, who lives with his unmarried step-children Coomy and Jal. It is a story of "not only a helpless old man's cross to bear but a burden to those who love him most" [Jha 2002:85]. They are scared of taking care of their step-father in his old age due to his unhealthy conditions and Parkinson's disease. Bharucha analyses this uncaring attitude of young generation of the Parsis as:

> **The fears of these two middle-aged siblings has to be seen in the context of the geriatric Parsi community in which there are today too few young and able members to care for the old and disabled.... late marriages and/ or a rampant individualism that does not brook the adjustments required within marriage, have led to most Parsis not marrying at all, or if married, either opting not to have children or being forced into a childless state**

> **by infertility caused by the advanced age of one or both spouses at the time of the marriage. There is also the fact that in the Parsi community thanks to economic pressures and general societed norms... unmarried adult children, continue to live with their parents. Those who do get married generally opt to move away and lead independent lives. Hence the burden of caring for aging, ill and often cantankerous parents falls on the unmarried offspring. This often results in feelings of resentment towards the married siblings who it appears have shrugged off their responsibilities towards ageing parents. [2003:171]**

It is this feeling of envy that Coomy grudges in her heart against Roxana and later on transfers Nariman to her flat and in course postpones Nariman's return to their house.

Mistry begins the novel with the discussions of post-Ayodhya riots. In Mumbai it was nowhere safe. Houses were set on fire, and minorities were being assassinated. Jal and Nariman discuss "the old Parsi couple" who died in their bedroom. ...The goondas who *assumed Muslims* were hiding in Dalal Estate and set fire to it?" (Emphasis added) (04). It suggest that the rioters were not real Muslim but fanatic Hindus. Jal provides one more example of an old lady from Firozsha Baag who was beaten and robbed inside her flat. Coomy's remark on ethnic riots depicts the sensitivity of such ethnic issues: "How often does a mosque in Ayodhya turn people into savages in Bombay? Once in a blue moon" (4-5). Mistry expresses the predicament of India and Maharashtra under BJP and Shiv Sena. Yezad calls the government as "the dogs ... and not well-bred dogs either, but pariahs" (31). BJP and Shiv Sena coalition is "a poisonous snake" (31). He blames these two parties for encouraging the Hindutva extremists to destroy the Babri Mosque. Further he lashes the Shiv Sena and Sena Supremo for spreading "all the hatred of minorities" (32) for the last thirty years. His observation aptly reflects the outlook of Shiv Sena:

> **"Senapati... the crackpot accuses people left and right of being anti-this and anti-that. South Indians are anti-Bombay, Valentine's Day is anti-Hindustan, film stars born before 1947 in the Pakistan part of Punjab are traitors to the country." (32)**

Nariman and Jal turn the Senapati as a butt of ridicule, one who works on whims:

> **"I suppose... if the Senapati gets gas after eating karela, the gourd will be declared as anti-Indian vegetable." "Let's hope his langoti doesn't give him a groin rash," said Jal. "Or all underwear might be banned." (32)**

Murad points out the duality of these leaders who object to anti-Indian attitude on the basis of culture and patriotism. Shiv Sena made an arrangement of "Michael Jackson concert" (32) for sheer financial profit. Jal criticized:

> **"Shiv Sena will pocket millions-they've obtained tax-free status by classifying it as a cultural event of national significance." (32)**

This extreme hatred has affected the sports also. For instance, whenever India and Pakistan play cricket, it is treated like a "war in Kashmir" (33).

Mistry portrays the picture of unsafe Bombay where decent people can't travel in the night. Some of the "Shiv Sena people" (44) harrassed Roxana questioning her: "Choli Kay Peechhay Kya Hai" (43). On resistence they threat Yezad: "Don't tingle-tangle with us, bavaji! We are Shiv Sena people, we are invincible!"(44). It suggests how minorities are insecure in the nation of majority. Here, Parsi existence is clearly marginalized. Parsis are considered as cultural and religious 'other' or subaltern.

Mistry highlights fanaticism and love for Marathi, or what can be said a fascination for 'swadeshi' names. Shiv Sena's insistance for Marathi names for the cities is shown when Mr. Rangrajan comments on suspicious atmosphere in Mumbai:

> **"...we Bombayites, Or should I say Mumbaikars" ... "These days you never can tell who might be a Shiv Sena fanatic, or a member of their Name Police. It is my understanding that some Shiv Sainiks have infiltrated the GPO, subjecting innocent letters and postcards to incineration if the address reads Bombay instead of Mumbai." (53)**

It raises the question of *lingual other*. Such *othering* results into the ethnic anxieties. Mr. Kapur was murdered by two Shiv Sainiks as he denied changing the name Bombay to Mumbai.

Mr. Rangrajan highlights the changing relations of India with other countries. In the countries like Russia, after the collapse of the Soviet Union, Indians were not welcomed as before. Mistry hails the present world leaders as "Nincompoops" (54). Rangrajan tragically expresses the helplessness of India. India had Five-thousand-year-old civilization and nine hundred million people but unable to produce one great leader. Instead of "a Mahatma" only "micro-mini atmas" (54) are available in India. Rangrajan criticizes the USA for its war against Kuwait. George Bush killed the Iraqis, and destroyed the job prospects in Gulf. But Rangrajan is optimistic to get job in US. In India political processions are normal. For the common man all the processions are the same: "It's hard to read the banners from here BJP, JD, CP, VHP, BSP, doesn't matter, they're all the same"(60).

Mistry focuses on the insecurity of the minorities under the fundamentalist majority rule. Majority kept close track record of their residence to harass them in times of anxieties:

> **Rubbish... Villie Cardmaster said he was most likely from Shiv Sena, listing names and addresses- that's how they had singled out Muslim homes during the Babri Mosque riots. Probably planning ahead for next time. (106)**

Because of threats of violence on businessmen, Vilas denied increase in letter writing charges. He was afraid if his clients asked any assistance from Shiv Sena shakha. They may even employ their "sticks-and-stones method of political persuasion, their fine art of scoring debating points of breaking opposition bones" (141). Hussain was the victim of Babri Mosque riots. He was hired under the program of Ekta-Samiti working for the rehabilitation of the Babri Mosque riots victims. Mr. Kapur and Yezad shared the common thought about Shiv Sena and Bombay. They lamented for Mumbai's slow death. It is destroyed "by goonda raj and mafia dons, as the newspaper put it, "in an unholy nexus of politicans, criminals, and police"" (151).

Mistry highlights the corruption and dictatorship of the government. Mr. Kapur read the news of shutting down of Shrikrishna Commission which was set up to investigate the Babri Mosque riots. Mistry criticizes that the guardians of the society are turned to be the destroyers. This action suggests that government took this action because everything was about to be exposed: "Shiv Sena involvement in looting and burning, police helping rioters, withholding assistance in Muslim localities" (154). Hussain called police as "budmaash!"(155). Mistry portrays the picture of Babri Mosque riots where Police itself vindicated the common people on the basis of their ethnicity:

> **...in those riots the police were behaving like gangsters. In Muslim mohallas they were shooting their guns at innocent people. Houses were burning, neighbours came out to throw water. And the police? Firing bullets like target practice. These guardians of the law were murdering everybody! (155)**

This is just one side of the story. As in such areas Hindus were also brutally killed but Mistry turns blind eyes to that. Mistry shows the paradox inherent in the politics that the rioters are now the makers of law and order which results into delayed justice or justice denied.

Vilas describes it aptly: "life is not an Amitabh Bachchan movie? That justice is a mirage?"(211). Shiv Sena is, "our greatest urban menace" (209), "Clowns and crooks. Or clownish crooks"(273). Muslims are "favourite scapegoat as usual" (273). Shiv Sena, saviour of Indian culture and values, censored the lives of minorities and restricted the freedom of expression. Mistry cites the examples of the Paintings of M.F. Husein whose paintings and Men's magazines were destroyed, for being nudity and moral degradation. Women were banned from working in bars and discos as it was against Indian family values.

Mistry's hatred for Hindu majority is clearly shown when he portrays Muslims as underdogs. At the same time, whenever Prophet is portrayed in humanshape, the whole Islamic world has caused great destruction to the civilization. So, what Mistry portrays here is a one facet of the problem. This may be the outcome of his Parsi-psyche which is affected by Hindutva extremism. Mr. Kapur comments on the arrogance and hooliganism smashing the people who stand in their way. Mistry laments for such destruction of his beloved city: "And poor Bombay has no champion to defend her. Unhappy city, that has no heroes" (336).

Mr. Kapur warns Yezad not to underrate these "Skinny...Baji Raos and Bhaji Khaos...are descendants of Marathas, tough as nails- though as that other spinach-eater, Popeye" (336). It reflects the anger due to oppression and suppression under majority.

Mr. Kapur's recollection of 1947 partition-riot made Yezad to think over the trauma and sufferings of uprooting and blood-sheding of millions:

> **Punjabi migrants of a certain age were like Indian authors writing about that period, whether in realist novels of corpse-filled trains or in the magic-realist midnight muddles, all repeating the same catalogue of horrors about slaughter and burning, rape and mutilation, foetuses torn out of the wombs, genitals stuffed in the mouths of the castrated. (151)**

Mistry's reference to "corpse-filled trains or in the magic-realist midnight muddles" (151) reminds the partition novels like Khuswant Singh's 'A Train to Pakistan' and Salman Rushdie's 'Midnight's Children'. Mistry compares these stories of Indian sub-continent's history with ethnic violence and sufferings of Jews from Europe:

> **...about the Holocaust, writing and remembering and having nightmares about the concentration camps and gas chambers and ovens, about the evil committed by ordinary people, by friends and neighbours, the evil that, decades later, was still incomprehensible. What choice was there, except to speak about it, again and again, and yet again? (151)**

Cherishing the memories from the old photograph collection of Mr. Kapur, who remembered how boys used to tease Shahrukh, a Muslim boy in the neighbourhood, to go Pakistan. He was teased for his circumcision as "an ABC... Adha Boolla Catayla" (227). Mr. Kapur regreted and wanted to undo the past by rewriting it neatly. He wanted to portray hormonious picture:

> **"...When I dream about my childhood, I wake up wishing I could find Shahrukh, tell him I'm sorry. The sad part**

> **was, later the family did go away to Pakistan, where they had relatives. We all felt guilty afterwards." (227)**

Mistry highlights the cricket teams in St. Xavier's school which used to compete for the championship with religious title like Hindus, Muslims, Parsis, and Europeans. It caused great sadness for Mahatma Gandhi who convinced that for national integrity and unity, cricket should not be played on the basis of "religious or ethnic divisions" (215). Father D'silva asked all the children not to think of as "Catholic or non-Catholic....no distinction of caste or creed" (215). But students categorised teams as vegetarians versus non-vegetarians, oiled hair versus unoiled and starched uniforms versus un-startched. The school was careful regarding communalism especially after the Babri Mosque demolition riots.

Mistry uses Mumbai as the character representing religious harmony, unity in diversity of India. Mr. Kapur's father came to Bombay and prospered. This city of love and longing was developed by Parsis and that's why this fascination for Bombay is recurrent in Mistry's works. Parsis are proud to be the makers of Bombay. They are "proud... being Parsi" [Pestonji 1999:30] for, "... Parsis built Bombay with the help of the British" [Ibid, 30]. He expressed his love for this symbol of unity:

> **Bombay endures because it gives and it receives. Within this warp and weft is woven the special texture of its social fabric, the spirit of tolerance, acceptance, generosity. Anywhere else in the world, in those so-called civilized places like England and America, such terrible conditions would lead to revolution. (159)**

After lashing Shiv Sena for its Hindu fanaticism, Mistry turns his discussion to analyse the true definition and nature of Hindu religion:

> **...Hinduism has an all-accepting nature, agreed? I'm not talking about the fundamentalist, mosque-destroying fanatics, but the real Hinduism that has nurtured this country for thousands of years, welcoming all creeds and beliefs and dogmas and theologies, making them feel at home. Sometimes, when they are not looking, it absorbs**

them within itself. Even false gods are accommodated, and turned into true ones, adding a few more deities to its existing millions. (362)

Mistry's nostaligia for Bombay has turned it into religion. Especially being a migrant he compares it with Hindu religion. It might be the result of the memory of getting boot out from Persia and seek refuge in India. Mr. Kapur used the simile of religion for Bombay:

Bombay is like a religion? Well, it's like Hinduism... Bombay makes room for everybody. Migrants, businessmen, perverts, politicians, holy men. Gamblers, beggars, wherever they come from, whatever caste or class, the city welcomes them and turns them into Bombayites. So who am I to say these people belong here and those don't? Janata Party okay, Shiv Sena not okay, secular good, communal bad, BJP unacceptable, Congress lesser of evils? (362)

Mistry talks about the real religious tolerance in general and particularly related with Parsis. Jehangir recites the history lesson on Shivaji:

Shivaji was born in 1627, and was the founder of the Maratha kingdom. He respected the beliefs of all communities, and protected their places of worship. In a time of religious savagery, Shivaji practised true religious tolerance. (444)

This is really mocking and ridiculous as a party like Shiv Sena respects this great leader as their ideal and the idol but behaves in complete contrast. Jal shows Murad and Jehangir holy pictures of Sai Baba, Virgin Mary, a Crucifixion, Haji Malang, several Zarathustra, Our Lady Fatima, and Buddha. Jal reveals that the pictures used to be hanged all over the flat: "You know how, in those days, it was usual for most Parsis to keep tokens of every religion" (485). Mr. Kapur declares to celebrate all the religious festivals like Divali, Christmas, Id, Parsi Navroze, Baisakhi, Buddha Jayanti, and Ganesh Chaturthi. Mr Kapur said "We are going to be a mini-Bombay, an example to our neighbourhood" (159).

He narrates the incident when one passanger was saved by the fellow passenger without any sense of caste, creed, race, religion while entering into the train:

> **Whose hands were they, and whose hands were they grasping? Hindu, Muslim, Dalit, Parsi, Chirstian? No one knew and no one cared. Fellow passengers, that's all they were. (160)**

Yezad made the analogy between the Santa Claus and Dustoorji. Both of them brought happiness into the lives of human beings. As Yezad witnesses the love of Murad for Jehangir in Santa Claus's gift so he found the peace of mind as he was at peace when Dustoorji prayed in the fire temple.

The downgraded conditions of the Parsis in post-colonial India compelled them to migrate to the West. Mistry talks about one more unsuccessful attempt of migration to the West (Canada). The dream of wealth, prosperity, status, respect is discussed brillantly. But to migrate one needs professional degree like computers or M.B.A., so Yezad advises his children to "Study useful things-computers, M.B.A. and they'll welcome you" (45). He wrote a letter full of figurative language as he was not "an engineer, nurse, technician, or anyone in high demand" (249). Yezad, like all immigrants, had a dream of the promised *home.* He aspired for clean cities, clean air, plenty of water, trains with seats for everyone, where people wait in queue at bus stops and behave courteously. He dreamt for "Not just the land of milk and honey, also the land of deodorant and toiletry" (137). He visualizes this utopian world to end "apeman commute" (137). The interview was a great fiasco and his fantasy about the new life in a new land had finished quickly. Yezad called it as a "naive nonsense" (250). Yezad convinced himself by comparing adverse conditions in Canada and India:

> **... unemployment, violent crime, homelessness, language laws of Quebec. Not much difference between there and here, he would think: we have beggars in Bombay, they have people freezing to death on Toronto streets; instead of high-and low-caste fighting, racism and police shootings; separatists in Kashmir, separatists in Quebec-why migrate from the frying pan into the fire? (137)**

Immigration has dark and bright aspects too. It is blissfull as one can enjoy the materialist pleasure as well as a curse when one has to live in alien land etc. Mistry highlights these two parts of immigration story. The first part deals with dream: the dream of prosperity, house, car, CD player, computer, clean air, snow, lakes, mountains, abundance and second part with reality that this dream was never going to come true. Yezad praised Canada's policies, its people, its geography and its place in the world:

> **...the munificence of Canada; multicultural policy, a policy that in the beauty of its wisdom did not demand the jettisoning of the old before letting them share in the new... The generosity of the Canadian dream makes room for everyone, for a multitude of languages and cultures and peoples. In Canada's willingness to define and redefine itself continually, on the basis of inclusion, lies its greateness, its promise, its hope. (249)**

While comparing American and Canadian policies towards immigrants, Yezad bitterly criticized the "American dream" (249) of immigration, its "melting pot" (249) theory which was "more a nightmare: a crude image better to sulphurous description of hellfire and brimstone than to a promised land" (249). Lashing American dream and favoring Canadian dream, Yezad wished to migrate to Canada with his family to share this "mosiac vision" (249) for its "nobility" (249) to sing "O Canada" (250) with all his hearts. Yezad described India as "this place of disaffection" (250) whereas praises Canada as "...where that values of compassion are paramount, where the creed of selfishness is caged and exterminated, where compromise is preferred to confrontation, and the flower of harmony is cultivated" (250). For the interview Chenoy family is all dressed up in western outfits. There were so many families in the immigration office like "a wedding party" (251). Yezad thought his surname "Chenoy" (251) as Canadian, when Yezad came to know immigration officer's name as "Mazobashi" (251), his hopes were destroyed. He found Canadians even more causal than Americans. Yezad's unawareness about Canada's geography, weather, and sports were responsible for the failure of his interview. At last, immigrant officer scolded him:

> **"'You Indians... You're so naive. You want to go and freeze your butts in a country you understand nothing about, just to make a pile of money. Well, thanks for your interest in Canada, we'll let you know.'" (253)**

Abraham Verghese writes a real incident about such interviews in New Yorker in an article entitled "Cowpath to America". He writes:

> **One morning, the visa officer turned down six consecutive doctors and told the seventh, who happened to be a friend of mine, and whom I'll call Vadivel, "Spare me the crap about coming back with specialized knowledge to serve your country. Why do you really want to go?" Vadivel, who held on to his American dream for so long that he could speak with the passion of a visionary, said, "Sir, craving your indulgence, I want to train in a decent, ten-story hospital where the lifts are actually working. I want to pass board-certification exams by my own merit and not through pull or bribes. I want to become a wonderful doctor, practice real medicine, pay taxes, make a good-living, drive a big car on decent roads, and eventually live in the Ansel Adams section of New Mexico and never come back to this wretched town, where doctors are as numerous as fleas and practice is cutthroat, and where the air outside is not even fit to breathe." The consul gave him a visa. The eighth applicant, forewarned, tried the same tactic but was turned down. [June 23 and 30, 1997]**

It depicts the variety of issues and dimensions of immigration. In case of Yezad, his frankness is not rewarded as his dual nature is completely displayed. He abused India as "place of disaffection" (250). Then, he abuses Canada and its policy that he regarded as "paramount" of "compassion" and "the flower of harmony" (250). He expressed his anger thus:

> **'You, whose people suffered racism and xenophobia in Canada, where they were Canadian citizens, put in camps like prisoners of war- you, sir, might be expected, more**

> **than anyone else, to understand and embody the more enlightened Canadians ideals of Multiculturalism. But if you are anything to go by, then Canada is a gigantic hoax.' (253)**

Mistry like Neil Bisoondath favours neither the American "melting pot" nor the Canadian "multicultural mosaic":

> **The American system likes to pretend that it is possible for individuals to shrug off their past, to pretend that it does not exist, and assume a new identity. Whereas the Canadian one says that it is possible to freeze the past and maintain it as it used to exist, while the country one left, by the way, continues to evolve. The melting pot and the mosaic- they're equally false. There has to be a middle way. And the first part is to have governments and bureaucrats get out of it...And so my attitude, simply put, is leave it to the individual. [1995:31]**

Yezad himself analysed the causes of failure. He thought his slamming of the American melting pot, could have gone against him. Mr. Mazobashi might have marked Yezad as "a radical, an America-hater or -baiter who might be trouble" (250). At the same time there was "a slight note of disloyalty to India?" (250). Thus, Yezad's Canadian dream was shattered. Nariman pointed out that Yezad's decision not to migrate to Canada was correct:

> **"I think emigration is an enormous mistake. The biggest anyone can make in their life. The loss of home leaves a hole that never fills." (254)**

Ashis Gupta reflects on the immigration dream of prosperity and comforts which is too fragile that immigrant find himself trapped in the host country. He explains this predicament: "When I use the words "in a venus-fly-trap" it is because often you get into that, a beautiful image of society, where you have every thing, all the comforts of the world, where every thing works. It is very easy to go complacent and sort of get lost in that without realizing, without sighting, like the fly there in a big jungle." [Ed. Jasbir Jain 2003:212].

Mistry's loss of home is clearly mentioned when Chenoy family approached Jehangir Mansion. Yezad sadly replied that his house was sold and now "strangers" (45) have inhabited his house. But this dream of immigration always made Yezad anxious about his present financial conditions. After knowing about the bribery of Jehangir, Yezad regretted over giving up on his Canadian dream. He believed that the racist immigration officer could not have closed his way forever. He imagined their happy life in Toronto, breathing the pure Rocky Mountain air instead of the "noxious fumes of this dying city, rotting with pollution and garbage and corruption" (283). Roxana argued the nature of Canadian policies and Yezad's general knowledge of Canada:

> **Canada was a land of living saints? And so far as she knew, the Rocky Mountains were still in Alberta, unless government had quietly shifted them to Ontario one night. (283)**

After so many years, Yezad was still unaware of Canada and its weather and geography as well. He is not satisfied with his present life in India.

Mistry deals with inter-faith marriage of Nariman Vakil. Vakil loved a Christian girl and faced opposition in marrying her just because she was a non-Parsi. Parsis are famous for the broad mindedness and they even encourage love-marriages but within the community. Nariman's father thought that his son is "*incapable of falling in love with a Parsi girl*" (14). Whenever his parents tried to findout a good match for him, people used to dig out his love affair with Lucy. His father blamed it for: "*Modern ideas*" (15) and his incapability to "*preserve that fine balance between tradition and moderness*" (15). It was impossible to find a perfect Parsi bride for Nariman so family selected a Parsi widow. He believed that "*the traditional ways were the best*" (16). Nariman was unhappy even after his marriage within the community. Mr. Arjani hired Lucy as an ayah to their grand-children. It was a kind of vengence on Nariman because his father filed a lawsuit against Mr. Arjani. A priest had performed a navjote ceremony for the son of a Parsi mother and non-Parsi father. It is forbidden for the orthodox Parsis. The event initiated debates and polemics and internal strife that infected "*the Reformists and the Orthodox from time to time, like the flu" (131).* Nariman's father wrote to Jam-e-Jamshed about the non-religious work of the "*misguided dustoor*" (132). Mr. Arjani debated over this issue through the letter in newspaper. The war of the letters fired between neighbours. Mr. Vakeel called Mr. Arjani as "*a prime example of the substandard mind whose cogitations were clearly worthless, unable to grasp the simplest tenets of the religion and the supreme significance of the navjote*" (133). Mr. Arjani slammed Mr. Vakeel and accused, "*...of being rabid racist who, in his maniacal quest for purity, wouldn't think twice about eliminating the spouses and offspring of intermarriage*" (133).

Mr. Vakeel denied invitation to Lucy on the grounds that she is not a Zoroastrian and not eligible to be Nariman's wife. She might be a wonderful, as gracious and charming as the Queen of England, but "*she was still unsuitable for his son because she was not a Zoroastrian, case closed*" (132). All these things ruined Nariman's family life and Yasmin's too. Nariman's father called Lucy a "*whore*" (267) and declared that such immoral attitude is "*destroying the Parsi community!*" (267) This is the way of abusing others and distancing them. Such efforts are made to bring about the break up the lovers to push the "non-Parsi girl...to a safe distance" [Pestonji 1999:152] which results into preserving the "self-image of being 'liberal modern Parsis'" [Ibid, 152].

Mistry has shown double-standards of some Parsis on the issue of morality when Soli said: "*Boys weal be boys, Marzi. Better that he has all his fun and froleek now. Afterwards, find a nice Parsi gull and settle down. Right, Nari? No hanky-panky after marriage*" (268). Further Soli humorously asked whether his girl friend confessed what they two did in the home. It is funny the way Parsis think of themselves as morally superior to Christians, their masters who claimed to be the only moral race in the world. He gives Nariman about the confessions made by Chiristian girls. Here, Mistry turns blasphemous as Mr. Soli narrates, "*I have it on good eenformation that these padres make the gulls tell all the juicy details- was he touching you, were you touching him, did he put it een?* (268). Obviously, in course of action Nariman married Yasmin, a window. But he did not forget Lucy either.

Mistry portrays changed Yezad who was liberal and have never gone to Fire Temple but in course of time he became "non-stop-praying stranger" (500) for Jehangir, "as though making up for lost time" (463). Yezad has been reading nothing but religious books and the holy cabinet contained the religious photographs. His bedroom also was full of religious books and the books on Parsi history. The drastically changed Yezad often attended The League of Orthodox Parsis and the Association for Zarathurstrian Education. He discussed these meetings with family. He told them about the incident that happended in 1818 of a Parsi bigamist who married a non-Parsi woman in Calcutta and a Parsi woman in Bombay. He was "excommunicated by the Panchayat" (466) for his crime. Panchayat threatened his father "to disown" (466) him otherwise he would be "excommunicated" (466). He humiliated himself by taking "a pair of shoes, one in each hand, and striking his head five times with them. Right before the assembly" (466-467). Panchayat members have agreed unanimously to follow the policy of excommunication strictly:

> **Parsi men and women, who have relations with non-Parsis, in or out of marriage, will suffer the consequences. Excommunication will be reversed if they repent publicly with the shoe punishment. (467)**

Yezad caught Murad kissing a "non-Parsi" (481) girl on the staircase. He told Murad about the impossibility of their relations as she was "a non-parsi" (481). He also tried to convince him of his wrong behaviour:

> **"Either she's your girlfriend, which is unacceptable, or you're having your fun with her, which is even more unacceptable.... The rules, the laws of our religion are absolute, this Maharashtrian cannot be your girlfriend. ...You can have any friends you like, any race or religion, but for a serious relationship, for marriage, the rules are different.... Because we are a pure Persian race, a unique contribution to this planet, and mixed marriages will destroy that." (482)**

Mistry has shown war of orthodox and modern Parsis on this issue. This alienation from Indain milieu is sympotomatic of superiority complex and sense of unrootedness, statless nation of Parsis. It suggests that they are still not melted into Indian life. Yezad expressed his opinions about the purity: "Inferior or superior is not the question. Purity is a virtue worth preserving" (482). Murad calls his father "a bigot" (482) and compares him with "Hitler" (482).

Roxana wanted to explain him the contrast between the moral behaviour of a Parsi and a non-Parsi girl. She unconsciously aligns her community as morally superior to non-Parsi communities. She convinced him that a Parsi girl would never behave in such a way as his Maharashtrian girl-friend did.

But Mistry also highlights paradox of the racial purity and moral superiority complex of the Parsis. Jehangir wanted to reveal that Parsi girls can behave the way Murad's Maharashtrian girl friend behaved:

> **...in the lift... we were holding each other tight, pretending to fight, pressing against each other and kissing, and I squeezed her breast. If the lift doors hadn't opened, she would have let me slip my hands inside her T-shirt. (483)**

Yezad denied premission to Murad's Maharashtrian girl-friend for the dinner. Murad considered Yezad as "fanatical" (486). As Yezad grew old his quest for spirituality has converted him from a liberal modern Parsi to an orthodox and fundamentalist Zoroastrian.

Purity as an essential religious element is ridiculed by modern day Parsis like Murad. He asked Yezad "Orthodox Parsis could invent a Purity Detector" to detect "an impure person" (486). Modern westernized Parsis think the issues like purity, the life and death of community as "a joking matter" (486). Murad views on these religious beliefs sound interesting:

> **"He started it. He's using religion like a weapon. Do you know the obession with purity is creating lunatics in our community? I'm never going to accpet these crazy ideas." (486)**

It is crucial to consider that important religious matters were ridiculed by modern day Parsis. It is what Firdaus Kanga says, "We Parsis don't take our religion too seriously, those who do are considered downright dangerous and little mad" [1991: 14]. Maya Jaggi in her article highlights the various developments that took place in the novel as well as in Yezad's character. According to her "Yezad's fundamentalism is born out of guilt" [2002], guilt of spending many years in irreligiousness, ridiculing his own religion as the religion of bigots etc... The interesting fact is Murad goes on the same track. Jaggi points out this aspect as:

> **There is also an echo of Sectarian intolerance in Orthodox Parsis' obsession with Purity, fearing extinction through inter-marriage or migration. The novel both affirms**

> **Zoroastrian ritual and derides bigotry. Though the sceptic Yezad returns to the fold, his insistence that his sons marry Parsis threatens in to replicate into Nariman's tragedy. [2002]**

In this way Mistry shows the predicament of orthodoxy within the Parsi community.

Mistry talks about the Parsi honesty. Mr. Kapur flattered Yezad for "the Parsi reputation for honesty" (156). Yezad tells his sons the story of his father who had jeopardized his life to save his name, and reputation for honesty of his community by saving money in the bank:

> **"When your grandfather was in danger of being killed, what concerned him most was not the loss of his life, but the loss of his good name. He always said, when he finished telling me the story, 'Remember, people can take everything away from you, but they cannot rob you of your decency. Not if you want to keep it. You alone can do that, by your actions.'" (234)**

Vilas believed Yezad's nature and trust in "integrity and fair play" (212). Yezad called it as "non-sense about Parsi honesty" (212). Vilas stretched the argument:

> **Not nonsense. Myths create the reality. Point is, there was a time when living according to certain myths served your community well. With the present state of society, those same myths can make misfits of men. (212-213)**

Parsi honesty really helped this community to survive the reign of every empire. Parsis believe in cleanliness and hygiene. Roxana counted old notes cautiously as it was unknown who might have touched or handled the notes and "how hygienic were their hands, did they wash twice with soap after going to the toilet?"(237). Parsi made fun of the Christians who did not follow the cleanliness and hygiene precautions. Soli passed insulting comments about "*ferangis who wiped their arses with paper instead of washing hygienically*" (15).

Mistry highlights the various religious beliefs of the Parsis. Parsis never keep cats. Cats are considered as "bad luck because cats hate water, they never take a bath" (162). Jehangir provides the scientific reasons about the cat's hygienic condition as cat licks itself. Nariman gives psychological explanation: "But beliefs are more powerful than facts" (162).

Parsis never kill spiders and male chicken. Nariman tells Jehangir that Spider spins the web and mends the chains that Zuhaak is about to break during night when Cock crows to keep the world safe again: "The Cock and Spider keep it safe for us, one day at a time" (164).

Parsis offer sandal wood and loban to fire on their religious occassions. The fragrance delighted Roxana. Yezad did not believe in these religious rituals. For him it was enough to go to fire-temple on Navroze and Khordad Sal and "loban smoke was merely one way to get rid of mosquitoes" (25). Modernized Parsis believe in the modernity and allow women and even teenagers to drink liquor. Nariman insists Roxana to drink on his birthday. Even her sons demanded that she must drink.

Mistry discusses the Parsi beliefs related with final rites. As per Parsi belief, funeral of the dead should not be delayed "beyond twenty-four hours from the time of death" (397). Navjote ceremony initiates the Parsi child into Zoroastrian fold. Yezad remembered about his Navjote:

> **The prayer cap his mother had bought for his navjote ceremony had been this very shade of marron. He was seven then - and how proud the family was that he had mastered the prayers already. Others had to wait till nine or eleven. (339)**

Palonji Contractor wished that his children should properly initiate into the Zoroastrian fold in his presence as his time was up:

> **...better for the father to witness the navjote, even if the initiates were a few verses short, so he could die secure in the knowledge that his progeny had been properly welcomed into the Zoroastrian fold. (28)**

Yezad hadn't visited Fire Temple in years and even not recited the prayers. He even had forgotten the tastes of "a chasni... paapri and malido" (306).

When he visits Fire Temple, he found it "cool" and "a real oasis in the midst of this big, mad city" (308). Non-Parsis are not allowed in the Fire Temple: "The sign said Admittance For Parsis Only - he was one, and entitled to go inside" (338). He is worried about the future of Parsis when he saw a young boy trained into his family business of selling Sukhad in Fire Temple:

> **Would there be a business when the boy became a man, wondered Yezad, the way the Parsis were dwindling in Bombay, and the way people like himself treated the faith? And the sandalwood trees fast disappearing, thanks to bandits and smugglers like Veerappan... (338)**

In the years of irreligiousness, Yezad forgot how to perform the kusti prayers. Prayers are sacred and can not be disturbed in between by "profane speech and unnecessary explanation" (340). In Zoroastrianism, common people and even dustoors are not allowed to enter into the interior sections of the Fire Temple: "only those in a state of ritual purity" (341) can go inside the interim sections of the Fire Temple and "the laity could not cross" (341) marble threshold. Parsis never extinguish fire as it is the symbol of sacredness and purity of God. Fire in the Fire Temple is continusously burning for almost a hundred and fifty years since it was built.

Fire is not polluted by human breath. So the priest lowered the protective square of mulmul from his head to cover his nose and mouth. According to Zoroastrian belief each day is divided into the *geh*. A Parsi priest performs certain ceremony for the changing geh:

> **...dustoorji stepped into the sanctum to perform the ceremony for the changing geh. Sunset, thought Yezad, and the fourth geh of the Zoroastrian day had commenced. He watched the ritual cleansing of the sanctum, the pedestal, the afargaan, the quiescent preparations before the offerings to the fire. (342)**

Yezad offered prayer for Nariman to soothe his anxious and unhealthy condition. But Roxana knew, he has abondoned prayers and "prefunctory observations" (444) and has not stepped inside a fire-temple in forty years because of the way his parents had treated Lucy. He used to call it "the religion of bigots" (444). Yezad is confident about the powers of Zoroastrian Prayers. He chanted the prayers loudly "Kemna mazda!" (445) by the time he finished the segment, Nariman became calm and quieter. Day by day Yezad grew more religious. He followed his religion very strictly. He yelled at Murad for entering into the holy place of prayer in his impure state after "a haircut" (462). Murad ridiculed Yezad's too much religiousness and minimum distance of pure prayer-zone: "This is twenty-first century… and you still believe such nonsense. It's sad… How did you get the exact figure? Did Zoroaster whisper it in your ear?" (463). These are stereotype reactions from younger generation who are exposed to science and technology. This irreligious attitude of Murad offended Yezad. He warned Murad not to use Zoroaster instead of Zarathustra. He also gave reference to the scripture: "Vendidaad, fargard XVII, explains the distance" (463). Murad was not ready to leave the argument. He called it "a rough estimate" (464) and would achieve "approximate purity" (464). Yezad was hurt and regretted that their "faith is a subject of ridicule" (464) for Murad. It is really tragic when Parsis, the younger generation, made fun of their own religion. Murad jokingly asked Yezad:

> **"What if an impure fly or mosquito or cockroach violates the sofa boundary? Do you check if they've showered? Maybe you should enclose your cabinet in a bubble." (464)**

Mistry discusses seriously with slight black humour about the future survival of his tiny community. Parsis believe in the values of individualism. Parsis suffer from typical diseases and one of them is Parkinson. Nariman suffers from this illness. Mistry aptly puts the frustration of such people and expects that "the new research in America would hurry up, something with foetal tissue, embryos" (357). Coomy calls Nariman "a walking medical dictionary" (34) suffering from "osteoporosis, Parkinson's disease, hypotension" (34). Dr. Fitter's anger shows the frustration due to the present day Parsi status and attitude of young generation: "Parsi men of today were useless, dithering idiots, the race had deteriorated" (51). This feeling of unworthiness and unimportance made Parsis what is called as "boring" and "…all doodh-paus. All flab, no muscle. No sex appeal" [Pestonji, Meher, 1999:63]. He compares them with the glorious past of the community. The Parsis brought luster and glory to the community through their dedication as the industrialists, the shipbuilders and the philanthropists. Parsis established the foundation of modern India.

They gave the sense of charity and social commitment to Indians by building hospitals and schools and libraries and bags.

Dr. Fitter is worried about the demographic decline in the Parsi community. He believes that his community is about to "doom and gloom" (51). He doubts whether his community would see the next century:

> **Demographics show we'll be extinct in fifty years. Maybe it's the best thing. What's the use of having spineless weaklings walking around, Parsi in name only. (51)**

Jal witnessed the hot discussion about the future of the Parsi community. They cover all topics regarding his dwindling community, like dwindling birth rate, interfaith marriages and the heavy migration to the West. If Parsi would extinguish: "Vultures and crematoriums, both will be redundant" (412). For Jal this was "explosive topic" (412). He admits the minority status of his community but they have survived, and prospered in course of time. Inspector Masalavala didn't want to "tolerate optimism" (412). Demographic experts predict the decline of the community in coming fifty years. This problem of survival is severe as the Parsis are not taking firm steps to prevent their extinction. Aditi Kapoor rightly says:

> **Unless something is done to augment their fast depleting numbers and to revive their religion the Parsis after an illustrious past could well just fade out in oblivion. ["The Parsis; Fire on Ice" in Times of India, 14th May 1989]**

If concrete decisions and active participation is not initiated then the possibility of extinction will be increased and the result will be that Parsi "will become a decadent community with a glorious past, a perilous present, and a dim future." [Palkhiwala 1994:320]

Dr. Fitter compares the extinction with dinosaurs. If people want to study Parsis they will have to study the Parsi bones. His humour characterized the Parsi spirit, the ability to laugh in the face of darkness. Dr. Fitter imagined the names given to Parsis skeletons like "Jalosauras", "Shapurjisauras", "Pestonjisauras", and "Whiskysauras" (413).

Mistry has highlighted that reasons like late marriages, individualism, westernization, modernization are responsible for the falling birth rate:

> **Our Parsi boys and girls don't want to get married unless they have their own flat. Which is next to impossible in Bombay, right? They don't want to sleep under the same roof as their mummy and daddy... These Western ideas are harmful. (413)**

Inspector Masalavala blamed the Parsis producing just one or two children: "Parsis seem to be the only people in India who follow the family planning message. Rest of the country is breeding like rabbits"(413). According to demographers another reason for low-birth rate is "the more educated a community, the lower the birth rate" (414). So they wanted to prohibit the Parsi from higher education:

> **Give them cash incentives to study less. And those who want to do post-graduates studies, tell them they will get no funding from Panchayat unless they sign a contract to have as many children as the number of people over age fifty in their family. Maximum of seven-we don't want to spoil the health of our young women. (414)**

He suggested that if Parsi couples face "medical problems, inability to conceive?"(414) then they can use "virto fertilization and all those mind-boggling technologies" that result in multiple births. But such large families would result in the evils like "- sickness, poverty" (414).

Inspector Masalavala rejects such possibilities as Panchayat has enough money for all the Parsis. He blames excessive individualism for this decline. Such ideas are "Poison...Pure poison" (414) for the Parsi community. He thinks that the extinction of Parsis would be a great loss to the whole world because "When a culture vanishes, humanity is the loser" (415). Assuming the end of Parsis they plan for:

> **...a time capsule for posterity. To be opened in one thousand years. Containing recipes for dhansak, patra-ni-machhi, margi-ni-farcha, and lagan-nu-custard... "How about including the Zend-Avesta, and words and music for Chhaiye Hamay Zarathosti?" a few old issues of *Jam-e-Jamshed*... Also, some cassettes of Adi Marzban's radio**

> **comedies... Complete instructions and explanations for all our rituals and ceremonies, ...a copy of our great Navsari epic, 'Ek Pila Ni Ladai'... With an English translation.**
>
> **As the evening wore on, the three of them filled their imagnary time capsule with their favourite items, ancient and modern, serious and frivolous, sacred and profane, till they ran out of ideas. (415-16)**

Inspector Masalavala sadly expressed the emotional bond between Parsis and Mumbai. Both prospered together and now for Parsis the city has just lost its old charm. For them Bombay is dying now, as their community is dying too. Parsis built this beautiful city and made it prosper. In a few more years, there won't be any Parsis left alive to tell this tale of great city and its grandeur. Inspector Masalavala concluded, "Well, we are dying out, and Bombay is dying as well ...When the spirit departs, it isn't long before the body decays and disintegrates." (416)

Mistry highlights *Anglomaniac* tendency of the Parsis. Using the Christian name is also the craze among the Parsis. Jehangir wanted to change his name to "John" (247). Yezad warns Roxana about Jehangir's becoming "a Christian" (247). Jehangir denied the possibility and convince them his Parsisness but just name will be slightly different. Roxana explained him:

> **Listen, Jehangla, your Christian friends have Christian names. Your Hindu friends have Hindu names. You are a Parsi so you have a Persian name. Be proud of it, it's not to be thrown out like an old shoe. (247)**

Mistry in a masterly fashion sketches the predicament of Parsis in post-colonial India with their downgraded economical status. Parsis are portrayed as middle class who are always in the financial crisis. It is very difficult for middle-class Parsis to manage the monthly budget. Coomy for this reason does not allow the use of ear-batteries to her brother Jal. Coomy was unable to cook "a decent dinner" (36) due to insufficient income. Coomy and Jal's damaged house can not be repaired due to the lack of money. Coomy took Nariman to a Parsi General Hospital to save money. Yezad was fade up of his life after Nariman's arrival in his house. Nariman's medical bills caused financial crisis. Such problems lead Yezad and his sons to indulge in corruption. Jahangir is made "a Homework Monitor" (31). While checking Ashok's incomplete homework, Ashok bribed Jehangir some cash. At first Jehangir denied but when:

> **He looked once more at Ashok's money. A small packet of butter. Or mutton for one meal. Or a week of eggs for Daddy's breakfast. (220-221)**

Roxana complained Yezad about the illness and payments of doctors. Yezad advised to plan accordingly as it was difficult to "buy both food and medicine" (96). Financial crisis in Roxana's family reached height when they have to cut on food too.

Insuffencient economic source and starvation of the whole family compelled Yezad to go to Villie Cardmaster to play the Mataka number. Jehangir thought of doing small jobs with Murad to earn money for his family. Yezad himself started playing Mataka. He won few times but at last when Police raided Mataka mafia, he lost all the money. Yezad thought of telling Mr. Kapur all about his present family condition. His financial condition would improve if Mr. Kapur gives him promotion otherwise the whole family would collapse. Thus Parsi community in Mistry's fiction suffers due to financial instability.

Rohinton Mistry in an interview highlights the predicament of the Parsi characters as per the choice, they made in their lives. Mistry highlights that the book supports the idea of destiny and show that everything happens as a consequence of what the character choose to do. Mistry says:

> **If Yezad had not undertaken the scheme with the actors, everything would have been different; Mr. Kapur would not have been killed. If Coomy had listened to her brother and said right, 30 years have gone by, it is time to forgive and forget, things could have gone differently. It is choice of each character that leads to the denouement. [Canadian Fiction Magazine, 2002]**

Mistry has very delicately interwoven the family saga of a Parsi family undergoing the drastic change in the times of political, financial and personal crisis.

*

Thus Mistry traced the ethnic anxieties as reflected his fictional world. Mistry's *Tales from Firozsha Baag* deals with the Parsi housing complex in Mumbai and its habitants. Mistry has bitterly and satirically commented on the ethos and paradoxes of the community. He focuses the themes of migration, inter-faith marriage, Parsi trusts and funds, poverty in the community, and unhygienic conditions of the Parsi colonies. *Such a Long Journey* explores the loss of innocence of the protagonist, Gustad Noble, as he attempts to define himself in relation to his family and his country during the chaotic times of 1971 India, during which India and Pakistan went on war over the liberation of the East Pakistan, or Bangladesh. He gives details of the lives of Gustad Noble and his family which serves as a contrast to outside world that disrupts the family order. Mistry presents the outside world as a rotten and corrupting force on even the most descent members of the inner sphere. It highlights various problems regarding the traditional dokhma, decline in vulture population and other important issues of Parsi community. *A Fine Balance* gives intense description of extreme poverty, and shows the bond that develops between four main characters, despite the barriers created by their differences in religion and social status. It shows the struggle of Parsi as well as other subaltern ethnic groups for their identity and survival. *Family Matters* portrays the Nariman Vakil, 79 year old Parsi patriarch and his family in overcrowded and politically corrupt Bombay. It is the comment on post-Babri Mumbai, where existence of minorities and Non-Maharashtrians is under threat. It also comments on the inter-faith marriage issues of the Parsis. Other Parsi customs, ceremonies, beliefs are also focused. It highlights the Parsi presence in Mumbai as *other.*

To sum up, Mistry has portrayed various anxieties of the Parsi Zoroastrian community. His portrayal of middle class Parsi community is a medley of post-colonial predicament of Parsi-Zoroastrian who is sidelined as a minority and 'other. At the same time, he highlights the various anxieties of this small ethnic group related with dokhma, prayers, conflict of national identity, recitation of prayers, vulture controversies etc. At last one can say that his novels will "preserve a record of how they lived to some extent," [Ali Lakhani] when the Parsis will disappear from the earth.

*

VI

Sidhwa & Mistry: A Comparison

This chapter aims at the comparative study of the two Parsi writers - Bapsi Sidhwa and Rohinton Mistry. Both differ from each other as they belong to two different geographical locations, Pakistan and India respectively. However, both are now settled in Canada. Since they belong to the sub-continental countries which were once united before acquiring status as independent states, they share the common element of religion and culture. Bapsi Sidhwa and Rohinton Mistry are the two crucial Parsi writers who focus on the problems of their microscopic community. They highlight the problems of survival in the cultural milieu they live in. Bapsi Sidhwa confronts the Muslim society in Pakistan and Rohinton Mistry experiences the Hindu ethos in India. The discussion here is aimed at the vivid facets of their skills as writers and the issues they dealt with. Both the writers write about their community at different point of time. So the problems faced by them are also rather different though not completely.

I

Every creative artist reflects his/her own world-view in his/her works. His treatment of his socio-religious, cultural, political, economical and environmental surroundings of his/her contemporary society contribute to the development of his/her fictional world. The artists' revelation of life aids him/her to recognize the things or incidents he/she faces in his/her life. Their treatment may differ regarding the similar tribulations. The thematic of the work can be dealt with several ways. The narration can either be in a tragic or a comic way. It is affected by the writer's feeling of endurance in the unsympathetic surroundings and recognition with the troubles and concerns following the resentment. Simultaneously, an author is considered in a way in which others identify him/her and situate him/her in a particular socio-cultural milieu. So the characters shaped by the author are fictional realities. If the writer belongs to a marginal ethnic group living on the periphery, indeed his/her fictional world is engaged with the tribulations that his/her ethnic group confronts. S/He handles the ensuing angsts of his ethnic group and obviously reveals the need for the continuance of the race of that ethnic group. Here the discussion is concerned about two Parsi writers. So their world view clearly mirrors the Parsi community. It highlights the various anxieties --- psychological or existential that Parsi community undergoes.

The world views of Bapsi Sidhwa and Rohinton Mistry are quite contrasting. However, the genderic difference is, to a large extent, responsible for their different outlook. Sidhwa analyses from the feminist point of view where as Mistry's work delineates the patriarchal ideology. Both have portrayed the public as well as private lives of their protagonists in accordance with their Parsi ethnic identity. Some times they are genuine representations, some times exaggerated exuberance of their Parsi psyche, and some times treated in ironic-satiric way or in realistic tradition. In this regard David Stouck has pointed out various modes of narrative. He writes:

> **Mode is a way of describing motivation in a work that is not contingent on time or place, that remains stable across the centuries and from culture to culture. It provides a basis from which we can relate to the experiences of people who lived hundreds of years ago or in totally different cultures at great distances from our own. One can identify four different modes. Briefly, *romances* are stories of individual adventures... while *pastrols* embody the individual's experience of remembering and sometimes grieving. *Satire and epics, on the other hand, serve the communal interests, epic celebrating the history of a community or***

> ***nation, satire criticizing its practices and exposing its shortcomings.* [Emphasis added] [David Stouck, 2003:64]**

It seems that the community as represented in Bapsi Sidhwa's fictional world has rather different problems than Mistry's depiction of his community. It may be because of the different dimension of their temporality. Some novels of Sidhwa display the traits of Mennippean satire. Mennippean satire is defined as:

> **... a form of intellectually humorous work characterized by miscellaneous contents, displays of curious erudition, and comical discussions on philosophical topics. [Baldic, Chris, 1990:132]**

Some of the features of such satire are varied as pointed out by M.H.Abrams:

> **A major feature is a series of extended dialogues and debates...in which *a group of loquacious eccentrics*, pedants, literary people, and representative of various professions or philosophical points of view serve to make ludicrous the attitudes and viewpoints they typify by the arguments they urge in their support. [M.H.Abrams 1993:189] (Emphasis added)**

Bakhtin too points out that Mennippean satire:

> **...is characterized by an extraordinary freedom of plot and philosophical invention... [while its] bold and unrestrained use of the fantastic and adventure is internally motivated, justified by and devoted to a purely ideational and philosophical end: the creation of extraordinary situations for the provoking and testing of a philosophical idea, a discourse, a truth, embodied in the image of a wise man, the seeker of this truth. [Cundy 134]**

Mennippean satire can easily be discerned in Bapsi Sidhwa's ground breaking Parsi novel *The Crow Eaters* which highlights the Parsi idiosyncrasy and paradoxes. The protagonist Freddy Junglewalla preaches the philosophy of survival to his young listeners.

> **...'The sweetest thing in the world is your *need*'... Need, I tell you – will force you to love your enemy as a brother! I followed the dictate of my needs, my wants- they make on flexible, elastic, humble. (TCE, 9-11)**

At the same time he talks about 'tiny spark' in every pure race, for the sake of racial purity. He debates over this issue with his son.

> **I believe in some kind of a tiny spark that is carried from parent to child, on through generations... a kind of inherited memory of wisdom and righteousness, reaching back to the times of Zarathustra, the Magi, the Mazdiasnians. It is a tenderly nurtured conscience evolving towards perfection. (TCE, 128)**

In *Ice-Candy Man* too, she highlights how Godmother talks philosophically on the feminine predicament on the eve of partition. At the same time, various characters from different ethnic groups discuss the survival in the frenzy of ethnic angst. *An American Brat* discusses the problems of insular-marriage where Sidhwa through Zareen's character wanted to prove the cultural dissimilarities by giving the horrible details in a comic and satiric way. On the other hand, Mistry's world view is very gloomy and tragic. He can be called as 'cynic' who believes that 'everything ends badly' and "there is a tiny piece of justice in the universe" (AFB, 680). Mistry's ideas about destiny are akin to Thomas Hardy. Hardy opines that man is bound to the wheel of destiny and therefore has to continuously struggle against the dictates of fate. Mistry's vision of life is dark and gloomy. For him, this cosmos is an unfriendly mechanism, heading for by some automatic principle of life, mysterious end, utterly uncaring to the feelings of human beings. One can say that human beings are toys in the hands of fate in his fictional world. Their actions are determined by fate, by an automatic and unsympathetic principle of life. Human action is not free but determined by the external forces acting on the will. Life to him is a lost, inglorious battle. His characters resist in vain against overpowering odds. His world is not the anvil whereon souls are beaten into shapes; rather they are crushed out of shape and broken. He bears a grudge against the universe which he could not throw off; he has a feeling of resentment at injustice and wanton cruelty heaped on human beings as Glouster in King Lear says:

> **As flies to wanton boys, are we to the gods,**
> **They kill us for their sport. [Act IV, Sc.1, line 43-44]**

The fictional world of Mistry created in *Such a Long Journey* is thus no utopia of any kind. It is a picture of the fallen world. Again, it is a world in which all forms of corruption, knavery, hypocrisy, tyranny, ugliness and decay have become the order of the day. The society depicted is completely deprived of resilience. Mistry's shock at the sight of stinking human condition and rampant corruption turns him into a realist, who is obliged to expose the world around him. His celebrated novel, *A Fine Balance*, is often called as cosmic tragedy, where all the characters are brutally crushed by the destiny. Honore de Balzac, *Le Pere Goriot* quoted at the beginning of the novel:

> **'Holding this book in your hand, sinking back in your soft armchair, you will say to yourself: perhaps it will amuse me. And after you have read this story of great misfortunes, you will no doubt dine well, blaming the author for your own insensitivity, accusing him of wild exaggeration and flights of fancy. But rest assured: this tragedy is not a fiction. All is true.' (AFB)**

In *Family Matters*, too, harsh realties compel the characters to shed off the innocence. Yezad engages in a fraud scheme, Jehangir is initiated into the world of crookedness and corruption. Mistry satirizes the survival scenario in ironical way when Dr. Fitter discusses it with other members of his community. Thus, both writers vary in their world view.

*

II

Literature serves both the purposes of delight and instruction. Sometime it delights through instruction and some time it instructs through entertainment. This edification and amusement is done through various characters that are situated in a particular socio-economic, culture-religious, national-political milieu. Hippolyte-Adolphe Taine realized that a literary work is "a transcript of contemporary manners" and from such "monuments of literature" one can understand "... knowledge of the manner in which men thought and felt." [1976:309]

Thus fiction, as a branch of the literature, is the expression of the most intimate social awareness of the society in which it is born and nurtured. As a creative process, fiction records the creative evolution of the society itself. Bhabani Bhattacharya highlights his view of the social consciousness in the novels. He says, "I hold that a novel must have a social purpose. It must place before the reader something from the society's point of view. Art is not necessarily for art's sake. Purposeless art and literature which is much in vogue does not appear to me as a sound judgment" [V. Venkata Reddy 1999:01]. Shyam Asnani finds that a writer is always "...seeking the strength and fertility of his own cultural sensibility and socio-cultural experience" in the literature [1985:4]. Literature highlights various social evils and problems like superstition, casteism, poverty, illiteracy, and many others. Society is torn by political maneuverings, social disparities, communal frenzy and corruption in bureaucracy. This stirs writers' imagination. In such a way, writers give artistic articulation to the problems that beset the common people and their joys and sorrows, the crusade against the tyranny of poverty, illiteracy, suffering, superstition, caste and sex, farmer, laborer, a factory worker, a patient, a virtuous woman, pitted against a zamindar, a landlord, a factory owner, or a ruthless callous hard-hearted man. In Joan Rockwell's opinion:

> **Fiction is not only a representation of social reality, but also a necessary functional part of social control, and also, paradoxically, an important element in social change. It plays a large part in the conduct of politics and, in general, gives symbols and modes of life...in those less**

> **easily defined, but basic areas such as norms, values, and personal and interpersonal behaviour. [1974:4]**

The social paradigm in the fictions of these two writers, Mistry and Sidhwa, is completely different from each other. Their fictions deal with different time and locations their community is placed in. Sidhwa highlights the law and order in Pakistan:

> **The Hadood Ordinance had been introduced by General Zia in 1979 without anyone knowing what they were. The Fedral Shariat Court, to oversee the Islamic laws, had also been established... *Zina* Ordinance... required the testimony of four "honorable" *male eye-withnesses or eight female eyewitnesses to establish rape* (emphasis added) The addition of *zina* altered the entire legal picture of sexual crime. The victim of rape ran the risk of being punished for adultery, while the rapist was often set free. Yet there were many apologists, upright men learned in jurisprudence, who agreed with the letter of the law, if not its spirit. They produced a litany of precedent and dire argument to support the verdicts. The gender bias was appalling. (AAB, 236-237)**

As Sidhwa herself worked on many committees' with Begum Bhutto, she had undergone so many experiences of poverty and the social-strata in Pakistan. Her shift to USA had opened the new world which also had its own 'dark-zones' or 'weak-pulses' where she found the Pakistan in USA with its disturbing conditions of the Blacks, the Hispanics and prevalent poverty:

> **They had their own vistas of uncompromising poverty and could not feel compassion for people in a distant, opulent country that had never been devasted by war, that greedily utilized one fourth of the world's resources and polluted its atmosphere and water with nuclear tests and poisonous pesticides that could serve as well obliterate Third World pests like themselves. Poverty had spread like a galloping, disfiguring disease. Every kind of poverty in**

> **the United States paled in comparison. Yet it did not mean that the condition of the poor in America was trifling, or the injustice there less rampant. Poverty, she realized, groping for expression, was relative. (AAB, 238)**

Sidhwa highlights the socio-economic conditions in Pakistan with a racist tone. Manek came back, on the way home driver applied his brakes behind a cyclist and blazed with anger,

> **"If you want to die, you black man, go and die beneath some other car!" The sun had set, and in the lingering afterglow made opaque by the dust and sooty emissions from the buses and mini-buses, it was impossible to tell the cyclist's color. But, then, had Snow White been the cyclist she would have been called "black man" also. The comment was not pertinent to color or sex. In the hierarchy of Pakistani traffic, truck and car are king; the cyclist, as possessor of an inferior vehicle, is treated with contempt. By the same token the pedestrian, whose only means of locomotion are his shoes, is more lowly. The lowest are the shoeless beggars who skip nimbly from the path of Toyotas driven by snobbish drivers. The racist overtones were provided by the legacy of the Khan's service in the British army during the days of the Raj. (AAB, 196)**

This reflects the social strata in the Pakistani society and how the whole nation was disillusioned and betrayed after the freedom. Mistry's world too had such undercurrents, especially, in his cosmic tragedy *A Fine Balance.* Mistry portrays the socio-religious scenario in the Indian villages:

> **...there are four varnas in society: Brahmin, Kshatriya, Vaishya, and Shudra. Each of us belongs to one of these four varnas, and they cannot mix. (AFB, 138)**

Sidhwa portrays the Parsi community in its highest development: Raj-*The Crow Eaters*), on the verge of Partition (*Ice-Candy Man*), community which faces the fundamentalism in independent Pakistan (*An American*

Brat). Mistry comments upon the Parsi community after 1960s - when large numbers of Parsis were migrating to the West. During post-Raj India, they were categorized as 'minority' and 'other'. He portrays the society which is threatened by the majorities like Hindus (Maratha) in *Such a Long Journey* and *Family Matters*. The Prime Minister is held to be responsible for the increasing fundamentalism in India:

> **At once she began encouraging the demands for a separate Maharashtra. How much bloodshed, how much rioting she caused. And today we have that bloody Shiv Sena, wanting to make the rest of us into second-class citizens. Don't forget, she started it all by supporting the racist buggers. (SALJ, 39)**

Sidhwa portrays the Parsis as having dignity, respect and awe in society-Godmother in *Ice-Candy Man* and Freddy in *The Crow Eaters*. In *Ice-Candy Man*, Sidhwa portrays Godmother as a kind of community chief who controls the nerves of the community. By her name only she commands respect from the community members and she is always taken seriously. Lenny talks about the arena and sphere of influence of the Godmother (ICM, 210).

On the other hand, Mistry portrays the Parsis who are considered as clowns and have become a butt of ridicule, who are losing their self-respect and dignity which have resulted into the westward migration. Mistry portrays Rustomji (*Tales from Firozsha Baag, 'An Inauspicious Occasion'*) who is humiliated publicly because he abuses the bus as well as the crowd when someone spat betel leaf juice on his white shirt (TBF, 17).

To save himself Rustomji made clown of himself. He removed his denture, "Look, such an old man, no teeth even" (TFB, 18). In this reference Bharucha writes:

> **It is this tragedy of shattered dreams and socio-political downgrading that lurks beneath Rustomji's comic mask and scatological humor, that ultimately makes the story come across as tender and sensitive discourse. [2003:78]**

Mistry portrays Dinshawaji's character in a caricaturesque style.

In this manner the social status of the Parsi community is incorporated in the fictional worlds of these two writers.

*

III

The political predicament in the novels of these two writers should also be taken into consideration. Literature is and always has been a social activity in reality. It is one aspect of the cultural superstructure which has its basics in the economic, political, social, philosophical and religious patterns of the time. It unravels multidimensional conscious and unconscious cravings of a society which are seeking happiness and realization in the world of actual reality. N. Shamota aptly points out that:

> **The soil which nurtures artistic talent is the culture of the people, the tastes spiritual demands and life of the artist's contemporaries. In other words, the artist is only the co-author of a magnificent creation known as the culture of the people. [1966:106-7]**

Stephen Spender opined that the political consciousness is aroused through the fiction [1935:19]. It suggests that literature can be used as a tool to preach the political ideologies. It helps people to understand the political turmoil in the specific country. According to Benjamin Disraeli, such consciousness is shaped by "a variety of influence- the influence of original organization, of climate, soil, religion, laws, customs, manners, extraordinary accidents and incidents in their history and the individual character of their illustrious citizens" [1967:21]. Thus literature can be seen as an organic part of the total cultural-complex in which it takes its origin. The organic nature of art makes it draw nourishment from diverse sources including politics, taken in its wider, elemental sense, as embracing the multiplicity of the contemporary scene with its economic, social, cultural and governmental aspects. Thomas Mann's growth from *Reflections of an Apolitical Man to Kultur and Politik* depended on realization that:

> **What is political and social is an indivisible part of what is human and enters into one problem of humanism, into which our intellect must include it and...in this problem a dangerous hiatus destructive for culture may manifest itself if we ignore the political, social element inherent in it. [1977:46]**

There could be isolated number of factors which 'politicize' literature and lend to the relationship between literature and politics a sharp possessive character. Jean Paul Sartre also thinks that literature is increasingly difficult to separate from the historical and the political events of its time.

So political aspect covers various issues related with the subjugation of Parsi community in the novels of these two writers. Both the writers have discussed the subaltern status of their community in the mainstream politics. The severity of the problems is sometimes exaggerated. The Parsi community in Sidhwa suffers the dilemma of political alignment whereas Parsi community in Mistry suffers the marginal existence on the periphery resulting into alienation from the national identity. Sidhwa's fiction has political overtones. She has positive approach in her depiction of Jinnah and Bhutto and she has tried to (re)construct ideal images. She assumes satiric tone while portraying the political figures such as Gandhijee and Nehru. She has tried to (de)construct them as common human beings having their own follies and simultaneously she criticizes the fundamentalism in Pakistan. Sidhwa describes Gandhijee as:

> **...a mythic figure... surrounded by women... small, dark, shriveled, old... He is a man who loves women. And lame children. And the untouchable sweeper - so he will love the untouchable sweeper's constipated girl best. (ICM, 85-87)**

Sidhwa further supports Pakistan's demands for Kashmir. While comparing Nehru and Jinnah in all their mannerisms and personality facets, Sidhwa writes, "the British favour Nehru over Jinnah. Nehru is Kashmiri; they grant him Kashmir" (ICM, 159). Sidhwa has compared Nehru and Jinnah:

> **Nehru wears red carnations in the buttonholes of his ivory jackets. He bandies words with Lady Mountbatten and is presumed to be her lover. He is charming, too,**

> **to Lord Mountbatten. Suave, Cambridge-polished, he carries about him an aura of power and a presence that flatters anyone he compliments tenfold. He doles out promises, smiles, kisses-on-cheeks. He is in the prime of his Brahmin manhood. He is handsome, his cheeks glow pink. (ICM, 159)**

Where as Jinnah is described as:

> **Jinnah is incapable of compliments. Austere, driven, pukka-sahib accented, deathly ill: incapable of cheek-kissing. Instead of carnations he wears a karakuli cap, somber with tight, grey lamb's-wool curls: and instead of pale jackets, black *achkan* coats. He is past the prime of his elegant manhood.Sallow, whip-thin, sharp-tongued, uncompromising. His training at the Old Bailey and practice in English courtroom has given him faith in constitutional means, and he puts his misplaced hopes into tall standards of upright justice. The fading Empire sacrifices his cause to their shifting allegiances. (ICM, 159-160)**

Sidhwa refers to the unfair portrayal of the Jinnah by the Western and Indian historians. Sidhwa as omniscient narrator writes:

> **And today, forty years later, in films of Gandhi's and Mountbatten's lives, in books by British and Indian scholars, Jinnah, who for a decade was known as 'Ambassador of Hindu-Muslim Unity', is caricatured, and portrayed as a monster. (ICM, 160)**

In *An American Brat*, Manek calls Bhutto as a "socialist bastard" (AAB, 100). Zareen calls him "... hero ... The champion of the poor, of women, of the minorities and underprivileged people - of democracy" (AAB, 175) and "a martyr!" (AAB, 21-22) "massiha" (AAB, 178) General Zia is described as 'the murder'-er and "a political rival" (AAB, 21-22)

Mistry's stance on politics has a satiric or to certain extent negative approach. He portrays the political figures such as Nehru, Indira Gandhi, and Balasaheb Thakrey in negative light. The approach must have been determined by his minority status and the exploitation perpetuated by these leaders on the community. He criticizes the corruption in Indian politics and its side-effects on his tiny endangered community. (Nagarwalla Case - Major Billimoria in SALJ). Dinshawji described Indira Gandhi as "a shrewd woman", "Saali" (SALJ, 38). Major Billimoria refers Indira Gandhi as "spy", "blackmail"(-er), "control"(-er), "very strong woman... very intelligent" (SALJ, 270) controller of "RAW, the courts, broadcasting... everything is in her pocket, all will be covered up."(SALJ, 278), "our leader" (AFB, 325), "mother India" (AFB, 329). Inspector Bamaji abuses the Pakistani leaders who are waging war against Bangladesh as, "Bastards", "Bloody bahen chod bhungees"(SALJ,295), Yahya Khan is "Drunkerd" (SALJ,307) LalBahadur Shastri is "a short man"(SALJ,114) who "command respect on the world stage", "Short in height but tall in brains is our Lal Bahadur" (SALJ,114) and "big little man" (SALJ,311). Sanjay Gandhi is "the car manufacturer" (323), "Son of India" (AFB, 329). America is "maader chod" (SALJ, 76). President Nixon is "chootia… licking his way up into Pakistan's arsehole" (SALJ, 76). Mistry describes politics as a "circus" (AFB, 324) and politicians as, "clowns, monkeys, acrobats, everything" (AFB, 324). Mistry very minutely describes the habits of famous leaders and their interpretations by common people (AFB, 324-325).

Mistry comments how popular leaders lost their image and worth in the eyes of common people due to their dictatorship. The big cutout of Prime Minister falls down:

> **Those in the vicinity of the cardboard-and-plywood giant ran for their lives. 'Nobody wants to be caught in the Prime Minister's embrace,' said Rajaram. 'But she tries to get on top of everyone,' said Om. (AFB, 330)**

Balasaheb Thakrey in *Family Matters* is portrayed as "Senapati" (FM, 32) and "the crackpot" (FM, 32). Further he is ridiculed and made as an object of the joke:

> **"If the Senapati gets gas after eating Karela, the gourd will be declared an anti-Indian vegetable." "Let's hope**

> **his langoti doesn't give him a groin rash," said Jal, "Or all underwear might be banned." (FM, 32)**

In *A Fine Balance* he is hailed as, "Thokray is the one in charge of this. He is wearing a badge, Controller of Slums. And Navalkar is Assistant Controller" (AFB, 364). Mistry shows the anger of suffering Parsi against the majority in Maharashtra. Dinshawaji calls the dubbawalla as "low-class people? No manners, no sense, nothing" (SALJ, 73). He holds "that bastard Shiv Sena leader" is responsible for this "who worships Hitler and Mussolini" (SALJ, 73). The cry "Maharashtra for Maharashtrians" of Shiv Sena is considered as "nonsense" and "Maratha Raj" is hailed as "real Gandoo Raj" (SALJ, 73-74).

Mistry expresses the predicament of India and Maharashtra under BJP and Shiv Sena coalition government:

> **Those two parties encouraged the Hindutva extremists to destroy the Babri Mosque. "And what about all the hatred of minorities that Shiv Sena has spread for the last thirty years"... Senapati... accuses people left and right of being anti-this and anti-that. South Indians are anti-Bombay, Valentine's Day is anti-Hindustan, film stars born before 1947 in the Pakistan part of Punjab are traitors to the country. (FM, 32)**

For Jal "Corruption is in the air" (FM, 31), and "nation specializes in turning honest people into crooks" (FM, 31). The country is governed by "pariah dogs" (FM, 31). Mistry calls the BJP - Shiv Sena coalition government as "a poisonous snake" (FM, 31).

Sidhwa sets her novel against the backdrop of politics - Raj period or colonized India in *The Crow Eaters*, freedom struggle and independence and consequent partition in 1947 in *Ice Candy Man*, fundamentalist and military-Raj of Pakistan and Bhutto's trial in 1970s in *An American Brat* whereas Mistry sets the background of his novels against the very crucial political phases of India: India-Pakistan war and independence of Bangladesh in 1971 in *Such a Long Journey*, tyranny of Indira Gandhi, emergency up to the riots after her assassination from 1978-84 in *A Fine Balance* and post-Ayodhya India of Hindu-fundamentalism after Babri Mosque demolition in *Family Matters* where each time his miniscule community suffered bitterly.

In Sidhwa's fictional world, Parsi community suffers the Prufrockian dilemma of politics in *The Crow Eaters* and *Ice Candy Man* but at the same time has the assurance of peace and prosperity as well as threat of Islamization as in *An American Brat*. Freddy assures the children about their safe future:

> **'But where will we go? What will happen to us?'... 'Nowhere, my children,'... 'We will stay where we are.... let Hindus, Muslims, Sikhs, or whoever, rule. What does it matter? The sun will continue to rise - and the sun continues to set - in their arses!' (TCE, 283)**

Whereas Col. Bharucha in *Ice Candy Man* cautions all the Parsis about miniscule nature of their community and instructs them to maintain low-profile:

> **'We must tread carefully... We have served the English faithfully, and earned their trust... So, we have prospered! But we are the smallest minority in India... Only one hundred and twenty thousand in the whole world. We have to be extra wary, or we'll be neither here nor there...' We must hunt with the hounds and run with the hare!'(ICM, 16)...** ***As long as we conduct our lives quietly, as long as we present no threat to anybody, we will prosper right here.'*** **(Emphasis added). (ICM, 40)**

All the adverse effects of General Zia's Islamization and Bhutto's hanging were described and Feroza wanted to know all these things to keep in touch with her own country which raised questions about her national identity:

> **"You should have sent me newspaper clippings," Feroza said to her mother. "I want to know what's going on here. After all, it's my country!" Zareen did not mention the innuendo, the odd barb, that had suddenly begun to fester at the back of her consciousness. The insinuation that her patriotism was questionable, or that she was not a proper Pakistani because she was not Muslim. What was she then? And where did she belong, if not in the city where**

> **her ancestors were buried? She was in the land of the seven rivers, the Septe Sindhu, the land that Prophet Zarathustra had declared as favored most by Ahura Mazda. (AAB, 237-238)**

On other hand, Parsi community in Mistry's fictional world suffers the identity crisis and the sheer existential problem. In one effective instance, he voices Gustad Nobel's acute pain with his son's disrespect for his helpless status as a minority in an ethnically chaotic society:

> **What kind of life was Sohrab going to look forward to? No future for minorities, with all these fascist Shiv Sena politics and Marathi language nonsense. (SALJ, 55)**

Dinshawji expresses his frustration of being classified as 'other', "Today we have that bloody Shiv Sena, wanting to make the rest of us into second-class citizens." (SALJ, 39)

In Sidhwa's fictional world Parsis never suffer socially, politically, and economically. In all walks of life they enjoyed the privileged status. Freddy who made the fortune by traveling from north-India to Lahore enjoyed the high-status on all levels in *The Crow Eaters*. Mr. and Mrs. Sethi and Godmother in *Ice Candy Man* have great respect and awe in the society. Zareen Ginnawalla herself has worked on many committees with Bhutto's wife in *An American Brat*. She had worked on many committees with Begum Bhutto for disadvantaged people, orphanage, "Destitute Women's and Children's Home" (AAB, 175). In this way both writers have described their tiny community under the political ethos of their respective countries.

*

IV

Literature deals with various economical strata living in the society. According to such economical status, characters fight against the financial inequality, poverty, subsequent subjugation which may result into the maladjustment of the characters trapping their lives in fraud, corruption, cheating etc, shedding their valuable innocence. Even writers are highly concerned about this social evil of poverty. It is aptly described in following words:

> **In these days of acute political awareness the love theme has lost its popularity. Readers tend to think that all love stories are deceptive and that their authors are enemies of the society. These are days for critics of institutions who condemn the feudal values in our society.... People have found out that it is the economic system that is at the root of all evil and that it can be corrected by collective action. [Buchibabu 1978:94]**

In this way, readers are also interested in the social realities of their times. It is necessary to see this economical aspect in these two writers. Parsis were considered as the most prosperous and rich community in the Indian sub-continent during the colonial India. But due to the loss of the elite status in post-colonial India and Pakistan, Parsis suffer from the severe problems of poverty and financial crisis. Both these aspects are highlighted by these two writers.

Sidhwa portrays the Parsi community which was on the peak of prosperity. At that time Parsis afforded the royal mansions as Sidhwa describes Easymoney's bunglow in *The Crow Eaters* and Feroza's haveli in *An American Brat*. Here Sidhwa presents the past glory of Parsis, especially in the colonial period, when they enjoyed the royal status, and were hailed as the close friends of the rulers. Easymoney's stately mansion is described as:

> **Rodabai led them into a handsome drawing room. It was a vast, cool room, lighted by crystal lamps and the sunlight that filtered through brocade curtains. One wall was hung with a huge French tapestry, and the dull gold furniture was of Louis XIV style. Carpets spread out beneath their feet a soft garden of Persian hunting scenes and flowers. (TCE, 199)**

On the other hand, Mistry's novels lack the royal descriptions of places. Mistry portrays the Parsi residential complex, bungalows in dilapidated conditions and adverse housing conditions as Parsis are downgraded financially in the post-colonial India. His descriptions of Parsi flats in *Tales from Firozsha Baag* (*An Inauspicious Occasion*), Khodad Building in *Such a Long Journey* (the wall, open public lavatory) the Chetau Felicity in *Family Matters* aptly reflects the Parsi status in the post-colonial India. Simultaneously, his descriptions of slums in *A Fine Balance*, prostitution in 'The House of Cages' in *Such a Long Journey* and the flat of Roxana and Coomy in *Family Matters* give nausea and the typical middle-class sense respectively. Mistry portrays the poor and unhygienic conditions of residents of the Baag. It is the result of lost glory of the Parsis in Post-Raj India where they became minority, and middle-class who suffer from many problems. As Rustomji complains about WC, "That stinking lavatory upstairs is leaking again!" (TFB, 04) Mistry describes Rustomji's flat,

> **The copper vessel was already filled with water. But someone had forgotten to cover it, and plaster from the ceiling had dripped into it. It floated on the surface, little motes of white.... Plaster had been dripping for some years now in his A Block flat. The building had acquired an appalling patina of yellow and gray griminess...during the monsoon season beads of moisture trickled down the walls, like sweat down a coolie's back, which considerably hastened the crumbling of paint and plaster. (TFB, 5-7)**

In *Lend Me Your Light*, like most immigrants, Kersi experienced the culture-shock after reaching Bombay: "He felt the contrast between the lush greenery of the West and 'the parched land, brown, weary, and unhappy' in India is striking" (TFB, 186).

In Sidhwa's works, Parsi community is shown as prosperous. Freddy (*The Crow Eaters*) is a business tycoon and has a chain of stores through the north India. Mr. and Mrs. Sethi (*Ice Candy Man*) can afford many servants. Feroza (*An American Brat*) is sent to USA for vacations and then for education.

On the other hand, in Mistry, Parsis suffered on all the fronts. Socially they are turned into the clown and buffoons (Rustomji in *Tales from Firozsha Baag*), politically they suffered being the minority community, (Major Billimoria as the victim of Indira's corruption in *Such a Long Journey*), economically too they went under drastic changes (Cavasji's complains to God are aptly comments on their poverty in *Such a Long Journey*). The nationalization of banks too is one of the major causes of their downgraded economical condition. Dinshawji expressed sorrow for the present condition of the Parsis and remembered:

> **'What days those were *yaar*. What fun we used to have. Parsis were the kings of banking in those days. Such respect we used to get. Now the whole atmosphere only has been spoiled. Ever since that Indira Gandhi nationalized the banks.'...'Nowhere in the world has nationalization worked. What can you say to idiots?' (SALJ, 38)**

Bharucha expresses the poverty among Parsis:

> **The Parsis in Firozsha Baag are middle class and like other middle class persons in Bombay have to engage in daily battle with intermittent water-supply, dilapidated homes, peeling paint, falling plaster and leaking WCs. [2003: 73-74]**

The troubles middle class and poor Parsis suffer from are also grudged through the complaints of Cawasji. Mistry's comments on the financial disparity among rich Parsis and poor, middle class Parsis are aptly put forth in complaints of old Cawasji at his second-floor window who used to yell through the window:

> **'To the Tatas You give so much! And nothing for me? To the Wadias You give, You keep on giving! You cannot hear my prayers? The pockets of the Camas only You will fill! We others don't need it, You think?' (SALJ, 87)**

Gustad had to sell his *camera* for Roshan's *medicine*. Dinlavaz sold her "two gold wedding bangles" (SALJ, 219). In *Family Matters*, Yezad indulges himself in Matka game, plans for fraud scheme; Murad walks to school to save his bus-fare to purchase Christmas-gift for Jehangir. Jehangir also engages himself in corruption by taking bribes to mark the homework. In *A Fine Balance*, Dina Dalal hires two tailors for her garment factory supply and accommodates a student- Manek to run the household budget.

Sidhwa comments on the American policy. She also highlights the status of Parsi in Pakistan.

> **...the zealous Islamization fostered by General Zia, which encouraged religious chauvinism and marginalized people like her- the minorities- and made them vulnerable to petty ill will. (AAB, 238)**

Feroza compared the poverty in America and Pakistan. She found the "Poverty... was relative" (238). She compared the minorities in USA ("the blacks and Hispanics" (238)) and Pakistan. Feroza criticized the policies of America but defended it for "Which other country opened its arms to the destitute and discarded of the world the way America did? Of course, it had its faults-- terrifying shortcomings-- but it had God's blessings, too" (239).

Parsi community in Sidhwa's fictional world is blessed with plenty. It never suffered financial anxiety. Sidhwa narrates the grandeur of the Parsis who lavishly spent money on their celebrations. Easymoney gave the grand party:

> **It was a memorable wedding. Years after people still talked about it. Hedges had been leveled in the compound of the Taj Mahal Hotel to clear parking space for carriages and limousines. Openings were dug in the walls dividing the banquet rooms, reception rooms, and lobby of the Hotel to accommodate guests and facilitate the flow of service. Flowers were commissioned from Banglore and Hyderabad, cheeses from Surat, and caviar from the Persian Gulf. There was lobster and wild-duck and venison. There was a bottle of Scotch and Burgundy for each guest; and ambulances, their motors idling, stood ready to convey the inebriated or overstuffed to their homes or to the hospital. Two hundred Parsi families living in a charitable housing scheme and not invited to the party were each given a sack of flour, a ten pound canister of rarefied butter, lentils and a box of Indian sweets. There was a Police Band, a Naval Band, a dance orchestra and an orchestra that played chamber music. There was singing. (TCE, 224)**

In this way these two writers displayed the financial anxieties of their ethnic community.

*

V

Religion is another important aspect that the creative artist deals with. Sculptor, paintings are other mediums where such creativity can be expressed. It is very difficult for the writer to write about another religion or culture without deep insight and insiders' perspective. It may cause the religious blasphemy resulting into the ethnic and religious anxieties. For the same reason, generally Christian writers deal with the Christian religion, African writers deal with their tribal religion, Muslim writers would highlight Islam and Indian writers focus on various religions like Hinduism. Literature by Zoroastrian writers have focused on their tiny endangered community. Here Mistry and Sidhwa, being Parsi and dealing with Parsi community in particular highlight many religious rituals and related issues in their fictions. Both the writers highlight various controversial issues like burial of the dead, fading away of the vultures and reciting of the prayers in English.

Parsi community does not allow insular marriage. In this regard, Sidhwa shows the orthodoxy in Parsis and appeals for reformation in her community. Zareen understood that the debate over reforms was inevitable. Zareen realized the wave of fundamentalism all over the world:

> **These educated custodians of the Zoroastrian doctrine were less rigid and ignorant than the *fundos* in Pakistan. This mindless current of fundamentalism sweeping the world like a plague had spared no religion, not even their microscopic community of 120 thousand. (AAB, 305-306)**

Later on, Zareen ponders over the need for reform in her community,

> ***Zareen wished David was a Parsee -- or that the Zoroastrians would permit selective conversion to their faith.* Zareen found herself seriously questioning the ban**

> **on interfaith marriage for the first time. She was not so sure anymore and felt herself suddenly aligned with the thinking of the liberals and reformists. It eased her heart to think that a debate on these issues was taking place. (AAB, 287-288) (Emphasis added)**

Parsi community in Sidhwa's fiction pants for Tower of Silences, as these are not available in cities like Lahore. In *The Crow Eaters*, Jerbanoo expressed the deep regret for the vultures on the top of a green tree: "What a pity. What a shame. These poor birds are permitted to starve despite all the Parsis we have in Lahore... all these vultures are going to waste - such a pity"(TCE, 50). Freddy described this absence of Tower of Silence as: "Vultures, vultures everywhere and not a body to share!" (TCE, 51) Mistry highlighted the low population of vultures as a cause of concern for Parsi community. The most important problem related with the *Dokhma* is the littering of the flesh by the vultures which troubled the clerk a lot as tenets from "luxury high-rises proliferating around Doongerwadi's green acres" (SALJ, 316) had often complained against vultures as it is described below:

> **'Your vultures!' the tenants complained. 'Control your vultures! Throwing rubbish on our balconies!' They claimed that the sated birds, flying out from the Tower after gorging themselves, invariably snatched a final bite to savour later. And if the tidbits were lost in mid-flight, they launched on the exclusive balconies. This, said the indignant tenants, was absolutely, intolerable considering the sky-high prices they had been charged for their de luxe flats. (SALJ, 316-317)**

On the other hand, relatives of the dead read about the skyscraper scandal and so they complained:

> **...they were not paying funeral fees to have their dear departed ones anatomized and strewn piecemeal on posh balconies. The bereaved insisted that the Punchayet do something about it. 'Train the vultures properly,' they said, 'or import more vultures, so all flesh can be consumed in**

the well. We don't want a surplus which can be carried off and lost in impure, profane places.' (SALJ, 317)

Sidhwa in *The Crow Eaters* shows that Parsis suffer from the lack of Tower of Silence. They have to compromise with mere burial. Modern day Parsis don't believe in 'nirang' bath of the dead. Alamai argued with the men who came to perform Dinshawaji's *suchkaar* and sponging the corpse with *Gomez*: 'All this nonsense with bull's urine is not for us,' she said. 'We are modern people. Use water only, nothing else' (SALJ, 246). Mistry also highlights the rigidity of Parsi community as Ghulam, being a non-Parsi, was denied entrance into The Tower of Silence: "Your Parsi priest's don't allow outsider like me to go inside" (SALJ, 322). These writers also focus the issues related with the prayer. Parsis think that Zoroastrian prayers are so strong and sacred that non-Parsi can't hear them. So they are not allowed inside the Fire Temple. Prayers are written in Avastan language and modern day Parsis don't know it, Gustad contemplates on his Kusti prayer in the Fire Temple "All his life he had uttered by rote the words of this dead language, comprehending not one of them while mouthing his prayers" (SALJ, 247-248). Feroza said tandarosti prayer- the happy little Jasa-me-avanghe Mazda prayer in Avastan language of the Gathas. She knew its meaning from the English translation in her prayer book:

Come to my help, O Ahura-Mazda!
Give me victory, power, and the joy of life. (AAB, 42)

In Zoroastrian religion common Parsis are not allowed in *Dungarwari* because, "only professional pall-bearers are allowed to witness the gory spectacle inside the Tower" (TCE, 46). But these people are treated as untouchables. Gustad points out this: "Silly customs, to have professional pall bearers. And on top of that, poor fellows treated like outcasts and untouchables" (SALJ, 252). Mistry talks about the continuous battle between the reformists and the orthodox Parsis. They fought over any topic with community interest like "the chemical analysis of *nirang*", "the vibration theory of Avesta prayers" (SALJ, 317). Dokhma is considered "both practical and hygienic" (TCE, 46). Parsi population is concentrated in the cities of Bombay and Karachi. There the Parsis have Doongarwari following traditional *dokhma,* but Parsis living in "far-flung areas have to be content with mere burial" (TCE, 46). At the same time tradition bound Parsis prefer dokhma irrespective of wants of the tower of silence. Slave-sister (Mini aunty) ridiculed such religious stands and retorted satirically: "...being devoured by vultures has nothing to do with the religion... Surely Zarathustra had more important messages to deliver" (ICM, 114).

In this way Rohinton Mistry and Bapsi Sidhwa have focused on various religious issues concerning Parsi community.

*

VI

History is often the subject of narratives. There is a whole array of historical novels. Histories are used as the source material for fictions. For instance, J.M.Coetzee's Booker winner book *Life and Time of Michael K* traces the history of its central character Michael K whereas Australian novelist Peter Carrey writes real life history of Kelly gang and its struggle under colonial rule in Australia in his Booker winner novel *The True History of Kelly Gang*. Salman Rushdie's *Shame* is called fictional/real history of Pakistan. Such fictions are called as historiographic metafiction that describes graphical history of imaginary country resembling real nation/state in fictional narrative and has the real/lifelike records. Rohinton Mistry and Bapsi Sidhwa have also used 'history' as a subtext in their fictions. They also have discussed the history of their 'Parsi ethnic' group on various occasions in their novels. Further one can say that both the writers have traced the history of their ethnic group in the background of national histories of their two nations. Analyzing the text of these two writers, it can be said that Bapsi Sidhwa's fictional world deals with the national history of undivided India in *The Crow Eaters* (colonial rule and Parsi community) and *Ice-Candy Man* (predicament of Parsi community with its ethnic counterparts i.e. Hindu and Muslim on the eve of partition). *An American Brat* deals with post-independent state of Pakistan. Sidhwa maintained the link between the private and national histories in her fiction. At the end of *The Crow Eaters,* Freddy curses Parsi leaders like Dadabhai Navroji for leading the freedom movement. In *Ice-Candy Man*, Sidhwa arranged a scene where Lenny meets Mahatma Gandhi, who was the leader of freedom struggle. In *An American Brat* too Zareen and Feroza visit Bhutto's sister. Mistry too, has utilized the history as a subtext in his fiction. His novels deal with the Indian history - *Such a Long Journey* (Nagarwalla Case, war with East Pakistan (Bangladesh freedom) in 1971); *A Fine Balance* (Internal emergency to assassination of Prime Minister and consequent anti-Sikh riots, 1978-1984) and *Family Matters* (Post-Ayodhya/post Babri mosque demolition riots in India, 1993). Mistry's characters were directly influenced by the contemporary historical events. Historical events are interwoven with personal events. In *Such a Long Journey,* Major Bilimoria is the fictive representation of Parsi RAW agent Nagarwalla, through whom Gustad's family is connected to the turmoil of Bangladesh freedom war led by Indira Gandhi. In *A Fine Balance,* all his characters suffer due to the emergency. Om and Ishvar were forced to attend the public meeting of Indira Gandhi (A Day at Circus…). In *Family Matters* his characters suffer from the Hindu fundamentalism of Shiv Sena leader Balasaheb Thakare and his *Maharashtra for Maharashtrians* agenda. A. Alvarez focuses the nationalist concern of the writers: "nationalism becomes a preoccupation of the writers… helping the nation to an awareness of itself, its aspirations, its troubles" [1967: x]. It highlights the writer's picturization of his nationality and its people. Sidhwa asserts her national identity as a Pakistani. Her positive affirmation of her Pakistani identity is clearly mentioned in *Ice-Candy Man* and *An American Brat* but at the same time she raises question over this national identity. Mistry is in conflict with Indian identity and has tried to escape it with unsuccessful attempts of migration to the West in *Tales from Firozsha Baag, Such a long journey*, and *Family Matters.*

Sidhwa portrayed the independent state of Pakistan as a drifting nation which has lost its ideals. Its growing fundamentalism is exactly contradictory to the ideas of Jinnah, who was "pukka-sahib" (ICM, 159) and advocated for the secular democracy. It was a utopian dream for future Pakistan and great disillusionment to Jinnah and Parsi community too, as Sidhwa exclaims, "Jinnah, too, died of a broken heart" (ICM, 100).

Mistry directly comments himself as a 'Tyresis' who suffered due to the guilt of migration (*Lend Me Your Light* in *Tales from Firozsha Baag*). The same vein was echoed in Kersi's preparation to immigrate to the USA. It is fully supported by his parents as foretold given his "education, and …westernized background, and fluency in the English language" (TFB, 178). The night before departure Kersi suffered from a searing pain in his eyes and wondered if he was being punished for his sin of migration:

> **...the sin of hubris for seeking emigration out of the land of my birth, and paying the price in burnt-out eyes, I Tiresias, blind and throbbing between two lives, the one in Bombay and the one to come in Toronto. (TFB, 180)**

Mistry's protagonists always plan for migration for better future prospects (*Such a Long Journey*, Gustad's dream plan of IIT for his son and then future migration, *Family Matters*, Yezad's dream to migrate to Canada, and last three stories of *Tales from Firozsha Baag*) are related to the problem of migration. But their migration brings failure which resulted into the loss of both 'homeland' and 'host land' (*Squatter* in *Tales from Firozsha Baag*). Nilufer Bharucha comments:

> **One can say that all of the Mistry's Canadian stories sketched "an unrelentingly dark and gloomy picture of Canada and even caution reader/listeners against the act of immigration." [2003:117]**

Sarosh returns home after his failure to cope with Canadian surroundings and mannerisms. But Sarosh once again uprooted from Canada was searching his roots in India where he was unable to find them:

> **Weeks went by and Sarosh found himself desperately searching for his old place in the pattern of life he had vacated ten years ago. The old pattern was never found by Sarosh; he searched in vain. Patterns of life are selfish and unforgiving. (TFB, 167)**

In *Family Matters* too, Mistry comments that, "...emigration is an enormous mistake. The biggest anyone can make in their life. The loss of home leaves a hole that never fills." (FM, 254)

Sidhwa explores the new possibilities of new life, new world when migrated. She discusses this aspect in her novel *An American Brat,* as:

> **From her visit to Lahore, Feroza knew she had changed, and the life of her friends there had also changed, taken a different direction from hers. Although the sense of**

> **dislocation, of not belonging, was more acute in America, she felt, it would be more tolerable because it was shared by thousands of newcomers like herself. It was not only that, Feroza thought in mild consternation. Like Manek she had become used to the seductive entitlements of the First World. Happy Hour, telephones that worked, the surfeit of food, freezers, electricity, and clean and abundant water, the malls, skyscrapers, and highway. (AAB, 312)**

Thus these novels turn up as a parallel history of the subcontinent - modern India and Pakistan. It is history from a writer's point of view that tries to (dis/un)cover the suppressed or neglected chapters of Indian history. By re-narrating history, the novelist constructs his/her story of his/her community and national-truth.

*

VII

Every writer has his/her own style of writing. It varies from writer to writer, shaped by influences on him/her and socio-political, culture-religious, economical atmosphere. A writer employs various devices of narrative structure as per his understanding of the surrounding. There are varieties of narrative techniques that a writer uses in his/her narrative like linear narrative where narrative develops in straight forward way. There is no interruption in between the narrative, whereas non-linear narrative allows a writer to shift his focus from past to present or from present to past. In such a case a writer uses techniques like ***Omniscient point of view, intrusive narrator, analepsis, prolepsis, "Flashback" "Anamnesis" "entrelacement", and intertextuality, story-telling.*** A brief look at these terms is imperative.

According to M.H. Abrams, the term *Omniscient point of view* means "a common term for the large and varied works of fiction written in accord with the *convention* that the narrator knows everything that needs to be known about the agents, actions, and events, and also has privileged access to the character's thoughts, feelings, and motives; and that the narrator is free to move at will in time and place, to shift from character to character, and to report (or conceal) their speech, doings, and states of consciousness." [1993: 166]

Within this mode, the ***intrusive narrator*** suggests the narrator/writer's peeping in the narrative to give his opinions, or comments on the happenings in the novel. It can be described as "one who not only reports, but also comments on and evaluates the actions and motives of the characters, and sometimes expresses personal views about human life in general. Most works are written in the convention that the omniscient narrator's reports and judgments are to be taken as the facts and values within the fictional world." [M.H. Abrams 1993:166]

Sidhwa sometimes peeps into the narrative (*Ice Candy Man*, when Lenny speaks about the Jinnah and *An American Brat*, the talk with an American who speaks with Zareen as genderless, etc.) Sidhwa as omniscient narrator writes:

> **'But didn't Jinnah, too, die of a broken heart? And today, forty years later, in films of Gandhi's and Mountbatten's lives, in books by British and Indian scholars, Jinnah, who for a decade was known as 'Ambassador of Hindu-Muslim Unity', is caricatured, and portrayed as monster.' (ICM, 160)**

Mistry, too, very rarely peeps into the narrative i.e. in *Family Matters*, where one of Yezad's friends comments on the Australian writer/critic Germaine Greer who in her interview on the BBC loathed the book and added that she did not find the India as portrayed by Mistry. Mistry peeps in the narrative as in *Family Matters* a character says:

> **"A while back, I read a novel about the Emergency. A big book full of horrors, real as life. But also full of life, and the laughter and dignity of ordinary people. One hundred percent honest- made me laugh and cry as I read it. But some reviewers said no, no, things were not that bad. Especially foreign critics. You know how they come here for two weeks and become experts. One poor woman whose name I can't remember made such a hash of it, she had to be a bit pagal, defending Indira, defending the Sanjay sterilization scheme, defending the entire**

> **Emergency- you felt sorry for her even though she was a big professor at some big university in England. What to do? People are afraid to accept the truth. As T.S. Eliot wrote, "Human kind can not bear very much reality." (FM, 210)**

While using nonlinear narrative writer uses flashback or flashforward techniques to shift the time in past and present. Flashback has been part of the narrative technique at least since Homer composed the Odyssey three thousand years ago. Linear narrative is so integral to our idea of a 'story' that we sometimes fail to realize we are not reading a beginning, middle, and end. This technique is popular in motion pictures and literature, narrative technique of interrupting the chronological sequence of events to interject events of earlier occurrence. The description of this technique goes as in:

> **The earlier events often take the form of reminiscence. The use of flashback enables the author to start the story from a point of high interest and to avoid the monotony of chronological exposition. It also keeps the story in the objective, dramatic present. In motion pictures, flashback is indicated not only by narrative devices but also by a variety of optical techniques such as fade-in or fade-out (the emergence of a scene from blackness to full definition, or its opposite), dissolves (the gradual exposure of a second image over the first while it is fading away), or iris-in or iris-out (the expansion or contraction of a circle enclosing the scene). [Encyclopedia Britannica 1994-2002]**

Flashback technique is also known as ***Analepsis*** which described as "...a form of anachrony by which some of the events of a story are related at a point in the narrative after later story events have already been recounted. Commonly referred to as retrospection or flashback, analepsis enables a storyteller to fill in background information about characters and events. A narrative begins in medias res will include an analeptic account of events preceding the point at which the tale began." [Chris Baldic 1990:09]. In flashback technique 'memory' is used as the mode of going into the past or present. ***Anamnesis*** is the technique which is "'a recalling to mind or reminiscence.' The word is from the Greek anámnesis 'to recall or remember'" [Encyclopædia Britannica 1994-2002]. Anamnesis is often used as a narrative technique in fiction and poetry as well as in memoirs and autobiographies. Memory, nostalgia, remembering are the modes used by diasporic writers. They are very useful in picturizing the various issues related with their homeland. Opposite to analepsis as a narrative technique, is ***Prolepsis***. It is often called as flashforward. It is described as: "...a 'flashforward' by which a future event is related as an interruption to the 'present' time of the narration" [Chris Baldic 1990:178] A writer intermingles many stories at a certain point in time in their narrative but before this writer presents a single story one by one. Then writer begins a major story. For this ***"entrelacement"*** is an apt term. It is described as "a literary technique in which several simultaneous stories are interlaced in one larger narrative. This technique allows digression and presents opportunities for moral and ironic commentary while not disturbing the unity of the whole." [Encyclopedia Britannica 1994-2002].

Sidhwa uses linear narrative where she tells the story in linear progression without shifting it often into past and present. She tells one story at a time. Her novels always contain one important story without the major interruption in the narrative. It is described as:

> **Bapsi Sidhwa does not follow the non-linear, non-realist narrative forms. The influence of Dickens and the nineteenth century novelists is obvious, as Bapsi Sidhwa firmly believes in the importance of a sound plot and gripping story in her novels. [Eds. R.K. Dhawan, Novy Kapadia 1996:13]**

She defends the importance of the linear realist narrative in the interview with David Montenenegro:

> **In the West storytelling has been lost in the byways of verbal acrobatics and the need to be smart and innovative in writing. The story element is very often lost in what they call 'literate fiction' in these parts of the world. [1989:47]**

Mistry uses nonlinear narrative. All his novels contain multi-stories. *Such a Long Journey* contains the story of Gustad as well as Major Billimoria connected together. *A Fine Balance* contains three major stories of Dina Dalal in Mumbai ("City by the Sea"), Om and Ishvar in the village ("In a village by a River") who suffered the problem of caste, Mike who lives in the hill station ("Mountain") and finally all these major character in Mumbai together ("Sailing Under One flag" and others). *Family Matters*, too, contains the story of Nariman Vakil's youth and his affair with an Anglo-Indian girl (which is given in flashback (Analepsis) and Mistry used italics mode for the writing) and the same Nariman with his old-age, and story of Yezad and his family. In *Tales from Firozsha Baag, 'Ghost of Firozsha Baag'* the narrator is a Goan ayah, who narrates two stories at a time about Seth from childhood up to present ghost and her own story from childhood to present time (prolepsis). Jaakaylee narrates the 'ghost' story in past which is given in 'normal' print:

> **But he did not come. Why, I wondered. If he came to the bedding of a fat and ugly ayah, now what was the matter? I could not understand. But when I said to myself, what are you thinking Jaakaylee where is your head, do you really want the ghost to come sleep with you and touch you so shamefully? (TFB, 50)**

She narrates the present events in italics:

> ***Time to cook rice now, time for seth to come home. Best quality Basmati rice we use, always, makes such a lovely fragrance while cooking, so tasty.*** **(TFB, 50)**

In the *Swimming Lesson, Tales from Firozsha Baag,* he reversed the technique. He uses normal print for present tense, "He does not call again. My Surf King is relegated to an unused drawer. Total losses...." (240) and italics for past events, "*The postman did not bring letter but a parcel, he was smiling because he knew that every time something came from Canada his baksheesh was guaranteed.*"(240)

Sidhwa has used flash back technique in *The Crow Eaters*. She begins the story of Faredoon Junglewalla, as a man of great honor and respect in Parsi community who preach the truths of the world to his young listeners:

> **In his prosperous middle years Faredoon Junglewalla was prone to reminiscence and rhetoric. Sunk in a cane-backed easy-chair after an exacting day, his long legs propped up on the sliding arms of chair, he talked to the young people gathered at his feet. (TCE, 9)**

On the next page only she begins the story of the novel with Freddy as a twenty three year old Parsi:

> **Faredoon Junglewalla, Freddy for short, embarked on his travels towards the end of the nineteenth century. Twenty-three years old, strong and pioneering, he saw no future for himself… (TCE, 12)**

Story-telling is an ancient narrative technique. While telling the story the attention of the reader is grasped totally by teller, who very interestingly tells various details with twist, turns, suspense etc. engaging the reader completely in the story. The listener is curious to know what will happen next. This suggests the total involvement of the teller and listener regarding the story. This is popular in the television world where daily soaps are eagerly watched by many. In such serials viewers are left with the frozen-screen at the end of the serial, to keep their interest for the next episode. This "what-nextism" [Rushdie 1983:39] is the secret of the popular Alf Lyla Wah Lyla, 1001 Arabian Nights stories. The female narrator interwoven one story into another and saved her own life as well as many others. The narrator was Scherazad, the queen of the king of Arabia. So this narrative technique is called as Scherazadic.

Mistry is a story-teller who follows the Alf Lalyah wa-Laylah, 1001 Nights, the Scheherazadic tradition of narration where story-teller always makes listener guess what next and prolongs the interest of the reader. This 'whatnextism' is the crux of this narrative technique. Storytelling is obviously a phenomenon of the oral tradition. In *Tales from Firozsha Baag*, Nariman Hansotia, a story-teller, of the story 'Squatter' tells the stories to the children of building. But Hansotia did not complete the tale nor did he take it up at another story-telling session. Nariman comes to the point for the beginning of a new story after arousing their interest by telling the moral of the last story, "Remember this, success alone does not bring happiness. Nor does failure have to bring unhappiness. Keep it in mind when you listen to today's story" (TFB,

153). The stories of the collection may not be a nostalgic writing but Mistry used the memory and remembering as narrative techniques. In *Such a Long Journey,* Peerbhoy Paanwalla also grasps the attention of his listeners with his 'paan-stories.' '*Squatter*' in *Tales from Firozsha Baag* is narrated by the master story-teller of Firozsha Baag, Nariman Hansotia in the Scherazadic narrative mode of the Arabian Nights. All the children of the Baag were always eager to listen to his well-told stories. Mistry describes him as a story-teller,

> **Nariman liked to use new words, especially big ones, in the stories he told, believing it was his duty to expose young minds to as shimmering and varied a vocabulary as possible; Jehangir, Kersi, and Viraf were familiar with Nariman's technique... Unpredictability was the brush he used to paint his tales with, and ambiguity the palette he mixed his colours in. Nariman sometimes told a funny incident in a very serious way, or expressed a significant matter in a light and playful manner. And these were only two rough divisions, in between were lots of subtle gradations of tone and texture. Which, then was the funny story and which the serious? Their opinions were divided, but ultimately, said Jehangir, it was up to the listener to decide. (TFB, 146-148)**

Sidhwa is a story-teller but does not follow the oral tradition of the Scherazadic tradition of narration. Though the stories of Freddy preaches the truths of the way of the world which are kind of edification for his listeners. He tells his young listeners:

> **I have never permitted pride and arrogance to stand in my way. Where would I be had I made a delicate flower of my pride- and sat my delicate bum on it? I followed the dictates of my needs, my wants- they make one flexible, elastic, humble. "The meek shall inherit the earth", says Christ. ... There is also a lot depth in the man who says, "Sway with the breeze, bend with the winds." (TCE, 11)**

Mistry describes Peerbhoy Paanwala as a story-teller who has a paan for all occasions with an interesting story for each: "to ward off sleep, to promote rest, to create appetities, to rein in an excess of lust, to help digestion, to assist bowel movements, to purify the kidneys, to nullify flatulence, to cure bad breath, to create seductive breath, to fight failing eyesight, to make well the deaf ear, to encourage lucidity of thought, to improve speech, to alleviate the stiffness of joints, to induce longevity, to reduce life expectancy, to mitigate the labour of birthing, to ease the pain of dying…"(SALJ,158).

Intertextuality is another narrative technique used in modern fiction. In this technique allusions to other literary works are given to underscore the meaning or otherwise to make reader aware about the scholarship of the writer. Sometimes such use of intertextuality shows the influences of those writers on the subject writer. These influences are no more called as plagiarism. Post-structuralism claims that a text cannot exist without a pretext. Every text is an intertext. But to establish their inter-relationship is the major difficulty of the writers. This 'intextextual' influence is aptly described as:

> **"…All literary texts are woven out of other literary texts, not in the conventional sense that they bear the traces of 'influence' but in the more radical sense that every word, phrase or segment is reworking of other writings which precede or surround the individual work." [Terry Eagleton 1993:138]**

Mistry gives references of Western classical music to heighten the poetic effect of the narrative. Mistry uses British and European poetry. He alludes to "The Rime of the Ancient Mariner" (FM, 55). The line "Human kind cannot bear very much reality" (FM, 210) echoes the line from T.S. Eliot's poem *Four Quartets*. While talking about the present scenario on Indian society, Mistry gives the various examples from European literature. Vilas talks about some actors who are "blind to real life with their intellectualizing. Stanislavsky-this and Strasberg-that, and Brechtian alienation is all they talk about" (FM, 211). To express his love for music he quotes: "If music be the food of love, play on, give me excess of it" (FM, 239). Coomy dreamt of "dancing in the ballroom of the Taj Hotel, a band was playing old-time favorites, "Fly Me to the Moon," "Tea For Two" in Latin rhythm, "Green, Green Grass of Home" (FM, 74).

To express the anxiety and nausea of nursing an ailing old man full of dirt and filth, Mistry (as Coomy and Jal talk) uses the Eliot's master metaphor **objective correlative** from Macbeth:

> **"If it is in your head, nothing will get rid of it. Like the damned spot on Lady Macbeth's hand, remember? All the perfumes of Arabia, all your swabbing and scrubbing and mopping and scouring will not remove it." (FM, 109)**

Yezad wished that Mr. Kapur should contest the election. So he discussed it with Gautam who expressed it in literary language by mixing quotations of W.B. Yeats' poem *The Second Coming* and mixing it with the traits of Aristotelian tragedy:

> **Understood... Basically, Mr. Kapur needs to experience an epiphany. So we must convey more than just present danger to him and his shop. We must transcend the here and now, move beyond this bank and shoal of time, and let him glimpse the horrors of a society *where the best lack all conviction while worst are full of passionate intensity...* We must move him beyond *catharsis, beyond pity and terror*, to state of engagement into the arena of epic realism, where the man of action... (FM, 332-333) (Emphasis added)**

The music was a blessing in disguise when Nariman was having a bad time-and when he heard Daisy's violin he felt calm. The moment her violin started, he grew calmer, as though he had taken a dose of medicine. Daisy provided the information about the music-therapy:

> **"I read a book about music therapy. It prescribed specific compositions for things like migraine, high or low blood pressure, stomach cramps... Bach was the one prescribed most often...from the *Well Tempered Clavier*." (FM, 239-240)**

Daisy played Mendelssohn's "*On Wings of Songs*" (FM, 240). Such influences of western literature can be described in following words:

> **There is the mushroom growth of so called 'influence' studies mainly dealing with Euro-American influences on Indian literatures. But the network of indigenous and alien 'texts' in a work of art remains still unexplored. Much fuss is made about alien allusions and quotations. In fact, over weighing alien allusions and quotations in our text should be considered a symptom of the alien oppressive forces in our literary culture. [Patil Anand B. 1999, 84]**

There are various examples of such influences in Rohinton Mistry's *Lend me Your Light* in *Tales from Firozsha Baag*, Malcolm and Gustad's reminiscence of their past in *Such a Long Journey*, Nariman's memories of violin and western classical music in *Family Matters*.

Memory is another mode of narration used in the narratives especially for the purpose of remembrance of the past. Mistry has brilliantly used "memory" and "remembering" as a narrative technique in his novels to express the nostalgia of beloved, happy past of his character. His writing can be called as 'Nostalgia Writing' [Bharucha 2003:73]. These techniques- memory and nostalgia – are used for what Craig Tapping has said: "Mistry is engaged in identity construction through the location of the present in the past" [Tapping 1992:39]. All his characters relished their sweet memories of the past. He aptly describes this reliving of the past as well as the nature of the memory:

> **How much Dina Aunty relished her memories. Mummy and Daddy were the same, talking about their yesterdays and smiling in the sad-happy way while selecting each picture, each frame from the past, examining it lovingly before it vanished again in the mist.... Memories were Permanent. Sorrowful ones remained sad even with the passing of time, yet happy ones could never be recreated - not with the same joy. Remembering bred its own peculiar sorrow. It seemed so unfair, that time should render both sadness and happiness into a source of pain. (AFB, 412-413)**

Mistry questions the existence of the memory and its fruitlessness:

> **So what was the point of possessing memory? It didn't help anything. In the end it was all hopeless.... No amount of remembering happy days, no amount of yearning or nostalgia could change a thing about the misery and suffering-love and concern and caring and sharing come to nothing, nothing. Everything ended badly. And Memory only made it worse, tormenting and taunting. Unless. Unless you lost your mind. Or committed suicide. The slate wiped clean. No more remembering, no more suffering. (AFB, 413)**

Maneck went to climb the hills with his mother and family friends. Mistry describes the past as the ghost. He writes, "The ghost from the past was greeted with delight by all who met it on its journey. Many decided to tag along, swelling the ranks of the spontaneous celebration" (AFB, 722). In *Family Matters*, Mistry has nicely woven the element of memory in the narrative of the text. Roxana observed Jehangir feeding his grandpa. Roxana captured the picture in her memory as "The balcony door framed the scene, nine-year old happily feeding seventy-nine" (FM, 113). Her eyes refused to give up the precious moment, for she knew on impulse that "...it would become a memory to cherish, to recall in difficult times when she needed strength. ... And for a brief instant, Roxana felt she understood the meaning of it all, of birth and life and death." (FM, 113)

Thus, one can say that Mistry is experimental while using the narrative techniques and Sidhwa is traditional in using linear narrative.

*

VIII

According to E.M. Forster, ***character*** is a crucial aspect of the novel. The writer develops the character according to the plot. While dealing with human lives, writers focus on the human characters, male or female, at the centre of the discussion. In course of action character develops and helps reader to understand the developments in the narrative. Many writers have written the character novels which picturized their journey of life. The narrative takes many turns as the character faces many troubles and harsh realities and overcomes many hurdles. These predicaments of the character differ from their gender. Writing about male hero was the trend followed by many of the narratives. But with the change of time, the literary scenario has also shifted its limelight from male to female protagonists. After recognizing the capability of women to join their counterparts in their fight against ignorance, superstition and backwardness, novelist instigated the reader to consider women as valid subjects for their purposeful social novels. Their effort was to be relevant to their culture by presenting characters and situations rooted in life. This is made clear by what Nayantara Sahgal proclaims:

> **To be relevant to his culture, a writer's imagination has to be able to create men and women and situations of the Indian environment and the Indian reality. If a writer can do this, make people feel with him, stimulate thinking, and inspire action because of what he writes, then he is fulfilling his function. [1971, v:5]**

Bapsi Sidhwa's main concern is with her female characters in almost all her novels except in *The Crow Eaters*. Mistry's main focus is his male characters in all of his novels. Sidhwa depicts the predicament of women in male-dominated society; her female characters strive for existence like Zaitoon in *Bride*, Feroza in *An America Brat* and sometimes just as the shadow of males like Putli, Tanya in *The Crow Eaters* and Mrs. Sethi and Ayah in *Ice Candy Man*. At the same time she portrays the female characters which are powerful and dominating like Godmother and caricatures like - Jerbanoo in *The Crow Eaters*. In *Ice-Candy Man*, Lenny's mother, and aunty rationed petrol and smuggled it to help those who needed timely help:

> **'We were only smuggling the rationed petrol to help our Hindu and Sikh friends to run away... And also for the convoys to send kidnapped women, like your ayah, to their families across the border.' (ICM, 242)**

Sidhwa portrayed her female character as Messiah of Hindus and Sikhs trapped in the burning city. Sidhwa also focuses on gender bias and related issues. Lenny enquired about the women in her courtyard. Hamida described them as "fallen women" (ICM, 214). Lenny innocently inquired about Hamida and Godmother explained that now she is a destitute as she was kidnapped and raped by Sikhs. Lenny said, "It isn't her fault she was kidnapped!", so Godmother answered, "Some folk fell that way - they can't stand their women being touched by other men" (ICM, 215). Sidhwa describes Godmother as powerful and all-knowing which means in real sense she is the Godmother who is controller of so many things around her:

> **And this is the course of her immense power: this reservoir of random knowledge, and her knowledge of ancient lore or wisdom and herbal remedy. You cannot be near her without feeling her uncanny strength. People bring to her their joy and woes. Show her their sores and swollen joints... She has access to many ears.... Godmother can move mountains from the paths of those she befriends, and erect mountainous barriers where she deems it necessary. (ICM, 211)**

Sidhwa in *The Crow Eaters* tells about women's status and position in India of those days:

> **In the India of Billy's days, girls, like jewels, were still being tucked away and zealously guarded by parents, brothers, grandparents, aunts and uncles. Every one kept a sharp eye out. Even the innocent horse-play of children was savagely punished, and a baby boy caught with his hand there, was promptly spanked on the hand. There were no salesgirls in shops and few women were to be seen on streets. There was but one co-educational school in Lahore and the only women a young man could talk to were those of his family. In this repressed atmosphere love grows astonishingly on nothing. It sprouts in the oddest places at oddest times and takes the most bizarre forms. This is most so among the Muslims and among the majority**

> **of Hindus who keep their women in purdah. There is no purdah at all among the Parsis- but the generally repressed air in India envelopes them. (TCE, 205-206)**

Sidhwa also points out the paradox of modern people like Billy who allowed their wives to interact among their friends but at the same time felt jealous and insecure as the result of their inferiority complex but a girl like Tanya retorts the suppression, "O.K., so you don't want me to look at their eyes! So where do you want me to look? At their balls?" (TCE, 246) But later on as he tames her she accepts herself as the shadow of her husband and follows the "commandments" (TCE, 278). Sidhwa writes, "Soon Tanya learnt to accost Billy directly. He forced her into adopting the strategies of a courtesan" (TCE, 278). Sidhwa also catches the veins of woman power where she can be 'durga' the warrior goddess who destroys evil and claims to be superior. It can be aptly described in Iqbal's couplet which she quotes in '*The Pakistani Bride*':

Khudi ko kar buland itana
ke her takdeer se pahele
Khuda khud bande se puche
bata teri raza kya hai. (TPB, 229)

This aspect of 'self-knowledge' of one's progress is portrayed in *An American Brat*, Zareen sent Feroza to USA where she enjoys the freedom and wants to live the life of her choice. She found herself misfit in a country which fitted her so well before coming to America. There would no going back for her, but she could go back at will:

> **If she flew and fell again, could she pick herself up again? Maybe one day she'd soar to that self-contained place from which there was no falling, if there was such a place. (AAB, 317)**

Sidhwa comments on the financial empowerment of the women that gives them the sense of power and control over their lives. Feroza expressed her enjoyment in earning money. Whereas Zareen, her mother, had never worked, so she was robbed of this thrill. Zareen understood the "thrilling" as "a sense of control over her life, a sense of accomplishment" (AAB, 240) where as Mistry's canvass is fully occupied by the male protagonists except Dina Dalal in *A Fine Balance*, but she too is a victim. Roxana, Coomy from *Family Matters* are in contrast, where as Roshan and Dilnavaz, her mother, are shadows of Nobel in *Such a Long Journey*. Roxana in *Family Matters* can be seen as the grown up Roshan who always acts as a peace-maker. Gustad Nobel (*Such a Long Journey*), Nariman Vakeel and the Yezad (*Family Matters*), Om, Ishvar, Mike (*A Fine Balance*) are the major male characters who overshadowed other characters in the respective novels. Mistry sketches Roshan as 'peace-maker' when her parents quarrel:

> **'Go kiss Mummy'... 'No, no, no. I cannot sleep till you kiss. Mummy will come here.' When Dilnavaz did not move, she went and began tugging at her arm, leaning on it with all her meager weight. Dilnavaz gave in. She looked coldly at Gustad and brushed his cheek cursorily. 'Not like that!' said Roshan, frustratedly, pounding the arm of the chair. 'That's not a real Mummy-Daddy kiss. Do it like when Daddy goes to work in the morning.' Dilnavaz rested her lips against Gustad's. 'Eyes closed, eyes closed!' yelled Roshan. 'Do it properly!' They obeyed, then separated. Gustad was amused. 'My little kissing umpire,' he said. Roshan somehow sensed that it took more than the joining of lips and closing of eyes to get rid of anger and bitterness. (SALJ, 167)**

Roxana has always worked as a peace-maker between Coomy and Jal, Yezad and Coomy. Dina Dalal (*A Fine Balance*) wanted to throw away the havoc of patriarchy and create a niche in her own life. She tries to grow independently without any help of her brother. But ultimately she has to return back to her brother after her loss of home. It destroyed her home. Nusswan found her very calm and submissive. Nusswan teased her but she did not retaliate:

> **There were times when he sat alone in his room, recalling the headstrong, indomitable sister, and regretted her fading. Well, he sighed to himself, that was what life did to those who refused to learn its lessons: it beat them down and broke their spirit. But at least her days of endless toil**

> **were behind her. Now she would be cared for, provided for by her own family. (AFB, 702)**

Mistry describes Nusswan as a dominant patriarch who controls everything very crookedly. Nusswan believed in discipline as his father did. He wanted to control and discipline everything in his house after his father, especially Dina. He scolded her:

> **...'You have always had the habit of blurting whatever comes into your loose mouth. But you are no longer a child. Someone has to teach you respect.' He sighed, 'It is my duty, I suppose,' and without warning he began slapping her. He stopped when a cut opened her lower lip. (AFB, 25)**

In *Family Matters,* Roxana is completely devoted to her family. She acts as the peace-make between the quarrels of Coomy and other members. Whereas Coomy is shrewd, calculated and talks with Nariman in terms of "flesh-and-blood" (FM, 07) terminology. Here one should note that the character of Jal has feminine overtones in terms of nature and thinking pattern, who very submissively acts on the whims of other's, first on Coomy's and later on Yezad's.

In this way, Sidhwa and Mistry have portrayed their characters according to their understanding of the world.

*

IX

Space is an important concept in post-modernism. Locale is often important character in the fictions of many writers like Thomas Hardy. A sense of place is one of the essentials of a writer's being, in imperative, increasingly being dislocated through extra-territoriality. Nineteenth century writing had privileged the sense of rootedness. Locating the site has become a narcissistic obsession with the postcolonial writer, especially the postcolonial immigrant writer. Exiled by choice or circumstance, the immigrant finds himself removed from his roots, his predecessors, and his Centre. He discards his colossal national and regional identity and becomes a storehouse of dualities and multiplicities. His position as the Outsider in the country of his adoption escorts him to create a discrete geographical and textual space that is contrary to the colonial discourse. These writers have consciously created a space that is rooted in a kaleidoscopic projection of the history and culture of the countries to which they belong to. Homi Bhabha, *The Location of Culture,* has pointed out that the creation of such a space disrupts "the logics of synchronicity and evolution which traditionally authorize the subject of cultural knowledge" [Bhabha, 1994:6]. Literary creativeness depends on the unconscious accumulation of local knowledge and the writer has only one source of unconsciousness material from which he has to accumulate the information about his cultural locale. Similarly Barry Lopez commenting upon "A Literature of Place" writes:

> **I want to talk about geography as a shaping force, not a subject... A specific and particular setting for human experience and endevour is, indeed central to the work of many nature writers, I would say a sense of place is also critical to the development of a sense of morality and of human identity.** [1996:7]

Natural surroundings influence artist's mind as well as his sense of identity. A sense of place that the imagination encounters imparts a sense of belonging and reduces the sense of being isolated. The expatriate writer moves from one kind of association (culture of origin) to another kind (culture of his adoption). When the writer creates a third space (memoryscape of his/her (imaginary) homelands in fictions), that is because he wants to escape from the conflict of situations and self-division, or may be as an attempt to negotiate alternate realities. Soja attracts the attention to the "ambivalent spatiality" of Foucault which was interconnected into "brilliant whirls of historical insight". Space and time are interrelated. History unfolds itself through constructions of space. Foucault explained that Heterotopia is to be distinguished from utopias. Heterotopia is a countersite like a resting place, a sanatorium, a prison or a theatre, a countersite where "all the other real sites that can be found within a culture are simultaneously represented, contested and inverted" [Foucault 1986:24-25] and where a juxtaposition of the otherwise incompatible can take place. The formation of this third space mirrors all these complexities. Thus, space offers in itself a dynamics for history. Writers from colonized countries and marginalized or interiorized societies are absorbed in a process of reconstructing both national and personal histories with the objectives of analyzing and understanding of their own past. As Edward Soja has pointed out, "The historical imagination is never completely spaceless and critical. Social historians have written, and continue to write, some of the best geographies of the past" [Soja 1997:14]. In order to test this hypothesis Abram's following definition of 'the regional novel' is of some help:

> **The regional novel emphasizes the setting, speech, and social structure, and customs of a particular locality, not merely as local color, but as important conditions affecting the treatment of characters their ways of thinking, feeling, and interacting…[1993:134]**

Parsis are always associated with Bombay, Karachi and Lahore. So it is important to focus on the cultural locale of these writers. Sidhwa's cultural locale is Lahore in *The Crow Eaters* and *Ice-Candy Man*. She shifts her locale from Pakistan to USA in her novel *An American Brat*. Mistry's fictions are preoccupied by his home city 'Bombay'. It is almost nostalgia and love for Bombay which compels Mistry to write about the Bombay and predicament of the minority community of Parsis in Bombay.

Sidhwa's fictional locale is historical city of 'Lahore', where she portrays the various parts of Lahore with vivid details like Hira Mandi, Warris Road, Garden, Mosque etc., as well as her fourth novel which is partly set in USA pictures the details of U.S.A.

Sidhwa describes Warris Road as the "compressed" (ICM, 1) world of Lenny. It is "lined with rain gutters, lies between Queens Road and Jail Road, both wide, clean, orderly streets at the affluent fringes of Lahore" (ICM, 1). She describes colonial rule in Garden in Lahore, "Queen Victoria, cast in gunmetal, is majestic, massive, overpowering, ugly. Her statue imposes the English Raj in the park" (ICM, 18). Sidhwa describes Hira Mandi as:

> **… into the blessed shade of the constricted gullies of the old city (ICM, 257) … a bazzar with rows of shops at the ground level and living quarters with frail arched windows and decaying wooden balconies teetering above… a stall overflowing with garlands of scarlet roses, jasmine and**

> **mounds of marigolds... Except for the betel-leaf and cigarette stalls and a few eating places where meat and *pakoras* are being fried... the mounds of rotting fruit and vegetables and the bones picked clean by the kites, their enormous wings stirring in the garbage: and the sudden yelp of kicked mongrels and raucous flights of crows and scraps of cardboard and rusted iron and other debris even the poor have no use for. (ICM, 258-259)**

Sidhwa gives the brilliant descriptions of America when Manek took Feroza on the tour of New York City. Sidhwa describes it as, "they embarked on cultural mission" (AAB, 75). They visited the Museo el Barrio, committed to Hispanic-American art, and the Jewish Musemum in the Warburg Mansion, the Museum of Modern Art and the Military Museum in the *Interpid* on the West side. Feroza noticed "a surrealistic impression of blurred images, a kaleidoscope of perceptions in which paintings, dinosaurs, American Indian artifacts, and Egyptian mummies mingled with hamburgers, pretzels, sapphire earrings, deodorants, and glamorous window displays" (AAB, 76). Sidhwa narrates the poverty of the USA at Port Authority bus terminal as:

> **She sensed the terminal was the infested hub of poverty from which the homeless and the discarded spiraled all over the shadier sidewalks of New York. Ragged and filthy men and women were spreading scores of flattened cardboard boxes to sleep on in the bus terminal. The smells disturbed her psyche; it seemed to her they personified the callous heart of the rich country that allowed such savage neglect to occur. (AAB, 81)**

At the same time she found that this dirt, filth, and poverty in USA were "alien" (AAB, 81) to her. Feroza saw the billboards as though "a stage set had been flipped around to reveal the glitzy and glamorous side of the ugliness and tawdry scenes they had witnessed on Eighth Avenue and on Forty-Second Street" (AAB, 82). Her dull heart thrilled to the rhythm of the bright lights, to the view of Japanese tourists taking photographs, the vendors showing jewelry, scarves, tacky T-shirts, and buttons. Feroza felt it all represented "a rich slice of the life and experience she had come to America to explore" (AAB, 82-83).

Sidhwa compares the two cities of pre-independent India, Lahore and Bombay. In their visit to India Billy found Bombay as "the bustling metropolis with its superb wide roads, tall stone buildings, buses and trams" (TCE, 195-96). It was the first impression of resident from the city like Lahore whose heart was "filled with awe and the beginnings of inferiority complex" (TCE, 195-96). Billy found himself "a country bumpkin" (TCE, 195-96) in Bombay. Sidhwa differentiates between USA and Pakistan in *An American Brat.* She calls Pakistan as "the land of poets and *ghazals*" (AAB, 311). USA is the land of the skyscrapers, glossy magazines etc.

Mistry differentiates Canada and India in *Lend Me Your Light* in *Tales from Firozsha Baag.* Like most immigrants Kersi experienced the culture-shock after landing in Bombay. He felt the striking contrast between "the lush… green… hopeful" (TFB, 186) West and "the parched land, brown, weary, and unhappy" (TFB, 186) India. He portrays the nostalgia of his home-metropolis 'Bombay' (Mumbai now) with its red light areas, slum areas, specially the colonies and buildings of the Parsis. Mistry describes Chor Bazaar:

> **…the maze of narrow lanes and byways that was Chor Bazaar. Where to begin? And so many people everywhere-locals, tourists, foreigners, treasure hunters, antique collectors, junk dealers, browsers. Away from the crowds swirls and eddies… a little stall selling a variety of used sockets and rusty wrenches. There were other tools as well: pliers, hammers with rough wooden handles, screwdrivers, a planer, worn-out files. (SALJ, 99)**

Mistry describes Dr. Paymaster's neighborhood as:

> **…a neighbourhood that had changed in recent years from a place of dusty, unobtrusive poverty to a bustling, overcrowded, and still dusty, nub of commerce. Crumbling, leaky warehouses, and rickety-staired, wobbly balconied tenements had been refurbished and upgraded, from squalid and uninhabitable to squalid and temporarily habitable. The sewer system remained unchanged, broken and overflowing. Water supply continued to be a problem. So did rats, garbage and street lighting. (SALJ, 155)**

The love and nostalgia for Bombay is expressed in *Family Matters* when Yezad saw a man trying to enter into the running-train and endangered his life but saved by fellow-passengers. The description was in contrast to Sidhwa's details about the social strata in Lahore in *An American Brat.* Mistry writes:

> **Whose hands were they, and whose hands were they grasping? Hindu, Muslim, Dalit, Parsi, Christian? No one knew and no one cared. Fellow passengers, that's all they were. And I stood there on the platform for a long time, Yezad, my eyes filled with tears of joy, because what I saw told me there was still hope for this great city. (FM, 160)**

Mistry has described almost all the major places in Mumbai at length in all his novels. It shows his deep rooted love and recollection of his past life in Mumbai. At the same time he also pictured Bombay's dark side i.e. extreme poverty in slum-areas in AFB. Mistry's cry for his lost city can be clearly seen in Family Matters where he compares Bombay to his beloved and complains that, "My beloved Bombay is being raped" (FM, 158).

Thus these two writers have shown their concern to their places of past as an indivisible part of their life left behind.

*

X

Different ethnic groups have been able to maintain their distinct ethnic identity due to the secular ethos of India. At the same time the convergence of different languages coupled with the impact of English language has led to the hybridization of language. Following is the brief analysis of Bapsi Sidhwa's and Rohinton Mistry's novels where hybrid language is used predominantly. Bapsi Sidhwa is influenced by Islamic culture in Pakistan while Mistry has impact of Hindu as well as other cultures in India. This has resulted into the liberal borrowing from all the Indian languages. The idea that Language is the constitutive agent of human consciousness received further impetus in the last century from Structural Linguistics. Language is understood to be anterior to the world. So what is called reality is a linguistically constructed artifact.

It is caused by different language systems people inhabit. Jacques Derrida's phrase "il ny a pas de hors-texte" [1976:157] reflects his view that language cannot adequately represent anything outside of itself. Human understanding of the world is necessarily mediated through language. But it does not follow that human are trapped within the 'prison house of language'. People of different nationalities are connected through long distance communication on the principle of a symbiotic relationship. In India, Standard English has been decentred and gave rise to a pluralistic use of English in India. Due to circumstances, largely facilitated by the spirit of globalization, the native/non-native binary in the use of English has collapsed on the Indian soil. As a result, a new variety of English is in the making. The ownership of English has been globally distributed by the inevitable dissolution of native vs. non-native equation. Language is another aspect with which an ethnic group maintains its distinct identity as an ethnic group. So Parsis too, have their typical accentuated Parsi-Gujarati language. The English used by Mistry and Sidhwa is totally different from each other. Various ethnic groups in India have led to the emergence of a multi-cultural scenario. The hybridity of Mistry's use of two separate discursive approaches can be seen as a political act to assert and conserve cultural territory for the Parsi. Simultaneously, the use of Parsi words has a nostalgic purpose of resituating the speaker in the Bombay of his childhood. The Parsi idioms momentarily de-center the English reader from his own culture. It insists on cultural difference, yet concurrently they centre the reader in the collective understanding of idyllic memory.

V.K. Sunwani has brilliantly highlighted on Mistry's use of language:

> **His language is full of for-the-nonce words which convey the exact meaning in the situation obtaining therein. It has a liberal sprinkling of Hindi words and Indianisms which have become an established part of linguistic repertoire of an Indian, educated or otherwise...Whereas English was a sign of linguistic imperialism, Hinglish has to survive in India and will continue to evolve and we will thus get rid of our linguistic slavery,. Secondly, Hinglish is a marriage of Indian culture and a Western language. [1997:110-11]**

Sidhwa's language has a polishing touch. She uses lots of Parsi-Gujarati words. In *An American Brat,* she has given special glossary of such words at the end of the novel. She uses some Punjabi, Urdu vocabulary as well. Sidhwa says, "After moving to America I realized that all my sentences in English were punctuated with Gujarati and Urdu words." [Jussawalla 1990:214]

Gujarati is the first language of Bapsi Sidhwa and most Parsis. It is one of the many Indian languages which voluntarily allow intricate word play. Bapsi Sidhwa's sentences in English are scattered with Gujarati and Urdu words. There are also Parsi maxim and Parsi-Gujarati modulations in her sentences. Sidhwa thinks that her technique is influenced by her manner of speaking, which she calls a "salad of languages" [Eds. Dhawan R.K. and Novy Kapadia, 1996:13]. In an interview with David Montenegro, she explains her motivations for juggling with words from three different languages in her narrative:

> **I think you just juggle for the best meaning, somehow. And certain words are so much more expressive in another language. Some thing that is zestful comes out so much better said in Punjabi, or something that is emotional or romantic comes out better in Urdu. Or certain Gujarati words carry so much more meaning. And you just automatically adopt this mixture to be more expressive. [1989:37]**

The verbal jugglery used by Sidhwa makes her writing style modernist or post-modernist. The language in her books is similar to the rhythms, styles and nuances of everyday language in the sub-continent. For Sidhwa life is like poetry comprehended through emotions, experiences sometimes brutal and philosophical. She often quotes Urdu Poets as in *Ice Candy Man.* The last few pages contain many couplets from the poets in Urdu with English translations. In *An American Brat* too there are Urdu couplets with English translations. Sidhwa's use of language is feminine and is very minute and brilliant whereas Mistry's use of language is rather rough and harsh and has masculine overtones. Sidhwa's vocabulary depicts her Pakistani citizenship as her works are full of Urdu words and couplets of Urdu Poets whereas Mistry's mixed code/hybrid language is, no doubt, the product of his home city, Mumbai, where a mini-India resides. His use of English poetry and songs shows his unfulfilled desire of being a singer and his degree in English Literature in Toronto. Mistry's use of a variety of languages shows multi-religious, multi-ethnic co-existence in India. His use of Marathi language and parodied dialect in Parsi-Gujarati or

English language shows his hatred for majority community and concern for marginalized existence of his community. Rohinton Mistry's fictional world is centered on Bombay and its variety of cultural, religious, economic, and social classes. So his language is the true picture of all these classes. Mistry in his novel *Such a Long Journey* gives the reference to "Barrere and Leland's Dictionary of Slang" (SALJ, 53). Following is a brief analysis of hybridization of the language as seen in the novels of these two writers.

Bapsi Sidhwa

Gujarati/Farsi words/phrases with English meanings:

An American Brat - Gathas-the song of Zarathustra (287), boochmai, an archaic Gujarati word for 'little girl' (69,78,123, 133,222)

English word with Hindi suffix:

An American Brat- lesson-walla (111)

Hindi word with English adjectization:

Ice Candy Man - goondaish (180,245)

Hindi-Punjabi sentence:

Ice Candy Man - 'Raj Karega Khalsa, aki rahi na koi!' (134)

Hindi-Gujarati word:

The Crow Eaters - Asha (12)

Hindi-English word/phrase and vice-versa:

The Crow Eaters - a betel nut paan (160)

Ice Candy Man- bodhi-hair (95), Paan spitting (245)

Urdu-Hindi words and vice versa:

The Crow Eaters- Fakir (33, 34), tonga (121), mela (229)

Ice Candy Man- Baijee (10,27,28,29,226-27,259,262), palloo(28,46), Angrez (28,63,129,92), bibi(29)

English-Urdu sentence:

The Crow Eaters – we were original non believing kafirs! (221)

Verbification of Hindi, Urdu words in English:

The Crow Eaters -salaamed (121), salaaming (235)

An American Brat - khoos-poosing (193)

Punjabi sentence with English meanings:

Ice Candy Man- 'O kee? What's that?'(96)

An American Brat - 'O menu ghoor-ghoor ke vekh raha see. He was making big, big eyes and staring at me.'(106)

English pluralization of Hindi-Urdu nouns:

The Crow Eaters- Toddywallas, Bankwallas, Bottiwallas and Chaiwallas (21) pyals (133) dains (159), patris (172,175), Mandirs (237)

Ice Candy Man- kebabs (44), tongawallah's (48), parathas (52,57,109), Congresswalahs (75), jalebis (106), pakoras (105,258), Mussulmans (122,128), ladoos (168-69), bodhis(175), haramzadas (180,249), kirpans (204), melas (209). Karmas (222) goondas (248,272), Shaitans (250)

An American Brat – mullahs (10, 11, 13), burqas (10), goondas (11,135,223), dopattas (19,48), gurudwaras (19), shalwars (21), Yathas (47), pakoras (36,38), heejras (78,79), gora-chittas (141), dhotis (106,217), jhuggees (238,239), mushairas (311), ghazals(s) (311)

Parsi/Gujrati with English plurals:

An American Brat- Ashem Vahoons (47), navjotes (204,293), pareekas (224)

Hindi-Urdu words/phrases/sentence with English meanings and vice versa:

The Crow Eaters- janam patris birth sheets (160-76), Agni puja (fire worshipping) (163), monkey-god Hanuman (237)

Ice Candy Man-

'Langer deen! Paisay ke teen! Tamba mota, pag mahin!'

'Lame Lenny! Three for a penny! Fluffy pants and fine fanny!' (3) electric aunt- bijli(21), a pahaliwan – a wrestler(27), 'Save me! Save me! Bachao! Bachao!' (30) Bitch! Haramzadi (45), Haramkhor! Slut (45), masti- a bit of naughtiness (48), phulkas (miniature chapatties) (49, 50, 58), Sikh priest, a granthi (54), 'Hasi to phasi! Laugh (and) get laid!'(55)

Chaudhary, a village leader (55,56,57,196-99,202), Janoo(a variation on Jana)(65,69), naswar (mixture of tobacco and Opium) (74), "Salaam-alekum mamajee [uncle]" (77),

'Siski hawa ne lee: Har Pati Kanp oothi.
The breeze sucked in his breath…
The leaves trembled, breathless (119),

putch-putch- kissing noises used to wheedle children dispatch on trivial errands(112), 'Pakistan Murdabad! Death to Pakistan' (134,144) tobacco-naswar (149); Kullah/kulla – around which turban is wrapped (152), achkan coats(160),

'Mere bachpan ke sathi mujhe bhool na jana
Dekho, dekho hense na zamana, hanse na zamana.
Friends from our childhood, don't forget us.
See that a changed world does not mock us. (159)

"Ghar ki murgi; dal barabar. A neighbour's beans are tastier than household chickens." (233) khut-putli- puppets (222), Hira Mandi means Diamond Market(240), Trouble Easers, the angels Mushkail Assan (241)

'Tum aye ho na shab-e-intazaar guzri hai-
Talash main hai seher baar baar guzri hai!'
You never came… The waitful night never passed.
Though many dawns have passed in the waiting.'(245)

'Kiya mujh ishq ne zalim ko aab ahista ahista
Ke aatish gul ko karti hai gulab ahista ahista.
Slowly, my love has compelled her, slowly-
The way the sun touches open the rosebud slowly.'(248)

'Hai ashqi ke beech sitam dekhna hi lutf
Mar jana ankhe moond ke kuch hunar nahin.
'Tis nothing… to roll up one's eyes and die.
endure my lover's tyranny wide-eyed. [263]

'La Ilaha Illallah, Mohammad ur Rasullallah.'
(There is no God but God, and Mohammad is his Prophet) (181)

<u>*An American Brat*</u> - heejra- a fifty-fifty (79), "Khush ho- Happy?" (241),
"Ulfat kee Naee manzil ko chalay:

Embarked on a new mission of love" (311)

Punjabi words/phrase with English meanings:

Ice Candy Man - kirpan-daggar (144)

Farsi with English plurals:

The Crow Eaters - kustis (56, 176)

Rohinton Mistry

Hindi and Marathi words made into English noun:

A Fine Balance - fakeologist (345) fakeology (599)

Mixture of Sanskrit and Hindi/slang :

A Fine Balance- 'Goluma Ekdama Tajidevum Chuptum Makkama Jhaptum (139)

Marathi, Hindi, English wording in the sentence:

Family Matters - Asaala kasaala karte? Maine tumko explain kiya, na, eleven o'clock ao. Abhi jao, ration shop ko jao. Paisa banao, later vapis ao (390)

Marathi sentence with Parsi accent:

Family Matters - Tumse lok aykat nai! Bai tumhala kai saangte? (389), Ai baba! Assa nako ghay (391), Assa Kai, Ganpat (392)

Gujarati asmai-kasmai code:

Such a Long Journey- "*Masmaybisme hisme wasmas skasmeepisming becasmecausemuse ismit wasmas raimainisming' (135*)

Gujarati-English words/phrases:

Such a Long Journey- A single paasri (240)

A Fine Balance- carrot-salad, carrot-ma-gose (252), prawn patia (734), Sudra and Kusti (712)

Marathi sentence with English word:

Such a Long Journey - Umcha section nai (132,330), O baba, arya ghay! Carefully, arya, arya (338)

Indianized spellings of English word:

Tales from Ferozsha Baag - phoren (183)

Gujarati sentences with English meanings:

Tales from Firozsha Baag- ayah no chhokro, ayah's child (46), "burgee nay dhoor thai gaya-corrupted to become useless as dust" (81)

English words/phrases with Parsi variation:

Tales from Firozsha Baag- Easy chairs-igeechur (44), French beans-ferach beech (44)

Hindi-English words and vice versa:

Such a Long Journey- *Angrezi* books (102), Head maalis? (102), jasmine and chamayli (157)

A Fine Balance- bulky samosa(38), shahenshahi calendar(31), No baba(82) twenty-five paisa(84), Two annas(129), One anna(129), drama and naatak(576), dal and chapati(151,407), earthen matka(203), open-air sundaes(205), The nussbandhi (215-16), Bhaji and chapati(220), Revolver Rani(344,346,348), Machine Gun Maharani (344,351,349), fifty paise(476), Two paisa(458), Maharishi carrot Baba(420), copra and kothmeer-mirchi(491), licence permit quota raj (501), saala idiot(515), Bilkool correct(521), Okay, batcha(526), Laddoo and jalebi, ras-malai(562), Saala murderer (607), ice-gola(629), the darkness of Kaliyug (636), karai chicken (746), a single paisa(752)

Family Matters- soup-chaaval (97,112) soo-soo bottle (119)

English sentence with Hindi/Marathi words:

Tales from Firozsha Baag- "...middle class people like us get the bamboo, all the way." (131), ghati-mentality (181)

Such a Long Journey- twenty naye paise (59), two paisa clerk (69), Ice-cold Paani, sweet-sweet paani(59), Spitting or playing satta prohibited(75), the all-clearfying testicular golaas(76)

Hindi sentence with English words:

A Fine Balance- Aray babu! O big paisawalla babu (341), Aray, hero ka batcha (425), saala shameless budmass (445)

Family Matters- chalo, sign ko string lagaake fix karo (363)

English - Parsi word and vice versa:

Tales from Firozsha Baag- Chicken-dhansak (151)

Verbification of Hindi/Marathi in English:

Family Matters - miaowing (489,550,555)

English Pluralization of Hindi/Marathi nouns:

Tales from Firozsha Baag- dharamsaalas (126), harijans (204), mawaalis (218), ghatis (17,35,176,178,183), ghatons(177)

Such a Long Journey- jhopadpattis(4), goondas(39), tohruns(284), devdasis(287), rundees, vaishyas(287); jhaarus(292), bahen-chod bungees(295), kholis(155), hijadaas (160,326)

A Fine Balance- pyjamas (21,65,66,138,305,585), kholis (81,499), beedis (94,98,100,102,345,379,382,484), gutters(103), jyotshis(105), pujas (122,381, 675), zamindars (126,182), puris (487,492), chapatti(s) (135,172,187,362, 408, 427,487,489,490,492,599,609,644,750), kurtas (585), ladoos (167), goondas (179,180,308,364,499,525,528,534-5,538, 543,549, 555, 599, 658, 694-95, 698), mullahs (181), coolies (186), pao-bhajis(478), massagwallas(508), jhopadpatti(s) (215,322,394, 398,465,676), jhopdi(s) (215,365), mathadis (319), sadhus (439), mohallas(445), wadas(491-92) Chawls (499) dhotis(501,641) Harijans (712)

Family Matters- mavaalis (23), chapatis (33), ghatis (52,389,395), chappals (74), goondas (144, 150, 334, 326), raakshas(204), sainiks (405)

English Pluralization of Parsi/Gujarati nouns:

Such a Long Journey -ghailchodias (214), khandhias (244),

Marathi with English meanings:

Such a Long Journey- asafoetida –hing (23)

Urdu with English Meanings:

Such a Long Journey- taveej, a protection (150)

Hindi with English meanings:

Tales from Firozsha Baag- garibi hatao-eradicate poverty (98)

Sukhi Sooraj, the strident paean to the rising sun (135), Sukhi Sooraj, the fervent tribute to sunrise (129)

Such A Long Journey- 'Humko kuch nahin maalom, we don't know anything' (14),

"Mere sapno ki rani kab ayegi tu, O
Queen of my dreams, when will you arrive" (165)
'Dil deke dekho, dil deke dekho, dil deke dekho…
Try giving your heart, give your heart away and see.'(201)

"Muncipality ki dadagiri nahi chalaygi- muncipalitys bullying will do not do" (325), Jis Deshme Ganga Bahti Hai-: the land where the Ganga flows and the Gutter overflows (325), palung-tode- bed breaker-paan (158,157,159, 160,192,306)

A Fine Balance- Meri dosti mera pyar…love and friendship (213),

Sagar-Darshan Ocean View Hotel (376), you are mad! Bilkool paagal (639)

Farsi with English meanings:

Tales from Firozsha Baag- "manashni, gavashni, kunashni, - good thoughts, good words, good deeds" (236)

English sentences with Gujarati meanings vice versa:

Tales from Firozsha Baag- a quiet good boy, aitlo dahyo (211), sidho-paadhro, to speak clearly (212)

Such a Long Journey- alive and squawking, jeevti-jaagti (19), fikko-fuchhuk, white as a ghost (35), "fire! fire! 'Aag laagi! Aag laagi" (168), "Kaakerya Kumar, ketlo bhaar? 'Munno bhaar' 'Ek uteri nay bagalma maar, taking turns and coercing each other with dire threats to retract the fists and stick it in an armpit" (191)

French with Gujarati meaning:

Such a Long Journey - fait-accompli. Jai thayu tay thayu (196)

Language is also an ethnic marker. It contributes to the ethno-culture ethno-religious connotations. Each ethnic group has its own vocabulary regarding the culture and religion as well as dressing and cuisines as a part of ethnic identity. In this way language signifies the typicality of that particular ethnic group. As these ethnic groups co-exist with other ethnic groups, the intermingling or exchange of habits, dressing code and cuisines is imperative. So vocabulary may belong to more than one ethnic group. Following is an approximate attempt to categorise the words within the ambit of particular ethnic group.

Bapsi Sidhwa

Edible items:

The Crow Eaters:

Paan (131,152,155)

Ice-Candy Man:

malida (33), kebabs (44), phulkas (miniature chapatties) (49,50,58)

parathas (52,57,109), pakoras (105,258), gulab-jamun (106), jalebis (106) ladoos (168-69), paan (126,135)

An American Brat:

dhan-dar (44), pakoras (36,38), dal (112,142)

Dressing:

The Crow Eaters:

lungi (120,151,171)

Ice-Candy Man:

kurta (133), khaddar (4), palloo (28,46), churidaar (105), rug (151), achkan coats (160), ghoongat (186-87,260,261), Chuddar (190-91,222,237), garara (260)

An American Brat:

burqas (10), dopattas (19,48), tanchoi (43), shalwar-kamiz (42,45,72, 122), lungi (19), shalwars (21,86), sudra (31,164,220, 278,317), kusti (31,41,164, 278,317), kamiz (74), dhotis (106,217), thaan (220), feta (248),

Hindu:

The Crow Eaters:

Hai Bhagwan (88) Mandirs (237) Hanuman (237) janam patris (160-76)

Ice Candy Man:

Arrey Bhagwan (76), Hai Ram (77,89,134), bodhi-hair(95), bodhi(117), karmas (222), bodhis (175), Kali yuga (148)

An American Brat:

Hai Bhagwan (252)

Muslim:

The Crow Eaters:

Hai Allah! (88,202), kafirs! (221) burqa (240) Fakir (33, 34),

Ice Candy Man:

Salaam (53) "Salaam-alekum mamajee ' (77), Ya Allah! (97)

Allah (98,111), Wah Allah! (99) 'Ya Allah! Ya Rahman! Ya Rahim!' (107) Mussulmans (122,128), nikah (250), Shaitans (250), Allah-ki-kasam (182), sehra (186-88), doolha (186-188), kalma (181), 'La Ilaha Illallah, Mohammad ur Rasullallah.' (181) Allah-o-Akbar! Ya Ali (135)

Allah-o-Akbar! (154,199) saalam ailekum (150)

An American Brat:

mullahs(10,11,13), sufi(19) maulvi(45), Aa-meen(46),

Allllh-ah (134), mushairas (311), mehfil (311)

Sikh:

Ice Candy Man:

Sikh priest, a granthi (54), granthi (56,106-8) Wah Guru! (107,203,204), kirpans (204), takth (223), kirpan (133), 'Raj Karega Khalsa, aki rahi na koi!' (134), Sat siri Akaal! Bolay Se nihal!' (134,154,199) kirpan (144)

An American Brat:

gurudwaras(19)

Parsi:

The Crow Eaters:

Asha (12), jashan (17), mathabanus (23, 59, 273), Dungerwaree (46) Atash (50) kustis (56, 176), sudreh (110), Navjote (124), pigani (52), rehra (67)

Ice Candy Man:

Dungarwadi (113-14), Shaitans (250), kusti(173)

An American Brat:

pahi (43,304), Yathas (47), Ashem Vahoons (47), agyari (40,41,278) atash(40, 41,47,257,317), sagan (44), madasara (223, 297) navjotes(204,293) dokhma(269), uthmna(270), Atash Behram(278) adarnee (297), pareekas(224)

Rohinton Mistry

Dressing

Tales from Firozsha Baag:

dugli (4,7,12,16-19,67), pheytoe (4,16,18), pyjama (5), paan ((18,67,86,156), kusti (67,110,120,221,236) choli (9,10), pugree (67,68,75) kurta-pyjama (210)

Such a Long Journey:

Kusti(1,4,5,14,15,39,137), Sudra (15) rajai (302), Duglo (130), jhabbho(210)

A Fine Balance:

sherbet (9,195), paan (11,317,524,526,638,639), pyjamas (21,65,66, 138,305,585) choli (147,148,165,345,502), kurtas (585) Salwar Kameez (379), ghaghra-choli (379), dupattas (683), Sherwani (699,432), sudra and kusti (712), kashmiri shawl (730), dhotis (501,641),

Family Matters:

pyjama (63,64) kurta (251) kusti (306-07,339-40,375,436,436,445)

Edible Items

Tales from Firozsha Baag:

dhandar-paatyo (7,20,32), Sali-boti (7), ailchee (9,) chasni (12), pupeta-na-gose (32), ferach beech (44), chai (45), dhansak masala (62,68,73)

jeeragoli (89), supari (89), aampapud (89), samosa, bhaijia, sev-ganthia (111), Chicken-dhansak (151), dhansak (151), daar-roteli (126), bhelpuri, panipuri, batata-wada, kulfi(182), chapatti(187), mithai (199), Shik-kababwalla (217), Shik-kabab (219), lungoatee (219),

Such a Long Journey:

subjo (16,77,87,127-128,163,208,299), kutchoomber (18,97), dhansak (18, 170, 270), Sev-ganthia (35), Paapud (56), Dhandar-paatyo (70), Paan (107, 158, 192-93, 195-96, 200, 205,313-14, 325, 308), buryani (145), bhakras (148), chana-mumra (163), murumbo (164), sataan (232), subjo (269), charbee (270), march ni bhukti, andoo, lassun, garam masalo (274)

A Fine Balance:

bulky samosa (38), soros-na-paatru (45), kabab (47), shish kabab (747), biryani (53,746), pulao-dal(54,57), bhakras, vasanu,...coomas (79), ghee(101), puris(487,492),, dal and chapati(151,407), ladoos(167)

pao-bhajis(478), Bhaji and chapati(220) carrot-salad, carrot-ma-gose (252), samosa (305), chutney (305), Burfi(397), Tamaater (431), masala wada (490,599), dal (491-92), wadas 491-92), chutney (491,492), copra and kothmeer-mirchi (491), paneer masala, shak-bhaji, aloo masala (492), Laddoo and jalebi, ras-malai (562), pakora (629), ice-gola (629), Unjir (629), bhajia (683), prawn patia (734), karai chicken (746), pakora, chutney, puri-bhaji(746)

Family Matters:

sarbut (25,26,30), chapattis (33), dhandar paatiyo (38,39), falooda (40), soup-chaaval (97,112), papayta-noo-gose (99), dhansak (127), pao-bhaji (150), Belgaum ghee (198), bun-muskaa (204,205), Chai (213), khichri (391), dhansak dhandar (414), Patra-ni-machhi (415), margi-nofarcha (415), lagan-nu-custard (415), ravo (487), jalebi (488,496), Sooterfeni (496), burfi (496), malai-na-khaja (496)

Parsis

<u>*Tales from Firozsha Baag*</u>:

Behram roje (3-7,11-12,11,12,15,20) Navjote (4,67) dustoorji (13, 53, 54,63,64,130), agyari (13,123,124,126,129,130), afargaan(13, 113), Dada Ormuzd (10,125), Bawa (11,138,74), Bawaji (17,35), Dustoor (13-4,19,20), jashan (54), Mathoobanoo (55,56,84,85,95,141,178,205 ,204), dusmoo (59,62,64,71), maasis (59), parvar Daegar (72), Sapaat (89) khoedai (85,100), roje (109) teelo(180) ghatis (17,35,176, 178,183), ghatons (177), loban (7,54),

<u>*Such a Long Journey*</u>:

sapaat (35) bawaji (71,83) dustoorji (39), Navjote (56)khandhias (244), bawa (244), bugalee (245,246,248, 252,255,315), gomez (246), suchkaar (246), kusti (246,269), loban (247,248,286,315), dustoorji (247,251,252, 316,318), char-chassam (251), dugli (251, 328), afargan (251,315), nasasasalers (252,253,255,316), atash-dadgh (254), nirang (317), pydaust (318), sudra (265,293)

<u>*A Fine Balance*</u>:

Dustoor (22,31,45,48,702), Sataan (26), afargan (45), baaj (45), faroksy (45), ashirvaad (45), Navroze (53), khordad Sal (53), kaaj (63) nirvana (589)

<u>*Family Matters*</u>:

Navroze (25), khordad Sal (25), loban (25), Navjote (28) bavaji (44) ghatis (52,389,395) manashni (307,340,375), gavashni (307,340,375), kunashni (307,340,375), Ahura mazda khodai, az hama gunah, patet pashemanum (307), navjote (339), Ahura Mazda Khodai (340), dustoorji (340,342,437), geh (342), atash-bahram (344), salaamati(412), Kem na mazda! Mavaite payum dadat, hyat ma dregvao (445), dusmoo (418), Pa name yazdan Ahurmazda khodai (446), Fravarane Mazdayasno Zarathushtrish (446), Ahunem vairim tanum paiti (447), Yashemcha vahmemcha aojashca zavarecha afrinami (447), Kerfti mozd gunah guzar eshnra kunam (447), Khshnaothra Ahurahe Mazdao! Ashem Vohu Vanishtem asti (445), Doongerwadi (476), afargaan (483), Avan Yazat (491), Komm (495)

Hindu

Tales from Firozsha Baag:
sadhu (150)

Such a Long Journey:
hing (23) boni (103) puja(138)

A Fine Balance:
karma (589), jyotshis(105), Yoga (398), sanyasi (583,592,593,594), pujas (122,381,675), kaliyug (122), Hai Bhagwan (125,230), Bhungi(136,163)
Hai Ram(127,164,186,229,332,472,517,575,637,647,657), Brahmin, kshatriya, Vaishya, and Shudra (138), Chit-pavan Brahmin(139), pujari (139), Sadhu (151,644) sati (175) Namaskaar (204, 317,477, 603)
Dhobi (237) swami(332) bhistee (425,450), sadhus (439) Ravan (445), Ram naam satya hai! (618) Harijans(712), kundalini shakti (726), Kaliyug (636), Mata ki sawari (644)

Family Matters:
mehetrani (76)

Muslim

Such a Long Journey:
Bismillah (21) salaam (33,135,139-40), namaaz (99), jhaanum (142) dojukh (153), zanaankhana (159) Jumma Masjid (183), mia-laanda (193)

A Fine Balance:
salaam (69) masjid(105), Inshallah (153,157,160,182, 632,643,645), Ya Allah (164), mullahs (181), salaam alaikum (187), salaam (32, 194), burkha (194,199), khuda hafiz (195), fakir (439,479)

Family Matters:
Adha Bolla Catayla (227) miyan (277,292,360,386) Salaam (402) salaamati (412)

Sikh

A Fine Balance:
kara (712-13,728)

This brief lingual analysis of novels of Rohinton Mistry and Bapsi Sidhwa suggest that Mistry's fictional world depicts the multi-religious and various ethnic groups whereas Bapsi Sidhwa's fictional world suggests the Islamic atmosphere in her novels.

*

XI

When a writer overcomes the boundaries of ethnicity, race, religion and nation the work has a universal appeal. Every work of art reflects human life in the abstract or concrete form. It appeals to various emotions of human lives. Literature attracts human beings all over the world apart from its lingual, regional, ethical, religious, national, cultural differences because it has certain universal appeal in it. This contains a variety of factors like philosophy of life, attitude towards a fellow human being. Though they differ in matters of culture, religion, color, race, geographical locale, they are connected at the level of emotions and thoughts. Literature has such universal appeal sans ethnicity or culture. As Bhabani Bhattacharya aptly says, "Art must teach, but unobtrusively, by its vivid interpretation of life. Art must preach, but only by virtue of its being a vehicle of truth. If that is propaganda there is no need to eschew the word"[1955:394]. For Romen Basu, "Fiction is a human document. For me, unless it has some bearing on real life it cannot be taken as a work of creation." [1922] Chaman Nahal is of the firm view that a novel must possess 'synchronic relevance,' and it must concern itself with "a specific community" a specific class, a specific society". He says:

> **The main point is that an artist should be able to associate himself with an identifiable community, or what Raymond Williams has called 'a knowable community' [1985:110]**

There is a universal appeal in the works of Rohinton Mistry and Bapsi Sidhwa. Rohinton Mistry deals with human destiny and infinite injustice of the lord of the life as well as the destruction of the natural resources and natural wealth. Bapsi Sidhwa concerns with the feminine predicament and their upliftment appeals the universal reader.

Sidhwa talks as a woman first and then as a Parsi. Her pleas for women's emancipation and freedom of 'choice' and a call for women's upliftment is clearly seen in all her novels especially in *An American Brat* when Zareen ponders over the need for reform in her community, But "*she argued this from a purely feminist and academic point of view.*" (AAB, 288) (Emphasis added).

Mistry talks more as a Parsi first and then as a 'Mumbaikar' who suffers from the nostalgia of his lost home, where he is left with a status of writhing insect striving for life and survival. Dinshawaji expressed his grief and rage against parties like Shiv Sena and its policies of renaming roads and cities:

> **'Why change the names? *Saala* sisterfuckers! Hutatma Chowk!' 'What is wrong with Flora Fountain?' 'Names are so important. I grew up on Lamington Road. But it has disappeared, in its place is Dadasaheb Bhadkhamkar Marg. My school was on Carnac Road. Now suddenly it's on Lokmanya Tilak Marg. I live at Sleater Road. Soon that will also disappear. My whole life I have come to work at Flora Fountain. And one fine day the name changes. So what happens to the life I have lived? Was I living the wrong life, with all the wrong names? Will I get a second chance to live it again, with these new names? Tell me what happens to my life. Rubbed out, just like that? Tell me.' (SALJ, 73-74)**

Dinshawaji's anxiety and anger aptly reflect the suppression of the marginal and minority communities under the majoritarian fundamental rule.

Sidhwa is never blasphemous though she is ironical or satirical. She highlights Parsi paradoxes with subtle humor: "Notorious misers, they are paradoxically generous to a cause" (TCE, 21). Sidhwa shows respect for the priests as in *An American Brat*, when Feroza while praying observes the priests in the Fire Temple:

> **Feroza also liked to watch the priest, luminous in a forth of starched white robes, decorously feed the fire with offerings of sandalwood from a long-handled silver ladle. (AAB, 41)**

Where as Mistry underscores the satire of human life in a very serious way though sometimes critically and comically. He turned to be a blasphemous sometimes as in *Tales from Firozsha Baag, 'An Inauspicious Occasion'*, when Rustomji talks about dustoorji's habit of passing comments on women between the prayers:

> ***Ashem Vahoo,***
> **See the tits on that chickie-boo... (TFB, 14)**

Rustomji charged all the dustoors as "masked bandits" (TFB, 14). It conveys decline in the religious ethos and increasing indifferent tendencies toward the religious cult among the Parsis living in the metropolis like Mumbai and abroad.

Mistry's characters fight against destiny, they strive for achieving something. They live in perfect dystopia where everything is unjust and merciless, full of chaos, wants and starvations. Mistry's narration is like a 'skull beneath the face'. Mistry's attitude is shaped by the experience he had from the majority community. He paints the grim realities in a straight forward manner.

A Fine Balance is full of tragedies of Dina Dalal, Om & Ishvar, Manek Kohlah and many *common human beings* who are striving for the mere survival while living on edge. Their tragedies are such that one can not forgive the writer for his realism in life where happiness is a rare dream. But after all the hurdles and tragedies, Dina Dalal, Om and Ishvar, tailors turned into beggars, still live a happy life because they maintained a fine balance in there life but Manek who could not put up with these tragedies commits suicide. What Mistry suggests is life is full of tragedies, compromises, and horrors but full of life. One has to live because it is not meant for making an end of it. *Family Matters* brings the typical family stories from every common man's life. Yezad and Roxana fight against all odds and come to terms with life.

Sidhwa's fictional world is Utopian, full of bliss and harmony. Sidhwa paints realities. Sidhwa's fictional world is full of happiness, celebration, relatives enjoying each other's family bonds, standing by each other during crisis. In *The Crow Eaters*, Freddy develops from nothing to a leader of his community. His next generation too, enjoys all kinds of pleasure without any difficulty. There are no financial crises or other problems related with family happiness. In *Ice-Candy Man* too, apart from the partition riots, there are no problems in the life of Mr. & Mrs. Sethi, and they did not even suffer directly from the partition riots. *An American Brat* portrays the Parsi family which is quite respectable without any suppression; it just suffers from the problems of insular-marriage.

For Mistry life is like jig-saw puzzles which can be comprehended in fragments and difficult to transform all fragments to make it a whole. In *A Fine Balance* the patches of various clothes of various colors in a blanket symbolizes the life in its various colors. In *Family Matters*, too, Jahangir and Murad's efforts to complete the jig-saw puzzle and their continuous efforts to complete it are described. For Mistry life is like Enid Blyton's series of children books searching for something which is hidden, absent, mysterious, and suspense. Jehangir was searching the piece to fit the fragment in his Lake Como jigsaw puzzle, the cardboard fragments to arrange accurately to see the beautiful complete Lake Como. Yezad advised his sons to enjoy their precious schools days. Jehangir as a teenager recapitulates his past life. He wanted to bring back his happy days from the past, his loving father turned stranger with his non-stop praying. He wanted to put together again all the fragments of his life. But it was just not possible, "Like some strange jigsaw puzzle of indefinite size. Each time I think it's done, I find a few more pieces" (FM, 491). Mistry heightens the present grotesque reality with the backdrop of blissful past. Mistry searches patches of beautiful life once lived in the past. For Mistry, "Life is not an Amitabh Bacchan movie? That justice is mirage?" (FM, 211) and "After all, our lives are but a sequence of accidents- a clanking chain of chance events. A string of choice, casual or deliberate, which add up to the one big calamity we call life" (AFB, 691). But he expects a kind of utopian world as expressed in *Family Matters*:

> **In a way, thought Jehangir, the Santa Claus story like the Famous Five books. You knew none of it was real, but it let you imagine there was a better world somewhere. You could dream of a place where there was lots to eat, where children could have a midnight feast and raid the larder that was always full of sumptuous delicacies. A place where they organized picnics to the countryside and had adventures, where even the smugglers and thieves they caught were not too dangerous, just "nasty customers" who were "up to**

> **no good", as the kindly police inspector explained at the end of each book. A place where there were no beggars, no sickness, and no one died of starvation. And once a year a jolly fat man brought gifts for good children. All this was what Murad wanted for him. (FM, 373)**

For Mistry life is also an infinite search. In the evening, by the sea, Gustad enjoyed the talk with Malcolm about the musical past and the present full of chaos and loss of rhythm. Both of them remembered about their fathers who always tried to search something in music and books, but could not. Gustad remembered Malcolm and his father playing violin and piano:

> **I used to love to see your father put rosin on the bow, his face was always frowning with concentration when he did that. Then he would start to play, his bow moving up and down with so much life and power - gave me a strange feeling. As if he was searching desperately for something, but always disappointed. Because the piece ended before he found it.' 'And the funny thing is my father had the same kind of look in his eyes. Sometimes, when he was reading- a kind of sadness that the book was finishing too soon, without telling him everything he wanted to know.' (SALJ, 229-230)**

For Sidhwa life is a journey, a search that is never complete. The journey as a search for life is expressed as:

> ***"Tum aye ho na shab-e-intezar guzri hai-***
> ***Talash main hai seher baar baar guzri hai!***
>
> **(You never came - The waitful night never passed-**
> **Though many dawns have passed in the waiting)"**
> **(ICM, 245)**

For Sidhwa life is the poetry of poets who search life in the present, the seen. One can enjoy the ecstasy and intoxication of highest pleasure:

> ***Ulfat Kee Naee Manzil Ko Chalay***
> **Embarked on a new mission of love. (AAB, 311)**

Mistry writes about the human life that has the same stereotyped incidents and story, only the characters and details are different:

> **"Everyone underestimates their own life. Funny thing is, in the end, all the stories- your life, my life, old Husain's life, they're the same. In fact, no matter where you go in the world, there is only one important story: of youth, and loss, and yearning for redemption. So we tell the same story, over and over, Just the details are different." (FM, 228)**

Mistry deals with the gay-homo-sexual themes. In the story "*The Collectors*", Eric promised Jehangir to give him stamps from the Patla & Jhaaria Babu stalls. For this Jehangir has to do some favor:

> **Eric found Jehangir's delicate hands and finger, his smooth legs and thighs very desirable. In class he gazed for hours, longingly, at the girlish face, curly hair, long eyelashes. (TFB, 90)**

The Eric-Jehangir pair earned the reputation of "moothya-maroo" (TFB, 93) in the class.

Sidhwa deals with lesbian-homosexual themes in *An American Brat*. Zareen appreciates Laura and Shirley as "decent girls" (AAB, 299). Feroza informed them as "lesbians" (AAB, 299) "lovers" (AAB, 300) and then explained:

> **Laura says, 'If Shirley gets my juices flowing, why should I mess around with boys?' (AAB, 300)**

Mistry's appeal to the world environment can be seen in his epic novel *A Fine Balance* where he talks about the coca-colonization and industrialization of the hill-station. This appeal to eco-criticism makes the novel universal as the whole world suffers from the ecological imbalance and consequent problems.

Mistry in *Tales from Firozsha Baag* highlights this problem when like most immigrants, Kersi, too, experienced the culture-shock after reaching the Bombay. He felt a contrast between the lush greenery of the West and 'the parched land, brown, weary, and unhappy' (TFB, 186) is striking. The city also seemed dirtier and more crowded. Kersi's reaction to a crowded railway station is given in a highly wrought passage. In *A Fine Balance* Mr. Kohlah was engrossed in observing the growth of development of the hills. He and his friends agreed that it was a nasty growth. The possibility of increased business at the General Store was no consolation. All his senses were being crushed by the invasion. The poisonous exhaust from Lorries was burning his nostrils, and the ugly excruciating of their engines was ripping his eardrums to shreds. Wherever he turned, he began to see the spread of shacks and shanties. Mistry describes it as:

> **The destitute encampments scratched away at the hillsides, the people drawn from every direction by stories of construction and wealth and employment. But the ranks of jobless always exponentially outnumbered the jobs, and a hungry army sheltered permanently on the slopes. The forests were being devoured for firewood; bald patches materialized upon the body of the hills. Then the seasons revolted. The rain, which used to make things grow and ripen, descended torrentially on the denuded hills, causing mudslides and avalanches. Snow, which had provided an ample blanket for the hills, turned skimpy. Even at the height of winter the cover was ragged and patchy. Mr. Kohlah felt a perverse satisfaction at nature's rebellion. It was a vindication of sorts: he was not alone in being appalled by the hideous rape. But when the seasonal disorder continued year after year, he could take no comfort in it. The lighter the snow cover, the heavier was his heart. Maneck said nothing, though he thought his father was being overly dramatic when he declared, 'Taking a walk is like going into a war zone.'(AFB, 264-265)**

For Mr. Kohlah long and solitary saunters were the immense pleasure of his life. Especially after winter, when every outing was graced by delicious uncertainty- "what lay round the next bend? A newborn rivulet, perhaps? Wildflowers he had not noticed yesterday?" (AFB, 265) But afterwards, every ramble was like a deathwatch to witness the destruction with naked eyes. Mr. Kohlah's intimate relationship with the hill-area and the trees is shown as:

> **Coming upon a favourite tree, he would stop under its branches a while before moving on. He would run his hand along the gnarled trunk, happy that an old friend had survived another day. Many of the rocky ledges that he used to sit on the watch the sunset had been removed by dynamite. When he did find one, he rested for a few minutes and wondered if it would be here for him the next time. Before long they began talking in town about him. 'Mr. Kohlah's screw is getting little loose,' they said. 'He speaks to trees and rocks, and pats them like they were his dogs.' (AFB, 265)**

When Maneck heard the gossip, he felt great humiliation and wished that his father would stop this embarrassing behaviour. He also blazed with anger on ignorant, insensitive people. One day Mr. Kohlah noticed that dusk had fallen: the sunset was forfeited behind the pall. The entire scene was so mean and squalid by twilight, so utterly beyond his ability to accept or comprehend:

> **He felt lost and frightened. Waves of anger, compassion, disgust, sorrow, failure, betrayal, love - surged and crashed, battering and confusing him. For what? Of whom? And why was it? If only he could....But he could make no sense of his emotions. He felt a tightness in his chest, then his throat constricted as if he were choking. He wept helplessly, silently. (AFB, 266)**

Then he decided to stop the walks. The construction of a road brought the complete disintegration of Mr. Kohlah who always thought of better future but now the darkness flooded the future which saw the decline in Mr. Kohlah's Cola. Mistry highlights the process of the coca-colonization of the hill-station and end of the local business. This disintegration brought the changes in the lives of Kohlahs. Maneck is sent to Mumbai for college-studies. The group of friends just reminisced about peaceful, happy past. But Maneck did not like to be in Bombay as it was thickly populated, polluted city. He decided to return to his home in the mountains after he finished college. Om and Ishvar are also not in favor of living in the polluted Bombay and wanted to return to their green and beautiful village by the river:

> **'We have also come for a short time only,' said Ishvar. 'To earn some money, then go back to our village. What is the use of such a big city? Noise and crowds, no place to live, water scarce, garbage everywhere. Terrible.' (AFB, 08)**

In *Family Matters* too, Mistry highlights the pollution of Mumbai as Yezad said, "They would all be living happily right now in Toronto, breathing the pure Rocky Mountain air instead of the noxious fumes of this dying city, rotting with pollution and garbage and corruption" (FM, 283). In such manner both the writers have portrayed their sentiments about their cultural locale.

*

XII

Today, the world suffers from the explosion of population. Countries like China and India face the problems of swelling population. Population of religions like Hindu, Islam, Christian and Buddhism is increasing day by day whereas the population of the Zoroastrian community is drastically declining. So it is a matter of concern for the community's survival in near future. It is the well-known fact that this community is on the verge of doom. It is an endangered species on the verge of extinction. Both writers have shown their deep concern for the declining demographic records. Mistry, in a very comic way, has prepared his mind for the retreat of his glorious and most ancient culture from this earth. In *Family Matters,* through the discussions of Jal and other Parsi members, it is clear that in the next millennium the religion is going to be the subject matter of museums and libraries where one can study the lost civilization and religion. On the other hand, Sidhwa is worried about the future of her community and suggests reforms for the survival of the community. Mistry in his *Family Matters* has described the future of the community very ironically. Dr. Fitter is angry over the present generation of the Parsis. He blames them as: "Parsi men of today were useless, dithering idiots, the race had deteriorated" [FM, 51]. He compares them with his glorious past:

> **When you think of our forefathers, the industrialists and shipbuilders who established the foundation of modern India, the philanthropists who gave us our hospitals and schools and libraries and baags, what lustre they brought to our community and the nation.(FM, 51)**

Dr. Fitter is worried about the demographic decline in the Parsi community. His community is about to "doom and gloom" (FM, 51). It is not sure that his community would see the next century:

> **"Demographics show we'll be extinct in fifty years. Maybe it's the best thing. What's the use of having spineless weaklings walking around, Parsi in name only." (FM, 51)**

Jal witnessed the discussion "about the future of the Parsi community" (FM, 412). They cover all topics regarding his dwindling community – "The orthodox and reform argument?... dwindling birth rate... men and women marrying non-Parsis, and the heavy migration to the West" (FM, 412). If Parsis would extinguish then "Vultures and crematoriums, both will be redundant" (FM, 412). Jal thought these things as "explosive topic" (FM, 412). He admits the minuscule status of his community "right from the beginning" (FM, 412). But still they have survived, and prospered. Inspector Masalavala didn't want to "tolerate optimism" (FM, 412). Demographic experts are certain that after fifty years there will be no Parsis left. Dr. Fitter compares the extinction with dinosaurs. If people want to study Parsis they will have to study the Parsi bones. "His humour epitomized the Parsi spirit, the ability to laugh in the face of darkness" (FM, 412). Dr. Fitter imagined the names given to Parsis like "Jalosauras", "Shapurjisauras", "Pestonjisauras", "Whiskysauras" (FM, 413).
Next they discussed the reasons for falling birth rate- like late marriages, education, individualism, westernization, modernization and says that "These Western ideas are harmful" (FM, 413). Inspector Masalavala blamed the Parsis producing just one or two children perhaps they are the only community who follow "the family planning message" (FM, 413). Another reason for low-birth

according to demographers is "the more educated the community, the lower the birth rate" (FM, 414). So they wanted to prohibit the youth to go beyond a bachelor's degree as well as further prepare different schemes to attract them:

> **"Give them cash incentives to study less. And those who want to do post-graduates studies, tell them they will get no funding from Panchayat unless they sign a contract to have as many children as the number of people over age fifty in their family. Maximum of seven-we don't want to spoil the health of our young women" (FM, 414).**

If there are "medical problems, inability to conceive" (FM, 414) then use "virto fertilization and all those mind-boggling technologies that result in multiple births. We can produce six and seven Parsis in one shot" (FM, 414). But Dr. Fitter rejects it as "that the evils that accompany large families do not creep in and ruin the joy and happiness" (FM, 414). Evils like "- sickness, poverty" (FM, 414).

Inspector Masalavala rejects such possibilities as Panchayat has enough money for all the Parsis. He blames too much individualism for this. For him it is "Poison. Pure poison, that's what these ideas are to the Parsi community" (FM, 414). He thinks that the extinction of Parsis "will be a loss to the whole world. When a culture vanishes, humanity is the loser" (FM, 415). Assuming the end of Parsis they plan for:

> **"...a time capsule for posterity. To be opened in one thousand years. Containing recipes for dhansak, patra-ni-machhi, margi-ni-farcha, and lagan-nu-custard... How about including the Zend- Avesta, and words and music for Chhaiye Hamay Zarathosti?... a few old issues of *Jam-e-Jamshed*... Also, some cassettes of Adi Marzban's radio comedies, Complete instructions and explanations for all our rituals and ceremonies, a copy of our great Navsari epic ... 'Ek Pila Ni Ladai' With an English translation.. As the evening wore on, the three of them filled their imaginary time capsule with their favourite items, ancient and modern, serious and frivolous, sacred and profane, till they ran out of ideas (FM, 415-16).**

Inspector Masalavala sadly expressed the relation of Parsis with their beloved city Mumbai:

> **"To think that we Parsis were the ones who built this beautiful city and made it prosper. And in a few more years, there won't be any of us left alive to tell the tale." (FM, 416)**

Dr. Fitter too, joined him by declaring the death of Parsis as well as Mumbai:

> **Well, we are dying out, and Bombay is dying as well... When the spirit departs, it isn't long before the body decays and disintegrates. (FM, 416)**

Here Mistry very comically explores the possibilities of extinction as well as suggests the alternate plan for survival. Where as Sidhwa's concern is grim and straightforward while suggesting the reforms in the rigidity of the community. She is not ready to tolerate the romantic fantasy about her community's survival. In *An American Brat,* she suggests the changes related with marriage problems for the continuity of her community. In course of her interaction with David she began to change the orthodox views and seriously thought over the reformation in Parsi Anjuman's laws about the marriage:

> **At such moments, Zareen wished David was a Parsee -- or that Zoroastrians would permit selective conversion to their faith. Zareen found herself seriously questioning the ban on interfaith marriage for the first time. She had often opined how unfair it was that while a Parsee man who married a "non" could keep his faith and bring up his children as Zoroastrians, a Parsee woman couldn't. And it didn't make sense that the "non" was not permitted to become Zoroastrian; one could hardly expect their children to practice a faith denied to their mother. *But she argued this from a purely feminist and academic point of view.* She had accepted the conventional wisdom and gone along with the opinion of the community because she had**

> **grown up with these precepts. She had never doubted that she would marry a Parsee. Till now these issues had not affected her. But with Feroza's happiness at stake and her strengthening affection for David, Zareen wondered about it. How could a religion whose prophet urged his followers to spread the Truth of his message in the holy *Gathas* -- the songs of Zarathustra -- prohibit conversion and throw her daughter out of the faith? (AAB, 287) (Emphasis added)**

Zareen knew that there was a severe controversy surrounding these issues in Bombay, as well as Britain, Canada, and America, where the Parsees had migrated in large numbers during the past few years. Bombay had sixty thousand Parsees which is fifty percent of the total world population of her community. Zareen had all along believed that the Parsee Panchyat in Bombay was the natural center of authority on community matters. She knew it also had an inclination to be conservative. Far away from Bombay she found distanced from such community matters in Lahore. But she was dimly sure that "the controversy would be resolved in an enlightened manner (after all, her community was educated and progressive) and that she could live with its decisions whichever way they went" (AAB, 287).

At this juncture Zareen found herself suddenly aligned with the thinking of "the liberals and reformists" (AAB, 288). She was happy that a debate on these issues was taking place. Perhaps the teenagers in Lahore were right. The Zoroastrian Anjuman in Karachi and Bombay should move with the times. Sidhwa here suggests that "The various *Anjumans* would have to introduce minor reforms if they wished their tiny-community to survive" (AAB, 288). Well known bollywood actress Perizad Zorabian has expressed the same thought that if community wants to survive Parsi Anjumans have to introduce certain minor changes concerning the marriage or other important issues.

Thus, Rohinton Mistry and Bapsi Sidhwa have various similarities concerning the issues of their community and differences concerning their treatment and narrative techniques.

It was exploration in fictional worlds of these two writers. The comparison of these two writers was based in terms of their vision of community, treatment of its problems and modes of narrative. Sidhwa deals with the Parsi community in Pakistan. She portrays the rich progressive, business Parsi families in her novels. She is a critique of Pakistani Parsi community. Sidhwa deals with three different phases: Pre-independent India, India on the verge of partition and independent Pakistan. Rohinton Mistry portrays the Parsi community in India. He shows the middle-class, working Parsi families in his fictions. He is predominantly a critique of Indian political situation and its adverse effect on his minority community. His novels mainly deal with a specific political period in Indian history.

Note: In this chapter abbrivations are used for the titles of the novels. Abbrivations are as follow:

Bapsi Sidhwa:

1. The Crow Eaters - TCE
2. Ice Candy Man - ICM
3. The Pakistani Bride - TPB
4. An American Brat - AAB

Rohinton Mistry:

1. Tales from Firozsha Baag - TFB
2. Such a Long Journey - SALJ
3. A Fine Balance - AFB
4. Family Matters - FM

VII
Conclusion

> *Man, this dialectical phenomenon, is compelled to be always in motion. Man, then, can never attain a final resting place and take up residence in God... How disgraceful, then, are all fixed standards. Who can ever fix standard? Man is a 'choice', a struggle, a constant migration. He is an infinite migration, a migration within himself, from clay to God; he is a migrant within his own soul. [Ali Shariati: 1979:92-93]*

The Parsi migration to India has caused great upheavals in their lives. The present study has focused on the issues related with Diaspora: exile, memory, nostalgia, homelessness, uprootedness etc. It discussed the resultant problems of diaspora like ethnicity and various factors related to ethnicity like culture and transculturalism, marginalization, nation and transnationalism, and intricacies of adjustment (assimilation, acculturation, alternation, multiculturalism and the fusion). Their reluctance to assimilate within the Indian milieu caused various problems and resulted into their ethnic anxieties. The community has suffered from within as well.

Contemporary literature strongly reflects these ethnic anxieties. Writers like Toni Morison and J.M. Coetzee have dealt with the black ethnicity. Writers like Mistry, Bapsi Sidhwa, Farrukh Dhondy, Ardshir Vakil, Boman Desai, and Dina Mehta continue themselves to Parsi ethnicity. There is not a great deal of focus on the Parsi ethnicity in the literature written by Parsis during the early and middle years of Indian-English Fiction. The Parsi identity as a separate ethno-religious minority in India is not recognized. It is only in the latest fictions by Parsis that one comes across an explicit declaration of ethnic identity. Writers like Bapsi Sidhwa, Farrukh Dhondy, Rohinton Mistry, Firdaus Kanga and Boman Desai, Meher Pestonji, Thrity Umrigar, Homi Sohrab Fracis focused on the ethnic distinctiveness of the Parsi community in their writings. They raised numerous significant issues asserting Parsi ethnicity.

Certain questions emphasize the need for distinct Parsi ethnic identity. If there is a Parsi identity, does it differ from an Indian identity and how? The affirmation of an ethnic Parsi identity also raises the associated links to assimilation into the Indian situation or in the context with Parsis living in the West, in an expatriate location. Essential sameness of the Parsi identity comprises its religious conviction, its ethnicity, its history and its perception of an elite status. It is in such a life-and-death circumstance that the Parsi community is making its final magnificent stand, affirming its splendid Persian past and its 1300-year-old Indian alliance. It is this contention of Parsi identity that is reflected in recent Parsi fiction. Parsis have preserved their ethnicity, racial uniqueness, in spite of their 1300 years on the Indian sub-continent. Even today, most Parsis desire to 'look different' from their fellow-Indians.

In addition to these traits, Parsis share a collective elite consciousness, which is developed from the colonial epoch when the Parsis were intimately allied with the British rulers of India. This Parsi identity compiled of religious exclusivity, ethnicity, common past and elitism has brought Parsis into divergence with the Indian identity. Even if Parsis like Dadabhai Navroji and Phirozsha Mehta joined the mainstream, the greater part of Parsis throughout the national movement in India experienced alienation from the India and sought an identity outside the Indian society. This quandary had not occurred earlier as a normally spelt out Indian identity. It was forged by Indian nationalists only towards the end of nineteenth century. The distinguished social position enjoyed by Parsis during the Raj, was thrashed in independent India. Parsis were marginalized as its elite status was not recognized by the new leaders of India.

The Parsis of India are the only existing Zoroastrians who accepted the ideas of Zarathustra. The Parsi Zoroastrians in India or the Western diaspora possess the similar ethnic group as the present day Islamic-Iranian but they are estranged by their religions and different civilizations. For the Parsis in Indian diaspora the fact of being a Parsi Zoroastrian is a racial as well as a religious identity. It is for this reason that their identity at once becomes national as well as transnational. These identities come in conflict with one another and are placed within private and public spaces. Such overlapping of spaces causes clashes between private and public histories as Chandra points out:

> **Ethnic anxieties arise out of a sense of ethnic identity. Such identity may be religious or secular. Anxieties, however, are compounded when the secular interests of two differing identities are seen to be divergent or threatening to one another. The threatening aspect of the 'other' or majority community becomes more pronounced in the case of economic or social backwardness. [Chandra, 1989:398]**

In this context, it seems that Parsi community has less ethnic anxiety. It is economically and socially most advanced community in spite of its minoritarian existence. Their religion is not under threat from the majority community or from any other community in India. But still a fact is that it is a dying community.

A well-known Parsi scholar Nilufar Bharucha [2003:28] has pointed out the diverse Diasporas that Parsis run concurrently. According to her, first migration/diaspora was from Iran under the shelter of Hindus, as a result of Muslim oppression. Then in Mogul era they once again felt threat of conversion. It was a double edged era; one of fear of renewed religious oppression and another of some regain of language and culture, as Moguls introduced Farsi as the major language. In British colonial rule they acquired the elite status, but it was the phase where they were alienated from India. Next in course of time after the Partition they were divided across new borders. Later in Postcolonial phase they lost the elite status, as well as social and economic status. Then they suffered once again in Post-Ayodhyian India which was the direct result of increasing fundamentalism and terrorist activities in Kashmir by Pakistan and resultant anguish of Hindu fundamentalists.

The successful Muslim conquest in the seventh century was not immediately disastrous for the followers of Zoroaster. They were given refuge in India on certain conditions. Parsis sincerely accepted all the conditions. Parsis adapted Gujarati language faithfully, forgetting their traditional language. Parsi women adopted Sari as the dress of the community. This sartorial custom has also been faithfully followed. Parsis respect cow and due to this tradition, Parsis still do not eat beef. Though there are no religious taboos against eating the beef. However, poor Parsis prefer beef as it is cheap. Parsis perform their ceremonies at night. This condition was imposed to distract local population from such a ceremony and hence the danger of conversion is reduced. Parsis do not allow outsiders in their Fire Temples, which is a further guarantee that they will not attempt any conversions to their religion. They do not allow insular marriage. The wedding ceremony is performed even today after sunset, and at least a part of ceremony is repeated in Sanskrit. Loyalty to the ruler of the day was a strong trait among the Parsis. They could preserve their faith due to the tolerant attitude of the Hindus, and they could maintain their identity because Hindu caste system prohibited insular-marriage.

These restrictive conditions have greatest impact on the Parsi psyche resulting into ethnic anxieties till now, even after 1300 years of their arrival in India. This led to a feeling of estrangement among them. It gave birth to 'the refugee and minority complex' and the resultant aggravated enthusiasm to achieve rigid religious identity. Adopting new cultural environment of the host country under the name of refuge and the act of benevolence was cultural persecution. Thus Parsis became 'a cultural hybrid minority community.' These uneven circumstances supplied fertile proliferation ground for the feeling of ambivalence, and isolation became exacerbated in the colonial period, when the Parsis were amid the first to cuddle education in English and became the most westernized Indian community. They became an intermediary linkage between the Indians and the Britishers. It divided their loyalty to India and the British. They settled down in Bombay which was more westernized and the center of British administration. Bombay, being a cosmopolitan town, provided them the correct surroundings to prosper and got freedom to practise their religion and customs. But independent India period, they suffered a remarkable social and economic humiliation directing them to the west. They migrated shedding off their Indian identity. Several migrated to the west in the 1950s and 1960s.

Those Parsis who have gone to the West also face problems. In the land of whites they are classified as the *other* brown races-the Asians. They tried to avoid this identity in India and it generates confusion and postpones assimilation into the new western context. The Parsis attempted to adapt the realities of the postcolonial India, but most of them experience a social and psychological alienation. They can not forget their Persian glory and their colonial privileges. They are too sophisticated and think of themselves as too cultured to mingle with the down-to-earth Indians. For them Indians are 'ghatis', people from the lower-society, who are coarse, unrefined, barbarians. Their Anglo maniac tendencies called as "anglophilia" persist strongly. Their Parsiness is fast dying out as the young generation prefers mixed marriages and migration to the West but there too they were not accepted in the mainstream. So one can say that migration is not the solution to escape the realities as it is described as:

> **Man, this dialectical phenomenon, is compelled to be always in motion. Man, then, can never attain a final resting place and take up residence in God... How disgraceful, then, are all fixed standards. Who can ever fix standard? Man is a 'choice', a struggle, a constant migration. He is an infinite migration, a migration within himself, from clay to God; he is a migrant within his own soul. [Ali Shariati: 1979:92-93]**

Even today, Parsis, as minority, are striving for the survival. They took efforts to cope with time. They have maintained their special ethnic identity, as a miniscule ethnic group.

The novels of Bapsi Sidhwa and Rohinton Mistry deal with various ethnic anxieties of the Parsi community. It may be external conflict of co-existence with other ethnic majority and its cultural milieu like Mistry's Hindu and Sidhwa's Muslim or community's own internal conflicts and anguish related with its survival and continuation in the future. This study has covered both the anxieties, psychological as well as physical. The physical anxieties comprises political passivity, subaltern status of Parsi community in the mainstream politics as well as in the context of ethno-religious, political-cultural existence. The psychological anxieties involve the downgraded condition of Parsi community in post-colonial era, superiority complex of the Parsis, financial poverty of the community, problems of inter-faith marriage and its increasing fad among young Parsis, debates over dokhma and other religious rites. It can be pointed out:

> **The factors which contribute to... ethnic atrophy are the Parsis's single-minded pursuit of prosperity, extreme**

> **individualism, craze for urbanization, late marriages, low birth rate, the rather high incidence of cancer, Alzheimers disease, osteoporosis, mental illness, and low fertility rate. [Eds. Novy Kapadia, Jaydipsinh Dodiya and R.K.Dhawan 2001:101]**

Bapsi Sidhwa depicts Parsis as cultural hybrids, sharing the traditions, languages, moral codes and cultural life of the Indians. The emphasis of Parsis on charity finds vivid expressions in the novel when Freddy preaches the importance of charity. Freddy and Yazdi indulges in every possible kind of charity. The virtue of cleanliness which is an important aspect of Parsi religion creates problems for Parsi characters in the novels during their visit to London. The unhygienic conditions in London detested Jerbanoo which indicates their inability to adopt to the new culture as well as their rigid observance of their religious values. Parsi people adopted the ways of the British people as they were intimately associated with them. This is evident in Freddy's character when he wanted to encash the insurance policy after setting his store on fire. The Parsi customs, ceremonies and beliefs also find a vivid reference in the novel. Parsi women were confined to the separate cells during their menstruation. In the menses, Putli retires to the other room respecting the tradition. Religious tolerance of Parsis is discerned as Freddy is shown to possess religious scriptures and literatures of most of the religions. Parsi marriage ceremonies, particularly of Billy and Tanya's showing the blend of Hindu and Muslim culture are colorfully described in the novel. Sidhwa also depicts the Parsi methods of cremation called as dokhma in the novel. Their benevolent attitude of offering their dead bodies to vultures and their rigidity to strictly follow religious funeral rites is mildly criticized. It is exemplified when Jerbanoo becomes restless and frustrated as she could not find Tower of Silence in Lahore. Sidhwa also deals with the issue of insular marriage. Yazdi's desire to marry Rosy Watson is frowned upon by Freddy. The opposition of the Parsis to insular marriages is depicted for the cause of racial as pointed out by Freddy. The depiction of the Parsis as an elite class who imitates their British Masters is hinted by Sidhwa in the novel as Parsis Freddy along with Putli attends the parties, as well as Billy and Tanya's mixed parties at home. However, Putli tries to preserve certain Parsi customs; she is labeled as backward by her own daughter. The demographic status of Parsi community is also highlighted in the novel. Freddy understands this harsh reality and made friendship with local people. He considers this as "a need to exist" (TCE, 12). Freddy's and Billy's recognition of their 'otherness' and as an ethnic group led them to be loyal to the rulers and ensure the security, peace and economic prosperity. Their alignment with the British emanates from their realization of their existence as minority. Freddy's abuses to patriotic Indian Parsis suggest his inclination with the Parsi neutrality towards politics. Freddy also assures his listeners about the future survival.

Ice Candy Man depicts the neutrality of Parsis and their Prufrockian dilemma to which community they lot their vote on the eve of partition. This is exemplified when they gather for the Jashan prayers at the Fire Temple in Lahore to celebrate the British victory in Second World War. This behaviour arouse from their recognition as a minority and subsequently their fear of being suppressed by Indian due to their loyalty to the British rulers. They could not rely on either the Hindu or Muslim rulers as they were oppressed by both. Col. Bharucha narrates the story of uprooting of Parsi people from Persia and subsequent settlement in India where their cultural annihilation was executed by the Hindu king by imposing certain conditions on Parsis which they followed sincerely. The constant fear of subjugation haunted Parsis so Col. Bharucha advised his community to align themselves with the people in power. The collective subconscious ness of Parsi community is revealed in the character of Lenny who lame which indicate the political passivity and neutrality. Thus ethnic anxieties are predominant in the novel. However, Sidhwa also describes some Parsi ceremonies, beliefs and prayers. The characters in the novel believed in God and would often conduct prayers. The final rites of Parsis are also discussed here. Orthodox Parsis Orthodox Parsis are reluctant to abandon their traditional dokhma where as modern Parsis are flexible. Godmother favored dokhma on ecological as well as religious grounds. Parsi community faced problems in Lahore as there was no Tower of Silence. Their insistence on getting dokhma in the tower of silence as per their religious rites is satirized when Slave-sister (Mini aunty) ridiculed this tradition. The discussion of dinning table is an important instance where Mr. Rogers, Mr. Singh and Mr. Sethi highlight the various facets regarding the partition of Indian subcontinent. In the heat of discussion Mr. Singh highlights the demand of Home-rule first and then the settlement of their ethnic quarrels. Mr. Rogers underlines the need of British government to keep the India together.

Lenny's identity as a distinct Parsi indicates ethnic group of Parsis as harmless. Lenny is appreciated by Sikh, Muslim and Hindus. Lenny as a member of Parsi ethnic group witnessed the harmony and peace in Lahore. She saw Ayah's group as a formulation of composite culture of India which includes Sikh, Muslim, Parsi, untouchable etc. Ayah is considered as the symbol unity. The group gathers in Lahore Garden in the beginning indicating the religious harmony in India. But as the waves of partition enveloped the whole country, the pattern of communal harmony is disturbed and there is gradual rising of ethnic anxiety among the members of group. It is symbolized by the shift in their meeting place. Later on group gathers in Wrestlers Restaurant which suggest that different ethnic group are at each others neck to hold the power. Sidhwa also highlights that hatred destroys all the human relations. Ice Candy Man to take the revenge of sister's killings, killed his friends. In course of action, he kidnapped Ayah, a Hindu, as well as murdered Masure his co-religionist. Through Ranna's story, Sidhwa also highlights that Muslim, too, suffered during partition. Parsi community in such communal rage has worked like ambassador of peace. Godmother rescued Ayah from prostitution and sent her across the border. Lenny's mother and her aunty helped their Sikh and Hindu neighbors by supplying petrol to send them India safely. Here, Parsi community is shown as a synthesizer between various ethnic groups of India. Parsi community accepts the change easily as they accepted the new Muslim, rulers of Pakistan. Thus this policy of acceptance of change has survived them.

In *An American Brat,* Sidhwa discusses the predicament of Parsi community in Pakistan. Parsi community was affected by fundamentalism in Pakistan. The novel also deals with Americanization of young Parsi girl, Feroza. Sidhwa deals with various Parsi beliefs, customs. Feroza visited fire temple regularly. Zareen's inability to visit the temple due to menses shows her belief in Parsi values. Feroza committed a sin of smoking and later on realized her guilt and offered prayers to purify herself. Zareen's worshipping of a Muslim saint Data Gunj Baksh reveals her effort to conform to religion of nation she lives in as well as the religious tolerance of the Parsis. Sidhwa also mentioned Parsi ceremony in the novel. The community's belief of the presence of a widow as inauspicious compels Khutlibai to remain behind when Good Luck ceremony is performed for Feroza. Sidhwa has given the detail of Manek's marriage ceremony. The problem of insular marriage is revealed in the novel. Feroza's education in America was opposed by Khutlibai as fears that Feroza would be Americanized and would probably choose a non-Parsi husband. The dilemma of Khutlibai show the rigidity of Parsi community who are tradition bound and do not marry out of their community. Feroza's decision to marry David is opposed by Manek as well as her family member. The refusal of the Parsi community to perform the final rites of Perin Powri who married a Muslim further highlights Parsi rigidity over marriage issue. Passion for racial purity of Parsis and opposition from Feroza's family led Zareen to seriously reflect over the reformation in Parsi Anjuman laws about marriage and conversion. Sidhwa also highlights the double standards of Parsi regarding the marriage of a Parsi male and a Parsi female to a non-Parsi. Zareen humiliated David because of his non-Parsiness by underestimating his Jew culture. The culture othering and differences led to the breakup of Feroza-David love affair. Zareen convinced him that cultural differenced mattered. Parsi community severely felt their identity fractured in Pakistani society. Feroza's making of Muslim friends suggests the attempts of minority to assimilate into majority culture. It depicts the marginal existence of Parsis amid Islamic majority in Pakistan where Feroza faces the problems of backwardness as well as of national identity. Feroza was not informed the details about Bhutto's death. She reminded her family that she too is Pakistani. Sidhwa highlights the question identity based on religious chauvinism. Feroza being Parsi has been doubtful about her Pakistani national identity because she was not Muslim. Sidhwa has also highlighted the east-west cultural encounter in the novel. Feroza during her stay assessed the American ways of life and found herself misfit in the country where she was fitted so well. Sidhwa focused various problems regarding the Americanization of Feroza. The novel also depicts the identity crisis of Feroza when she migrates to America. She sheds her Parsi identity as well as Pakistani cultural identity. She adopts the American way of life and even defends it.

Thus, Sidhwa has focused various issues regarding her miniscule community i.e. insular marriage, dokhma problems, conversion, minority, subaltern status, political passivity, post-colonial crisis of identity etc. which caused the ethnic angst for her community.

Rohinton Mistry has also depicted the problems and predicament of the Parsi community in his novels. His collection of short stories *Tales from Firozsha Baag* depicts the idiosyncrasies of Parsis in Mumbai. **Auspicious**

Occasion highlights the identity construction of the Parsis. The religious festival day of *Behram Roje* is described where Mehru is shown to celebrate it with great devotion. The Parsi ceremonies are also described in detail. The attitude of the Parsis towards the Indians and their superiority complex, which reflects anglomaniac tendencies, is also portrayed. **One Sunday** shows the Parsi community's effort to merge with different subaltern group in India. The Boyce family eats beef which align them with Muslims. Tehmina drinks wine which associated them with Christians. The humiliation of Parsi boys in the story further suggests that the Indians still recognize them with other ethnic group. **The Ghost of the Firozsha Baag** highlights the hybridity of language used by Parsi. It also shows the influence atmosphere on Jaaklee and other characters. **Condolence Visit** deals with the beliefs related with final rites of the Parsi. Daulat decided to donate all the items of Minocher after his death which is in accordance with the Parsi tradition of charity. It also highlights the decadence of Parsi culture regarding the traditional dressings of Parsi as a result of westernization. **Of white hair and Cricket** highlights the gluttony and other Parsi issues. Grandmother of Kersi, like other Parsis, is convinced that hair is evil and source of Black magic. She thinks that Kersi's father is committing a sin by forcing Kersi to pull his hair. She is a devout Parsi who spun wool for Kusti. The game of Cricket brings forward the colonial association of Parsi with British rulers and their royal stature. It is contradicted by the present poverty of the Parsi families in Firozsha Baag. **Paying Guest** deals with the problems of evacuation of the paying guest the space trapped Bombay. Boman and Kashmira suffered due to their paying guest. No Parsi family is ready to help him in court. Only a Muslim tenant offers himself readily. But Boman avoids his help for the reasons of inherited enmity. **The Exercisers** highlights the inscription of Hindu spiritualism in Parsi community. Mr. & Mrs. Bulsara seek the help of family guru Bhagwan Baba to convince Jehangir how unsuitable the girl was for him. **Squatter** reflects the pride of Parsis and their contribution to modern India. This is evident in Savukshaw's behaviour when he single handedly won the match for Indian Cricket Team. The eating habits of Parsis people are also focused as Mrs. Savukshaw is shown to be a master in cooking Parsi dish *dhansak.* The inability of Sarosh to assimilate in Canadian culture and his identity crisis is also depicted. **Lend Me Your Light** focuses on complex issues related with Parsi diaspora, identity crisis and assimilation. The three Parsi protagonists show different dimensions of these problems. Jamshed's character portrays the alienated Parsi who desires for elite status and hence migration to West. Kersi also migrates but he is confused with his new host land. He does not want to lose his identity and always feels guilty of living India. Percy shows the complete assimilation into Indian milieu as he works for the betterment of the villagers. **Swimming Lessons** reflects the dilemma of Parsi immigrant. Kersi's failure to swim in beach of Bombay chowpatty and swimming pool in Canada shows his inability to assimilate into either Indian or Canadian culture. It also highlights the various issues regarding the diasporic writers need to be different. It shows the rising Hindu fundamentalism in Mumbai.

Such a Long Journey reflects how contemporary politics affected Parsi community in India. The novel depicts the lives of Gustad Nobel and his family who resides in Khodadad building, a Parsi housing complex. The changing behaviour of Jimmy, an honest Parsi, suggests the adverse effect of dictatorial political rule of Indians on minority community like Parsis. Parsi attitude of religious tolerance is also hinted in the novel. Mistry also focuses on religious beliefs, ceremonies and customs of the Parsis. The rigidity of the Parsi community is also highlighted as Ghulam, a non-Parsi, is denied entry into the Tower of Silence. Final rites of Dinshawji are also described. The problems related with dokhma and the suggestion of the reforms to improve it is also mentioned. The littering of the flesh by vultures troubled the tenants of flats around the Tower of Silence. Mistry also deals with religious issues and other values which are responsible for the distinct identity of Parsi as an ethnic group. Mistry also highlights Parsi paradoxes related with the ideas modernity and orthodoxy. Dinshwaji's wife refuses to clean the body with bull's urine and insists on the use of water only whereas she begins to cry when dog gives no hint of life. Mistry focuses the subaltern status of the Parsis in Hindu majority as Dinshawji expresses his anger on Shiv Sena's policy of changing road names and Maharashtra for Maharashtrians.

Mistry also highlights the religious tolerance through the character of wall on which pavement artist has drawn the deities, Gods and Goddess, saints from all religions. Mistry also highlights the economical condition of the middle-class Parsis who are trapped in financial crisis. Gustad could not afford even the basic facility in life. The plight of Cawasji and his prayers to God to take care of poor Parsis reflect the financial crisis and economical problems of the poor or middle-class Parsis. Thus the novel portrays the political financial and racial problem that Gustad Nobel and his family faces.

A Fine Balance highlights the emergency period during 1977 in India and it focuses on the contemporary political scenario and its adverse effects on the middle class and poor people in India. Mistry dexterously has shown the attitude of common people towards politics. In such atmosphere, Mistry has woven the four different stories into one and the tragedies of Om, Ishvar, Dina Dalal Manek Kohlah at the end of the novel. Mistry shows the Parsi patriarchy where Nusswan controls the life of Dina. Dina as a widow suffers the financial crisis and hires two tailors and a paying guest to lead an independent life. Manek Kohlah belongs to the mountain region where his father's business is destroyed by the multinational company. Om and Ishvar challenged age-old caste hierarchy by changing their traditional profession of cobbler to a tailor. It raged great ethnic violence and upheaval in village where family is burnt out in night. Mistry critically portrays the Hindu caste system in India. He also vividly sketches the injustice done to lower caste people by upper caste Hindus.

Together in Mumbai, these all character support each other to lead a happy life. But destiny destroys their happiness. Om and Ishvar in sterilization camp were operated very badly that later they became beggars. Dina without any financial support returned to her brother and became dependent on him. Manek migrates to Dubai, but after returning could not cope with the change and commits suicide. These all characters fall prey to the political turmoil of the contemporary India.

Mistry also focuses the problems of dokhma in the far away regions of mountains where unavailability of Tower of Silence and Fire Temple result into want of proper Parsi ceremonies for Manek's father. His father, Farrukh, wished to be cremated. It caused opposition to perform prayers for him by Parsi dustoors. Other Parsi ceremonies, customs, beliefs are also discussed by Mistry. Dina was denied indoor cutting as it is considered sin and evil bringing bad luck. Mistry highlights the professional jealousy of Parsi priests. Dustoor Dab-Chaab expresses his unhappiness because he was not hired to perform Dina's marriage ceremonies. Mistry criticizes the Parsi dustoors for their sensual approaches to young women. He also highlights that Parsi community is forward and modernized as it allows the remarriage of widow when Nusswan plans the second marriage of Dina. Mistry also highlights the gora complex of Parsis when Nusswan's wife was treated badly as ayah by his grandfather because her skin was not fair. Thus novel portrays the battle of Dina Dalal, Manek and Om and Ishvar against the destiny to maintain a fine balance.

Family Matters deals with the middle-class Parsi who is trapped into the financial worries due to the insufficient economic sources and burdened by the medical expenditure of old man. Mistry deals with the problems of ageing parents in the Parsi community where individualization modernization results into late marriage and subsequent problems of old age. Nariman Vakil suffers so many diseases typically associated with Parsi community. Mistry also highlights the insular marriage issue of Nariman Vakil with Lucy. Later, Yezad also preaches the racial purity to his son Murad who has befriended with a non-Parsi girl. Mistry highlights the rigidity and orthodoxy of Parsi community. Mr. Vakil slammed the dustoor who performed Navjote to a non-Parsi. Yezad also talks about Anjuman's policy of debarring from community. Yezad's too much religious rigidity concerning cleanliness, purity; scripture are ridiculed by Murad as bigoted religion. Dr. Fitter, Jal and Inspector Masalavala talked at length about the future extinction of Parsi community and the reasons of demographic decline. They blame individualization, late marriages, westernization, diseases, and too much education for this. They also suggest some reforms regarding marriages and other rigid issues of the community. Mistry also highlights the subaltern and marginal status of Parsi community under Hindu majority in India. Yezad's dream to migrate Canada and unsuccessful attempt is also discussed at length focusing the various aspects and tribulations concerning the migration. Mistry highlights the religious tolerance of the Parsis. He portrays the Bombay city and Hindu religion in their tolerant attitude towards all religions. Parsi community also suffers from severs economical problems. Yezad plays matka to earn extra money. Jahangir is corrupted due to financial anxieties of his parents who accepts bribe to mark homework.

Mistry portrays the Mumbai after Babri mosque demolition and resultant ethnic riots. He portrays Hindus as fundamentalist causing pain to all the minorities in India. Muslims are portrayed as scape-goats.

Thus Mistry portrays his Parsi community under various political phases in India suffering from the marginal existence. Mistry has depicted various anguishes of the Parsi Zoroastrian community. His depiction of middle class Parsi community is a combination of post-colonial predicament of Parsi-Zoroastrians who are sidelined as a minority and 'other. Simultaneously, he highlights the various angst of this small ethnic group related with dokhma, prayers, conflict of national identity, recitation of prayers, vulture controversies etc.

Highlighting these various ethnic anxieties, internal and external, both the writers have also given the universal truths that human love, compassion, brotherhood are the essence of life and if the people of all the religions and ethnic groups consider themselves as the citizens of the universe shedding off the cultural, religious, racial and geographical differences there is a possibility of blissful harmonious life on this earth.

Sidhwa is meticulously feminist whereas Mistry is completely male chauvinist. Sidhwa is a traditional story-teller who uses linear narrative. On the other hand, Mistry is experimental who employs narrative techniques like multi-stories, intertextuality, Scherazadic method of story-telling. He evokes the racial pride of his Parsi community in the stories like **"Squatter"** using the narrator Nariman Hansotia. Sidhwa is a humorous Parsi with picaresque and ironic tone whereas Mistry is a cynic, pessimist and tragic writer. Sidhwa asserts her Pakistani identity whereas Mistry escapes from his Indian identity. Mistry indulges into the religious blasphemy as in *Tales from Firozsha Baag* ("**Auspicious Occasion**"), *A Fine Balance* and *Family Matters.* Rustomji, in Auspicious Occasion**,** criticizes Dustoor Dhunjisha for taking advantage of his respected image one who fondles with young women. He calls them as masked bandits. The Parsi community is endangered in coming years, as Rohinton Mistry comments in *Family Matters.* They are also prepared to retreat leaving back the cultural capsule to be opened in thousand years containing all Parsi cultural and religious heritage.

So it can be concluded that though these two Parsi writers belong to two different nations, these differences prove as overt because they write about their common Parsi-Zoroastrian religion and ethnicity which had suffered same problems in the Indian subcontinent and in the West with slight changes. It can also be noticed that Mistry slightly exaggerated the ethnic anxieties whereas Sidhwa has tried to put them straightly as they are. One can say that these two writers have proved to be the representatives of their tiny community, as it is said, "… Parsis all over the world find in him [Mistry] a spokesperson of their anxieties, fear, and frustrations." [Ed. Novy Kapadia, Jaydipsinh Dodiya, R.K.Dhawan 2001:104]

Thus Parsis should forget their post-colonial grievances and merge in the national realities as it was asserted by Behram Malbari who was charged that he was only Parsi and not to meddle into the Hindu affairs like *sati pratha*, Malbari wrote in the Indian Spectator:

> **If my Hindu friends take this line of argument—that I am "only a Parsi", I will be forced to reply that I am as good as a Hindu any of them, that India, is as much my country as theirs, and that if they do not give me a *locus standi,* in the case, I will take my stand on the higher ground of humanity… [Bharucha 2003:37]**

In the end one has to agree that ethnic group of Parsi Zoroastrians is an endangered species. Aditi Kapoor writes in her article "The Parsis; Fire on Ice" in Times of India: "Unless something is done to augment their fast depleting numbers and to revive their religion, the Parsis after an illustrious past could well just fade out in oblivion" [14th May 1989]. The community has a glorious Iranian past because in those times they were the ruling class, but even in Iran today they are in minority and living on the margin.Hence it is futile to expect to return to their original homeland. It is debatable whether the Parsis of today are pure Zoroastrians. So Parsis should learn the following attitude:

> **It is therefore, a source of great virtue for the practiced mind to learn, bit by bit, first to change about in visible and transitory things, so that afterwards it may be able to leave them behind altogether. The person who finds his homeland sweet is still a tender beginner, he to whom every soil is as his native one is already strong; but he is perfect to whom the entire world is as foreign place. The tender soul has fixed his love on one spot in the world; the strong person has extended his love to all places; the perfect man has extinguished his. [Hugo of St. Victor: 1961:101]**

Parsis are stuck up with their colonial prosperity. They were the pioneers in the fields of anthropology, ship building, libraries etc… If the community is to survive, it has to learn to change with changing times and mould themselves as per the requirements forgetting all those air of colonial superiority and conditions of the refuge and allow conversions. They need to mix with their national, geographical and cultural realities with active participation in all walks of the life. Infact, they have contributed in tremendous way for the development of India coming out of their cocoon existence. They should accept the truth what Uma Parameswarn says 'Home is where your feet are, and may your heart be there too'. It is painful reality that people who followed the teachings of Zarathustra are in crisis. The religion of Zoroaster based on his teachings is about to disappear from the universe. The religion of Zoroaster is existential with the choice of good and evil. It can be said that it is a religion which is not limited only to those who are born out of Zoroastrian parentage but all those who choose between good and evil. As Feroza says, "as for her religion, no one could take it away from her, she carried its fire in her heart" [AAB, 317]. It can be said that one who has girded his/her loins to serve the betterment of humanity fighting against the evil to make this world a happy place to live is a Zarathusti because the religion is based on relation of cause and effect. It means if you choose right thing you will be benefited with goodness and if you choose wrong you will face its results. One who is carrying the fire of goodness and charity in his heart can be called a Zarathusti. Nargis Dalal contemplates in one of her articles:

> **His (Zarathustra's) beautiful religion was for everyone who was prepared to join the fight of good against evil and live by three guiding principles – good thought, good words, good deeds. The fire which stands at the centre of the religion was considered only as the symbol of Ahura Mazda, the light and the truth. ["The Parsis as an endangered Species", in Times of India, 24/01/95]**

It can be supported by what A.R. Wadia wrote:

> **During its triumphant career of over two millennia, it (Zoroastrianism) came into living contact with millions of people both to the east and west of Iran and in this period it transferred a good deal of its moral and spiritual vigour to other people. The Hebrews, the Christians and the Muslims, have all drunk deep, consciously or unconsciously at the**

> **founts of Zoroastrianism, and the best of Zoroastrianism lives in the best of other religions...A flame that has passed on its light to countless other flames must disdain so sordid a feeling of jealousy. Good thoughts, good words and good deeds are not the monopoly of Zoroastrians. In the dim antiquity Zoroaster preached it and his reward is that it has become the common inheritance of all humanity. [A.R. Wadia 1973:466]**

Though Parsi community suffers from the ethnic anxieties within the community and from other external factor, they have to come to terms with the present realities and prosper with other ethnic groups of the world allowing certain changes in the ethnic norms if they want to survive in the next millennium.

Primary Sources

Mistry, Rohinton. *Tales from Firozsha Baag,* Faber & Faber: London, 1987.

----------------. *Such a Long Journey,* London: Faber & Faber, 1991.

----------------. *A Fine Balance,* London: Faber & Faber, 1996.

----------------. *Family Matters,* London: Faber & Faber, 2002.

Sidhwa, Bapsi. *The Crow Eaters,* New Delhi: Penguin Books India Ltd., 1990.

---------------. *The Pakistani Bride,* New Delhi: Penguin Books India Ltd., 1990.

---------------. *Ice-Candy-Man,* New Delhi: Penguin Books India Ltd., 1989.

---------------. *An American Brat,* New Delhi: Penguin Books India Ltd., 1994.

Secondary Sources

Ali, Shariati. *On the Sociology of Islam: The lectures by Ali Shariati.* Trans. Hamid Algar. Berkeley: Mizan Press, 1979.

Alvarez A. *Hungarian Short Stories.* London: Oxford University Press, 1967.

Anzaldua, Gloria, *'Borderlands/ La Frontera'*, 1987. Eds. Julie Rivkin and Michael Ryan Literary Theory: An Anthology, Blackwell Publishers, 1998.

Ashcroft, B., G. Griffiths and H. Tiffin. *The Post Colonial Studies Reader.* London: Routledge, 1995.

Asnani, Shyam M. *Critical Responses to Indian English fiction.* Delhi: Mittal Publications, 1985.

Atwood, Margaret. *Surfacing.* Toronto: General Publishing, 1983.

Basch Linda, Nina Glick Schiller and Cristina Blanc Szanton. *Nation Unbound: Transnational Projects, Post-colonial Predicaments and Deterritorialzed Nation-States.* Langhorne. PA: Gorden & Beach, 1994.

Barnes, Julian. *The Sense of an Ending. Jonathan Cape:London, 2011.*

Bhabha, Homi. *The Location of the Culture.* London: Routledge, 1994.

Bharucha, Nilufer E. *Rohinton Mistry-Ethnic Enclosures and Transcultural Spaces.* Jaipur and Delhi: Rawat Publication, 2003.

Bharucha, Perin. *The Fire Worshippers*. Bombay: Strand Books, 1986.

Bhatnagar, M.K. *Political consciousness in Indian English Writing*. Bahri Publicaiton, 1991.

Bisoondath, Neil. *Digging Up the Mountains*. Toronto: Macmillan Paperbacks, 1985.

Brass, Paul. *Ethnicity* Delhi: Sage Publication, 1990.

Brenann, Timothy. *Salman Rushdie & the Third World - Myths of Nation*. London: The MacMillan Press Ltd. 1989.

Butler, Judith. *The Psychic Life of Power: Theories in Subjection of Identity.* New York: Routledge, 1990.

Chandra, Bipin. *India's Struggle For Independence.* New Delhi: Penguin Books India Pvt. Ltd., 1989.

Christophe, in Aime Cesaire's Le Roi Christophe. Qt. In Salman Rushdie and Third World. Timothy Brenann, London: MacMillan Press Ltd. 1989.

Dabu, K.S. *Message of Zarathustra, IInd ed*. Bombay: The New Book Co., 1959.

Darling, M.L. *The Punjab Peasant in Prosperity and Debt*, London, 1925.

Dass, Veena Noble, R.K. Dhawan Eds. *Fiction of the Nineties*. New Delhi: Prestige Books, 1994.

Dawson, M.M. *The Ethical Religion of Zoroaster.* New York: AMS Press, 1969.

Derrida, Jaques. *Of Gramatology.* Tr.G.C.Spivak, Baltimore, 1976.

Derrida, Jacques. *Specters of Marx: The State of the Debt, the Work of Mourning and the New International*. Trans. Peggy Kamuf, New York: Routledge, 1994.

Desai, S.F. *A Community at the Cross Road.* Bombay: The New Book Co., 1948.

DuBois, W.E.B. *The Soul of Black Folk*. New York: Fawcett, 1961.

Dhalla, M. N. *History of Zoroastrianism*. Bombay: The K.R.Cama Oriental Institute, 1963.

Dhawan, R.K., Novy Kapadia, Eds. *The Novels of Bapsi Sidhwa.* New Delhi: Prestige books, 1996.

Dhondy, Farrukh. *Bombay Duck*. Calcutta: Rupa Indian Paper, 1991.

Disraeli, Benjamin. Qt. by Karl W. Deutsch in Nationalism and Social Communication. Cambridge:Massachusetts Institute of Technology Press, 1967.

Dodiya, Jaydipsinh. Ed. *The Fiction of Rohinton Mistry- critical studies*. New Delhi: Sangam Books, 1998.

Dwivedi, A.N. *Indian Writing In English: Part II- Genres other than Poetry*. Delhi: Amar Prakashan, 1991.

Fanon, Frantz. *Black Skin, White Masks*. Tr. Charles Lam Markmann. London: Pluto, 1986.

Fanon, Frantz. *The Wretched of the Earth*. Trans. Constance Farrington. New York: Grove Press, 1968.

Fishman J.A. *The Rise & Fall of the Ethnic Revival: Perspectives on Language & Ethnicity*. Berlin & New York: Mouton, 1985.

Fuss, Diana. *Essentially Speaking: Feminisim, Nature & Difference*. New York: Routledge, 1990.

Gallant, Mavis. *Home Truths: Selected Canadian Stories*. Toronto: MacMillan, 1981.

Gupta, Ashis. *The Toymaker from Wiesbader*. Surrey: Spantech and Lancer, 1993.

Hans, Kohn. *Nationalism: Its Meaning and History*. New York and Cincinati, Ohio: D. Van Nostrand, 1965.

Hartman, Geoffery. *The Fateful Question of Culture*. London: Routledge, 1994.

Hegel, G.W.F. *The Phenomenology of Mind*. Tr. J.B. Baillie. New York: Harper and Row, 1931.

Herodotus, *Book One: Section 136*.

Herodotus, *Book One: Section 138*.

Hodivala, S.M. *Studies in Parsi History*. Bombay, 1920.

Howell, Coral Ann. *Private and Fictional Worlds*. London: Methuen, 1987.

Hugo of St. Victor. *Didascalicon*. Tr. Jerome Taylor, New York: Columbia University Press, 1961.

Huntington, Samuel. *The Clash of Civilization and the Remaking of the World Order.* Delhi: Viking, Penguin Books of India, 1997.

Iyengar Srinivasa K.R., Prema Nandakumar, *Indian Writing in English.* New Delhi: Sterling Publishers Pvt. Ltd., 1985.

Jackson, A.V. Williams. *Zoroaster, The Prophet of Ancient Iran.* New York: Columbia University Press, 1898.

Jain, Jasbir. Ed. *Writers of Indian Diaspora: Theory and Practice.*

Jaipur & New Delhi: Rawat Publication, 2003.

Jain, Jasbir, Veena Singh Eds. *Contesting Postcolonialisms.* Jaipur and Delhi: Rawat Publication, 2000.

Joel, Kuortti. *Fictions to Live In.* Peter Lang: GMBH, 1998.

Khalidi, Tarif. *Classical Arab Islam: The culture and Heritage of the Golden Age.* Princeton, N.J.: Darwin Press, 1985.

Kamleshwar, *Partitions.* Penguin Books: New Delhi, 2006, Tr. Ameena Kazi Ansari

Kanga, Firdaus. *Trying to Grow.* New Delhi: Ravi Dayal Publishers, 1991.

Kapadia, Novy, A.G. Khan Eds. *The Parsis Madyan to Sanjan.* New Delhi: Creative Books, 1997.

Kapadia, Novy, Jaydipsinh Dodiya and R.K.Dhawan. Eds. *Parsi Fiction Volume 1&2* New Delhi: Prestige Books, 2001.

Karka, D.F. *History of the Parsis.* London and Bombay: MacMillan. 1884.

Koran Chapter 10, Sura 9.

Kristeva, Julia. *About Chinese Women.* Tr. Anita Barrpws. London: Marion Boyars, 1977.

Kulke, Eckhard. *The Parsees in India.* Delhi: Vikas Publishing House, 1974.

-------------------. *The Parsis in India: A minority as Agent of social change.* Delhi: Bell Books, 1978.

Kumar, V.S. *The Whiner's Plaint. In search of Identity (or Who am I).* Pune: MSBS, 1996.

Kupiainen, Jari, Erkki Sevanen and John A. Stotesbury Eds. *Cultural Identity in Transition.* New Delhi: Atalantic Publishers, 2004.

Lodge, David. *The Modes of Modern Writing.* London: Arnold-Heinemann, 1977.

Luhrmann, Tanya. *The Good Parsi: The Fate of Colonial Elite in a Postcolonial Society.* Delhi: Oxford University Press. 1996.

M.T. Ansari, Deepa Achar. Eds. Discourse Democracy and Difference-Perspectives on Community, Politics and Culture. Sahitya Akademi:New Delhi, 2010.

333Mattelart, Armand. 'Introduction', *Communications and Class Struggle, Vol. 2.* New York: International General, 1983.

Mitapalli Rajeshwar, Alessandro Monti Eds. *Post-Independence Indian English Fiction.* New Delhi: Atlantic Publishers, 2001.

Modi, J.J. *A Pahlevi text quoted in Moral Extracts from Zoroastrian books.* Bombay, 1925.

Moares, Dom. *My Son's Father.* Delhi: Vikas Publication, 1990.

Mohanty, Satya. *Literary theory and the Claims of History:*

Postmodernism, Objectivity, Multiculturalism Politics. Ithaca: Cornell University Press, 1997.

Moraga Cherrie, Gloria Anzadua. Eds. *This Bridge called my back: Writings by Radical Women of Color-2nd edition.* New York: Kitchen Table Women of Color Press, 1983.

Moya, Paula M.L. & Michael R. Hames-Garcia. Eds. *Reclaiming Identity-Realist Theory & the Predicament of Post-Modernism.* Hyderabad: Orient Longman, 2000.

Mudimbe. *The Invention of Africa.* Bloomington & Indianpolis: Indiana University Press, 1988. Qt. in Fractured Identity Fractured Idenitity. Jaipur and Delhi: Rawat Publication, 2003.

Mujeeb M. *Indian Muslims.* London, 1967.

Mukherjee, Bharati. *Darkness.* New Delhi: Penguin India, 1985.

Mukherjee, Bharati. *The middleman ad other stories,* New Delhi: Prentice Hall of India, 1989.

Nahal, Chaman. *The New Literatures in English,* New Delhi: Allied Publishers, 1985.

Naik, M.K. *A History of Indian English Literature.* New Delhi: Sahitya Akademi, 1982.

Nanavutty, Pillo. *The Parsis.* New Delhi: National Book Trust, 1977.

Okri, Ben. *Mental Fight.* London:Phoenix, 1999.

Palkhiwala, Nani. *We the Nation: The Lost Decades.* New Delhi: UBSPD, 1994.

Pangborn, C.R. *A Beleaguered Faith.* New Delhi: Vikas Publishing House Pvt. Ltd., 1982.

Patil, Anand B. *The Whirlgig of the Taste: Essays in Comparative Literature.* New Delhi: Creative Books, 1999.

Pestonji, Meher. *Mixed Marriage and Other Parsis Stories,* New Delhi: Harper Collins India, 1999.

Portes, Alejandro. *Globalization from Below: The Rise of Transnational Communities,* 1997. Qt. in Fractured Identity Fractured Idenitity. Jaipur and Delhi : Rawat Publication. 2003.

Prett, J.B. *India and its Faiths: A Traveller's Record.* New Delhi: SBW Publishers, 1987.

Rama, Angel. *Transculturacion narrative en America Latina.* Mexico City: Siglo Veintiuno Editors, 1982.

Rao P.M., R.Mittapalli, K.D.Rao. Eds. *Postcolonial theory and literature.* Atlantic Publication: New Delhi, 2003.

Raymond, Williams. *The Year 2000.* New York: Pantheon Books, 1983.

Reddy Venkata K., P. Bayapa Reddy Ed. *The Indian Novel with a social Purpose.* NewDelhi:Atlantic Publishers, 1999.

Rivkin Julie, Michael Ryan Eds. Literary Theroy:An Anthology. Blackwell Publishers, 1998.

Rockwell, Joan. *Fact In Fiction: The use of Literature in the Systematic Study of Society,* London: Routledge & Kegan Paul, 1974.

Rodriguez, Richard. *Days of Obligation: An Argument with My Mexican Father.* New York: Viking, 1992.

Romen, Basu. *Letter dated. May 19, 1922.*

Rushdie, Salman. *Grimus.* London:Alfred Knopf, 1975.

----------------. *Imaginary Homelands.* New York: Viking&Granta, 1991.

----------------. *Midnight's Chidlren*. London & New York: Viking, 1983.

----------------. *The Satanic Verses*. London: Viking, 1988.

Said, Edward. *Beginning: Intention and Method (1975)* reprinted New York: Columbia University Press, 1985.

--------------. *Culture and Imperialism*. London: Vintage, 1994.

Schermerhorn. *Comparative Ethnic Relations: A Framework for Theory & Research*. New York: Random House, 1970.

Shamota, N. *On Artistic Freedom*. Moscow: Progress Publishers, 1966.

Shukla, Sheobhushan, Anu Shukla. Eds. *Indian English Novel in the Nineties*. New Delhi: Sarup & Sons, 2002.

Singh R.S., Gulab Vazirani, Arnold, *Indian novel in English*. New Delhi: Heinmann Publishers, 1977.

Singh, Randhir Pratap. *Bapsi Sidhwa*. Delhi: Ivy Publishing House, 2005.

Sinha, M.P. *Research Methods in English*. New Delhi: Atalantic Publishers, 2004.

Soja, Edward W. *Postmodern Geographies: The Reassertion of Space in Critical Theory*. Jaipur: Rawat Publications. 1997.

Sollers, Werner. *The Invention of Ethnicity*. New York: Oxford University Press, 1989.

Spender, Stephen. *The Destructive Element*. London: Jonathan Cape, 1935.

Stewart, S.M. *Citizenship & Belonging: Local Expression of Political & Economic Restructering*. Transnational Communities Programme, 2001.

Thomas Mann's growth from Reflections of an Apolitical Man to Kultur and Politik Qt. by Yuri Barbash in Aesthetics and Politics Moscow: Progress Publishers, 1977.

Varma J. Sushma and Seshan Radhika Eds. *Fractured Identity- The Indian Diaspora in Canada*. Jaipur and New Delhi: Rawat Publication, 2003.

Vertovec, Steven and Robin Cohends. Eds. *Migration, Diasporas and Transculturalism*. Cheltenham:U.K.:Edward Elgar Publications Ltd.1999.

Yasna xiii Verse 23.

Yasna 30 Verse 03.

Yasna 31 Verse 08.

Yasna 31 Verse 11.

Yasna 31 Verse 20.

Yasna 43 Verse 05.

Yasna 45 Verse 02.

Wadia, P.A. et al. *Parsis Ere the Shadows Thicken.* Bombay: P.A.Wadia, 1949.

Zaehner, R.C. *The Dawn and Twilight of Zoroastrianism.* New York: G.P.Puntam's Sons, 1961.

Articles

Abraham, P.A. "Crisis of Unbelonging in Some Expatriate Stories from the Canadian and Indian context" Ed. Jasbir Jain, *Writers of Indian Diaspora:Theory and Practice.* Jaipur & New Delhi: Rawat Publications, 2003.

Alcoff, Linda Martin. "The Elimination of Experience in Feminist Theory." Paper presented at the women's studies symposium, Cornell University, February 3, 1995.

-------------. "Who is afraid of Idenitty politics?" in *Reclaiming Identity-Realist Theory & the Predicament of Post-Modernism.* Eds. Moya, Paula M.L. & Michael R. Hames-Garcia. Hyderabad: Orient Longman, 2000.

Bavadam, Lyla. "Thus Spake Zarathustra?" *Sunday Magazine* (Anand Bazar Patrika Group) May 1995.

Bhabha, Homi. "On the Irremovable Strangeness of Being Different", PMLA 113, January 1998:34.

Bharucha, Nilufer. "The Parsi Voice In Recent Indian English Fiction: An Assertion of Ethnic Identity", *Indian-English Fiction 1980-90: An Assesment,* Eds. Nilufer E. Bhrucha, Vilas Sarang. Delhi: B.R. Publishers, 1994.

----------------. "Reflections in Broken Mirrors: Diverse Diasporas in Recent Parsi Fiction", *Wasafiri,* 21 (Spring 1995).

----------------. "When Old Tracks are Lost: Rohinton Mistry's Fiction as a Diasporic Discourse", *Journal of Commonwealth Literature,* Vol. XXX No.2, 1995.

-------------. "Stereotyping the Orient", *The Independent,* 29 Oct. 1992.

Bhatt, Indira. "Journey towards Freedom: A study of Bapsi Sidhwa's An American Brat", *Parsi Fiction*, Vol 2.

Bhattacharya, Bhabani. "Literature and Social Reality", *The Aryanpath*, Vol. xxvi. No.9 (Sept. 1955).

Blumer, M. "Key Variable in Sociological Interventions", *Race & Ethnicity*. Ed. R.G. Burgess, London: Routledge, 1986.

Bisney, J.R. "Losing Count", *Parsiana*. November, 1994.

Bisoondath, Neil. "Building on Common Ground", *Canadian Literature* 147, 1995:127-35.

Buchibabu, "Nirantara-trayam" Kalalo Jarina Kanniror (Vijaywada:Adarsa Grantha Mandali, 1969) tr. From original Telgu by Velcheru Narayan Rao and qt. in his article. "The Political Novel in the Telgu". *Politics and the Novel in India*, ed. Yogendra K. Malik New Delhi:Orient Longman, 1978.

Buford, Bill. "Editorial, The New Yorker. Special Fiction Issue", June 23-30.

Cama, Lovji. "The Little boat and the sinking ship", *Parsiana*. November, 1994.

Chandra, Subhash "Bad Faith in Rohinton Mistry's "*Lend Me you Light*", *India in Canadian Imagination, The commonwealth Review*, Vol. 12 no.2. 2002.

Cundy, Cathrine. ""Rehearsing Voices": Salman Rushdie's Grimus", *Journal of Commonwealth Literature*, 134. Originally in Mikhail

Bakhtin, "Problems of Dostevsky's Poetics, from Theory and Literature Vol 8. Ed. & Trans. Caryl Emerson, Manchester: Manchester UP. P.114.

Dalal, Nargis. "The Parsis an Endangered Species", *Times of India*. 24 Jan. 1995.

Daruwala, Jehan. "Truth changes with Time", *Editorial of Bombay Samachar*. August 28, 1977.

Daruwalla Keki N. *The Hindustan Times*, New Delhi, Sunday, May 26, 2002.

Dasenbrock, Reed Way. "Intelligibility and Meaningfulness in Multicultural Literature in English." *PMLA* 102, 1987.

De Souza, Eunice. "Four Expatriate Writers", *JSL*. Winter 1976-77:54-60.

Desai, S.F. "History of the Bombay Parsi Punchyet: 1860-1960", *Parsiana*. July 2004.

Dhalla, H.B. "Proselytism, then what?" *Memorial Volume*, Golden Jubilee of the Memorial column at Sanjan 1920-1971, Eds. N.E. Turel, K.C. Sheriar, Bombay: Zoroastrian Jashan Comittee, 1971.

Dharan, N.S. "Ethnic Atrohpy Syndrome in Rohinton Mistry's fiction", *Parsi Fiction Vol.2* Eds. Novy Kapadia, Jaydipsinh Dodiya, R.K.Dhawan. New Delhi: Prestige Books, 2001.

Didur, Jill. "Cracking the Nation: Gender, Minorities, and Agency in Bapsi Sidhwa's Cracking India", *ARIEL*, Vol. 29, No. 3 July, 1998.

Dipanjali, June-December, 1996.

Dr. Mallikarjun Patil, "Nargis Dalal- The Woman Writer", *Feminist English Literature*, New Delhi: Atlantic Publishers, 2002, Ed. Manmohan K. Bhatnagar.

E.H. Erikson, "Identity and Life Style", *Psychological Issue*, I (1959).

Eagleton, Terry. Qt in Anand B. Patil, "A Comparative Study of Nativistic Intertextuality in Indian Fiction", *The Whirlgig of the Taste: Essays in Comparative Literature*. New Delhi: Creative Books, 1999.

Foucault, Michel. "Texts/Contexts: Of Other Spaces", *Diacritics*, Spring 1986.

Franco, Jean. "Beyond Ethnocentrism: Gender, Power, and the Third World Intelligentia", in *Marxism & the Interpretation of Culture*. Eds.

Cary Nelson & Lawrence Grossberg. Urbana & Chicago III: University of Illinois ress, 1988.

Gajendrakumar Ed. "Rohinton Mistry's "A Fine Balance: A Slice of Middle Class Life", *Indian English Literature- A New Perspective*, New Delhi: Sarup and Sons, 2001.

Gandhi, Keki J. Cited in *FED Newsletter* No. 138, *The Federation of Parsi Zoroastrian Anjumans*, April 1995.

Ganguly, Keya. "Mirgant Identities Personal Memory and the construction of Selfhood", *Cultural Studies*, 6. 1 Jan. 1992.

Garcia, Michael, R. Hames-, "Who are our own People? (Challenges for a theory of social identity", Eds. Moya, Paula M.L. & Michael R. Hames-Garcia. *Reclaiming Identity,* Hyderabad: Orient Longman, 2000.

"Ghidhade ghtahet", *Maharashtra Times*, Mumbai, Saturday 23 April 2005.

Ginwalla, N.S. "A Peep into Parsi life" *Journal of the National Indian Association*. No. 110, Feb. 1880.

Gooding-Williams, Robert. "Race, Multiculturalism, and Justice", *Constellations*. 5.1 January 1998.

Hall, Stuart. "New ethnicities," Black Film/British Cinema, ICA Document 7. London: Institute of Contemporary Arts, 1988.

Hanchard, Michael. *Identity, Meaning, and the African American Social Text 24,* 1990.

----------------------."Racial Consciousness and Afro-Diasporic Experiences", Antonio Gramsci Reconsidered." *Socialism and Democracy* 3 (Fall 1991)

Haraway, Donna. "A Manifesto for Cyborg: Science, Technology, & Socialist Feminism in 1980s", *Feminism/Postmodernism*. Ed. Linda J. Nicholson, New York: Routledge, 1990.

Harold R. Isaacs "The House of Mumbi", *Washington Monthlly* 3, Dec. 1971.

Heidegger, M. "Building, Dwelling, Thinking", in *Poetry, Language, Thought.* New York: Harper and Row, 1971.

Hippolyte-Adolphe Taine "From the Introduction to the History of English Literature" *Twentieth Century Criticism- The Major Statements*, Eds. William J. Handy and Max Westbrook, New Delhi:Light and Life Publishers, 1976.

Howe, Irving. "The Limits of Ethnicity", *Ethnic America*, Ed. M. Weiser. New York: The H.M. Wilson Company 1978.

Hurston, Zora Neale. "How It Feels to be Colored Me", *I love myself when I am laughing. A Zora Neale Hurston Reader.* New York: The Feminist Press, 1979.

Isjaw, W.W. "Definitions of Ethnicity", *Ethnicity* (1) 2, 1974.

Jagdev Singh, "Ice-Candy-Man: A Parsi Perception", *Novels of Bapsi Sidhwa*, Eds. R.K. Dhawan and Novy Kapadia, New Delhi: Prestige, 1996.

Jaggi, Maya. *The Guardian, Satuarday*, April, 13, 2002.

Jain, Madhu. "Sensitive Servings: Deshpande and Sidhwa Fetch Notice," *India Today*, September 15, 1989.

Jain, Madhu. Review "The Parsi dilemma is: whom do they cast their lot with?" "Sensitive Servings: Deshpande and Sidhwa Fetch Notice," India Today, September 15, 1989, P.47)

Jenny, Bourne. Homelands of the Mind: Jewish Feminism and Idenitity Politics', *Race and Class*, xxix,1987:1

Jha, Parmanand. "Ties and Trials in Rohinton Mistry's Family Matters" India in Candian Imagination. *The Commonwealth Review*. Vol. 12 No. 2, 2002.

Kakar, Sudhir. "The psychological origins," *Seminar*, 307 (November) 1991.

Kanga, M.F. "The conception of an Ideal Priest", *Iran Society Silver Jubilee Souvenir Vol. 1944-1969* No. 1, Calcutta: Iran Society, Nov.1970.

Kapadia, Novy. "Theme of Marriage in An American Brat". *Novels of Bapsi Sidhwa*, Eds. R.K. Dhawan, Novy Kapadia, New Delhi: Prestige books, 1996.

Kapadia, Novy. "The Parsi Paradox in The Crow Eaters" *Novels of Bapsi Sidhwa*. Eds. R.K. Dhawan and Novy Kapadia, New Delhi: Prestige, 1996.

Kapoor, Aditi. "The Parsis; Fire on Ice", *Times of India,* 14 May, 1989.

Karkhanavala, M.D. "Parsis, be true Mazdayasnian-Zarathostis', *Memorial Volume, Golden Jubilee of the Memorial column at Sanjan 1920-1971*. Ed. N.E. Turel, K.C. Sheriar, Bombay:Zoroastrian Jashan Comittee, 1971.

Kaufnan, Michael T., "Author from three countries", *New York Times Book Review*, 13 November 1983.

Khan, A.G. "Rohinton Mistry alias Peerbhoy Paanwala", *Canadian literature and Indian Literature*, Creative books: New Delhi, 1995.

Khullar, Ava. "Let the boundaries give way", *Parsiana*. November, 1994.

Kumar, Shiv P. "Towards a Transnational Protocol in the Postcolonial India", Eds. Rao P.M., R.Mittapalli, K.D.Rao. *Postcolonial theory and literature*. Atlantic Publication: New Delhi, 2003.

La Framboise, Teresa, Hardin Coleman and Jennifer Gerton. "Psychological Impact of Biculturalism, Evidence and Theory", *Psychological Bulletin*, 114(3)

Levit, Peggy. "Towards an understanding of Transnational community: Forms and their Impact on Immigrant Incorporation", Harvard

University: Winter Workshop University of California at San Diego, 19 February 1999.

Lloyd, David. "Ethnic Cultures, Minority Discourses and the State." Colonial Discourse/ Postcolonial Theory. Eds. Francis Barker, Peter Hulme and Margaret Iversen. New York: Manchester, University Press, 1994. Pp-221-38.

Lopez, Barry. "A Literature of Place", *A sense of Place: Regional American Literature.* Delhi: USIS, August. 1996.

Lugones, Maria C. "Purity, Impurity, and Separation", Signs 19.21, 1994. Garcia Papers. Rare and Manuscript collection #7574. Carl A. Kroach Library. Cornell University.

Malak, Amin. "Images of India". *Canadian Literature.* No. 119 (Winter) 1988.

-------------. "The Shahrazadic Tradition: *Rohinton Mistry's* Such a Long Journey and the Art of Storytelling", *Journal of Commonwealth Literature*, Vol xxix No.2, 1993:108-118.

Marg: Persepolis Vol. XXIV No. 4, September 1971.

Markham, S.F. "Welfare:Creating professional Beggers", Parsiana, July, 2004.

Marshall, R.R. "Parsi Population Problem, Rahe Asha (The Path of Righteousness)", *Federation of the Parsi Zoroastrian Anjuman of India*, June 1977. Memorial column at Sanjan 1920-1971, Ed. By N.E. Turel, K.C. Sheriar, Bombay: Zoroastrian Jashan Comittee, 1971.

Minocher, Homi Homji B. "O Whither Parsis placate and perish or Reform of flourish", *A Study of Community Introspection.* Karachi, 1978.

Mishra, Charu Chandra. "Ecology and Identity Crisis in Rohinton Mistry's *A Fine Balance", The Commonwealth Review*, No. 12.2, 2002.

-----------------. "Modes of Resistance in Rohinton Mistry's 'Such a Long Journey'", Ed. Amarnath Prasad, *Indian Novelist in English: Critical Perspectives.* New Delhi: Sarup&Sons, 2000.

Mithe, Stephen. "Three from Here". *Quill & Quire.* Vol. 61. No.9 (September 1995)

Modi, J.J. "The Parsi Priesthood", *Journal of the K.R. Cama Oriental Institution*, Vol. XXXI, 1937.

Oberoi, Nirmaljeet. "Intertextuality in the Poetry of Indians in Canada," *Indian Journal of Canadian Studies*, IV 1995, p.68.

Pandit, M.L. "Fiction across Worlds: Some writers of Indian origin in Canada", Ed. Dodiya Jaydipsinh, *The fictions of Rohinton Mistry: Critical Studies*, New Delhi: Sangam Books, 1998.

Pandit, Santishree D. "Tamil Diaspora in Canada" Eds. Sushma J. Varma and Radhika Seshan. *Fractured Idenitity.* Jaipur and Delhi: Rawat Publication. 2003.

Paranjapae, Makarand. "Early Novels of Bapsi Sidhwa" *The Novels of Bapsi Sidhwa*, Eds. R.K. Dhawan and Novy Kapadia New Delhi: Prestige, 1996.

Pathak, R.S. "Minority Discourse: Inlets to the Parsi Sensibility", *Modern Indian Novel in English.* New Delhi: Creative Books, 1999.

Pavri, Jal Dastur Curestji. "The Zoroastrian Doctrine of a Future Life", The Columbia University Indo-Iranian Series IInd Edition, Vol.11. Ed. Jackson. New York:AMS Press, 1965.

Paymaster, Feroza. "Would you marry out of the Community?" *Parsiana.* Dec-Jan 1975.

Pharand, Michael W. "The Road to Salvation: Mythological and Theological Intertextuality in Rohinton Mistry's Such a Long Journey". Open Letter. Eighth Series, No. 8 (Winter) 1994.

Purushotham K. and N.S. Rahul. "'First World' Within The 'Third World': The Universalist Fallacy In Criticism." Eds. P.M. Rao, R.Mittapalli, K.D.Rao. *Postcolonial theory and literature,* New Delhi: Atlantic Publication, 2003.

Qt. In Pesi Muncherji. "The Sacred and Reverent Fire of Zarathustr", Parsi Fiction Vol.I Ed. By Kapadia Novy, Dodiya Jaydipsinh, Dhwan R.K. New Delhi:Prestige Books, 2001.

Qt. In The Parsis Madyan to Sanjan, Ed. By Novy Kapadia & A.G. Khan, in "Ashem Vohu: Blessed is the Virtue", New Delhi:Creative Books, 1997.

Ramanathan, Malathi. "Voices from within: Diaspora and women writers", Eds. Sushma J. Varma and Radhika Seshan. *Fractured Idenitity.* Jaipur and Delhi : Rawat Publication. 2003.

Rao, K. Damodar. "Oridinariness of Dreams, Longevity of the Journey: Story, Statement, and Allegory in Rohinton Mistry's Such a Long Journey", *The commonwealth Review*, Vol. 5 No.1. 1994.

Rao, Venkat D. "Political *Returns: Abuses* of the Academy", Eds. Rao P.M., R.Mittapalli, K.D.Rao. *Postcolonial theory and literature*. Atlantic Publication: New Delhi, 2003.

Reddy, V. Venkata. "Introduction" *The Indian Novel with a social Purpose* Eds. K. Venkata Reddy, P. Bayapa Reddy. New Delhi: Atlantic Publishers, 1999.

Renan, Ernest. "What is a Nation?", in Homi Bhabha Ed. *Nation and Narration*. London: Routledge, 1990.

Report. Trustees of the Parsi Punchayet Funds and Properties, Bombay, 1970.

Rivkin, Julie and Michael Ryan Eds. "Introduction: The politics of Culture", *Literary Theory: An Anthology*. Blackwell Publishers, 1998.

Robert E. Park. "Human Migration and the Marginal Man", American Journal of Sociology, 33 (1978) p.892

Rushdie, Salman. 'Imaginary Homelands', London Review of Books, October, 1982.

Sahgal, Nayantara. "The Indian Writer and the English Language", *The statesman*, 9 May 1971 (Sunday edition) p. v: 5.

Schermbrucker, Bill. "Live from Khodadad Building", *Event*. Vol. 21 No. 1(Spring) 1992.

Schemerhorn. "Ethnicity in the perspective of the sociology of Knowledge", *Ethnicity (1)* 1 April 1972.

Scott, Joan. "The Evidence of Experience", *Critical Inquiry* 17. 1991. "Seeking new directions", *Parsiana*, Jan. 2001.

Sidhwa, Bapsi. "Groping in the New World," *Indian Review of Books* 2.4 Jan.16, Feb.15, 1993.

Singh, A.K. "Community in the Parsi Novels in English" *The Parsis Madyan to Sanjan*, Eds. Novy Kapadia, A.G.Khan, New Delhi: Creative Books, 1997.

Spivak, Chakravoty Gayatri. "Can Subaltern Speak?" *Marxism and the Interpretation of Culture*. Ed. Cary Nelson and Lawrence Grossberg. Urbana: University of Illinois Press, 1988.

Spivak, Chakravorty Gayatri. "Explanation & Culture:Marginalia"(1979), *In Other Worlds: Essays in Cultural Politics.* New York: Routledge, 1988.

Sunwani, V.K. "Ronhinton Mistry's A Fine Balance: A Critique" *The Journal of Indian Writing in English*, Ed. G.S. Balarama Gupta, Vol. 25, Jan-July, 1997 no. 1 & 2, Gulbarga.

Stouck, David. ""Hanji" means "Yes Sir": Reading Sameness and Difference in Canadian Writing" Ed. Jain, Jasbir. *Writers of Indian Diaspora: Theory andPractice*. Jaipur & New Delhi: Rawat Publication, 2003.

Tapping, Craig. "South Asia/North America: New Dwellings and the Past", *Reworlding: The Literature of the Indian Diaspora*, Ed. Emmanuel S. Nelson, New York: Greenwood Press, 1992.

"The Weaker Sex?" Editorial Viewpoint. *Parsiana*, Feb. 2004.

Townsend, David. "Multiple Pleasures in Mistry's Journey", *Quill & Quire*, Vol. 57, No.3 March 1991.

Trikha, Pradeep. "Rohinton Mistry's A Fine Balance: An overview", Novy Kapadia, Jaydipsinh Dodiya, R.K.Dhawan Eds. *Parsi Fiction Volume 1&2* New Delhi: Prestige Books, 2001.

Umrigar, K.D. "Are the Parsis Dying out?" *The Illustrated Weekly of India*, August 29, 1971.

Vakil, S.R. "The Future Shock", *Parsiana*, Nov. 1973.

Vertovec, Steven. "'Three Meanings of Diaspora' Exemplified among South Asian Religions", *Diaspora* 6, 1997.

Verghese, Abraham. "Cowpath in America", New Yorker, June 23 and 30, 1997.

Vimadalal, J. R. "Power of Prayer", *Memorial Volume.* Op cit., 1971.

Walia, Shelley. "Postmodernism, Discourse and The Colonial Perspective", Eds. Rao P.M., R.Mittapalli, K.D.Rao. *Postcolonial theory and literature.* Atlantic Publication: New Delhi, 2003.

Wasi, Muriel "Putting Magic into Realism," *The Hindu* (Literary Review), July 4, 1993.

Webliography

"A distinctive minority dwindles in India, A group apart/Parsis or Sparsees?" 15 Sept. 2003. <http://www. infoplease.com/ce6/society/A0837727. html>

"Aryan history", 9 June 2004. <http:// www.Parsicommunity.com/Religion /Aryan history.html>

"A Race nearly finished the remarkable Parsis helped build modernIndia, but their old-fashioned ways now might doom them", 15 Sept. 2003. <http://www.infoplease.com/ce6/society/A0837727.html>

"A tribute to the Parsi community, Business India", 15 Sept. 2003. <http://www.infoplease.com/ce6/ society/ A0837727.html>

Birodkar, Sudheer. "Zoroastrianism", 2 June 2004. <http://hindubooks.org/Sudheer_Birodkar/hindu_history/ Zoroastrianism. html>

Chothia, Fali S. "Getting to know the Zoroastrians", 9 June 2004. <http://www.Zamwi.org/ religion/getting.html>

Dr. Kevala, Rustom. "Religion after the Fall of the Sassanians", 9 June 2004. <http://www.Zamwi.org/ religion/sassanian.html>

Dr.Varza, Bahram. "Zoroastrian faith and Parsi philosophy", 3 Jan. 2004. <http://www.Zoroastrianism.com>

"Features:Parsis face success, survival", 15 Sept. 2003. <http://www.infoplease.com/ce6/ society/ A0837727.html>

Hashmi, Alamgir. "Current Pakistani fiction", SPAN: Journal of the South Pacific Association for Commonwealth Literature and Language Studies 33 (1992)

Neo-Colonialism. Ed. Kathryn Trees. 20 Jan. 2004 <http://www.google.com >

"India's Parsi population on verge of Extinction", 15 Sept. 2003. <http://www.infoplease.com/ce6/ society/ A0837727.html>

Life of Zarathustra, "Zarathustra's Birth", 9 June 2004. <http://www.Parsicommunity.com/Religion/Zarathustra/Lifeof ZarathustraBirth.html>

"Parsis, a bright people passionate about their faith, concerned with their dwindeling numbers (Ap Worldstream)", 15 Sept. 2003. <http://www. infoplease.com/ce6/society/A0837727.html>

"Parsis Divided over funeral rites (Ap Online) 15 Sept. 2003. <http://www.infoplease.com/ce6/ society/ A0837727.html>

"Profile: Parsi People of India nearing extinction", 15 Sept. 2003. <http://www.infoplease.com/ce6/ society/ A0837727.html>

"Rare Birds Indeed: India's Parsi community is struck particularly hard by a mysterious disease afflicting local Vultures", 15 Sept. 2003. <http://www.infoplease.com/ce6/ society/ A0837727.html>

Shamsie, Muneeza. "At the new threshold", 20 Jan.2004 <http://www. google.com>

--------------------. "They made their mark." 20 Jan. 2004. <http://www.dawn.com>

Shroff, K.B. "Zoroastrianism Under the Achamenians", 9 June 2004. <http://www.Zamwi.org/religion/Achamenians.html>

Shroff, K.B. "Mankind and the freedom of Choice in Zoroastrianism Scripture", 9 June 2004. <http://www.Zamwi.org/religion/human_rights.html>

Srinivasa, Seetha. "Post-colonial Hybrid mindscape", *The Hindu*. Sunday, Feb. 02-2000. Internet Surfing - 19/04/2004. <http://www.google.com>

T. Kumar. "India's Unfinished Agenda: Equality and justice for 200 million Victims of the caste system"-, <www.amnestyusa.org> pg.1-2, 6 October 2005, surfing date-25th August 2006.

"Threat to Parsi death rite as Vultures die off", 15 Sept. 2003. <http://www.infoplease.com/ce6/society/A0837727.html>

"Zarathustra, Zoroastrian Faith and Philosophy", 3 Jan. 2004. <http://www.zoroaster.net/index.html>

Dictionaries and Encyclopedias

Robinson Mairi, George Davidson Eds. *CHAMBERS 21st century Dictionary*, New Delhi: Allied Chambers, 2000.

Hornby, A.S. *OXFORD Advanced Learner's Dictionary*, Ed. Jonathan Crowther, Oxford: Oxford University Press, 1996.

Ashcroft, Bill, Gareth Griffiths, and Helen Tiffin. *Key Concepts in Post-Colonial Studies*. London and New York: Routledge, 2004.

Abrams, M.H. *A Glossary of Literary Terms- Sixth Edition,* Banglore: Prism Books Pvt. Ltd. 1993.

Baldic, Chris. *Oxford Concise Dictionary of Literary Terms*. New York: Oxford University Press, 1996.

Encyclopædia Britannica Deluxe Edition CD-ROM. 1994-2002

Encyclopedia Wikepedia. <www.google.com>

Wolfreys Julian, Ruth Robbins and Kenneth Womack. Eds. *Key Concepts in Literary Theory*. Atlantic Publishers, Edinburgh University Press, 2005.

Interviews

Ali Lakhani, Interview with Rohinton Mistry at the Vancouver International Wrtiers' Festival, The Long Journey of Rohinton Mistry.

Gibson, Stacey. "Such a Long Journey", *University of Toronto Magazine*, Summer 2002.

Gokhale, Veena. 'How Memory Lives and Dies," *The Sunday Review, The Times of India,* October 27, 1996.

Hancock, Geoff. "An Interview with Rohinton Mistry." *Canadian Fiction Magazine* No. 65, P.143-150, 1989.

Janet, Chimonyo. "An Interview with Rohinton Mistry", *Canadian Fiction Magazine,* No. 65. 1989.

Jussawalla, Adil. "Writers Aren't Self-Centered", *Midday,* September 9, 1988.

Lambert, Angela. "Touched with Fire", *The Guardian*, April 26, 2002.

Mc Lay, Robert. "Rohinton Mistry Talks to Robert McLay", Wasafiri, No.23, Spring 1996.

Montenegro, David. *Points of Depearture – International Writers on Writing and Politics*. Interview with Bapsi Sidhwa, 1989.

Padgaonkar, Nikhil. "An Interview with Edward Said", *Doordarshan's Metro Channel,* December 6, 1998.

Sangari, Kumkum. "Consent, Agency and Rhetorics of Incitement", *Economic and Political Weekly*, 1 May 1993:867-82.

Saraiya, Indu. "Luck Played a Great Part", *The Independent*, August 4, 1991.

Sidhwa, Bapsi. Interview with Feroza Jussawalla. *Interviews with Writers of the Post-Colonial World.* Eds. Feroza Jussawalla and Reed Way Dasenbrock, 1990. Jackson and London: University Press of Mississipipi, 1992, 198-221.

----------------. "On the Writers' World". Interview with Naila Hussain. *The Nation*. 26 May, 1993:8, 19.

----------------. Interview with Aisha Fayyazi Sarwari. *Pakistan News Service.* 14 August 2002. <http//versa.paknews.com/rm_files/Bapsi_sidhwa_html>

----------------. "Ice Candy Man" Interview with Bachi Karkaria. *The Times of India*. 19 Feb. 2005, Lucknow ed.:4.